D1317823

buying
the best

hugo arnold

buying
the best

**how to shop and cook with
the world's best ingredients**

with photography by
Ray Main

Kyle Cathie Limited

for my family, my sternest critics and most faithful admirers

First published in Great Britain in 2000 by
Kyle Cathie Limited,
122 Arlington Road,
London NW1 7HP

ISBN 1 85626 333 9

All rights reserved. No reproduction, copy or transmission of this publication may be made without written permission. No paragraph of this publication may be reproduced, copied or transmitted save with written permission or in accordance with the provision of the Copyright Act 1956 (as amended). Any person who does any unauthorized act in relation to this publication may be liable to criminal prosecution and civil claims for damages.

Text © Hugo Arnold 2000
Photography © Ray Main 2000
Project Editors: Kate Oldfield &
    Lewis Esson
Designer: Paul Welti
Editor: Lewis Esson
Food for Photography: Hugo Arnold and
    Jane Suthering assisted by
    Olivier Laudus
Styling: Róisín Nield and Penny Markham

Hugo Arnold is hereby identified as the Author of this Work in accordance with Section 77 of the Copyright, Designs and Patents Act 1988.

A CIP catalogue record for this title is available from the British Library.

Printed and bound in Toledo, Spain, by Artes Graficas
Colour separations by Colourscan
D.L. TO: 1354-2000

Throughout the recipes in this book both metric and imperial quantities are given. Use either all metric or all imperial, as the two are not necessarily interchangeable.

contents

preface

I shop for food almost every day, take pleasure from an empty fridge and generally have a vegetable bowl brimming with onions and garlic and the odd squash, but not much else. I go to a supermarket once a month, and even that has been curtailed, the Internet being a much more satisfactory way of sourcing tissues and washing-up liquid.

How do I find the time? I have no idea. Certainly working from home helps, but I cannot imagine any other way. I am lucky, too, with the shops I have nearby: a fishmonger, a butcher, a cheese shop and an Italian delicatessen, that not only does a mean line in salamis and hams, but also buys vegetables from Sicily.

I realize that not everybody wants to – or can – shop daily, but it is increasingly possible to shop more frequently, and for better ingredients, than was once the case. Where city-centre retail space was, at one time, the preserve of clothes and electrical goods, food has found a role, and late-night corner stores have moved on from pot noodles. Unfortunately, we are still not quite as civilized in this respect as the French, Spanish or Italians, but things are improving.

Finish working in almost any area of Paris, or any other city throughout that gastronomic country, and it is to the *boulangerie*, *pâtisserie*, *charcuterie* or *traiteur* that most people head. No other country separates its food shopping in quite the same way – it's a great shame that this tradition is on the wane. Yet an Italian *salumeria* can yield the same thrill; trays of stuffed ravioli, sausages in every shape, size and colour, more pasta shapes than you can ever tire of. There is no real need to cook, supper is there in front of you, a mere saucepan of boiling water away. This is the kind of convenience shopping I want, and am quite prepared to pay for.

I shop because I love to cook and what I cook is usually dictated by what I can buy. Do I build my menu round what looks good? Perhaps, but I am more concerned with the inspiration derived from the experience, the exchange, which is why I like small shops.

Patricia will have well over 100 cheeses on sale at any one time, so I want to know from her what is particularly ripe and ready for eating, but I want the chat and gossip too. Chris, who sells me my meat, has a definite opinion on the various cuts sitting behind his impeccably managed chill cabinets, but he is also keen to know what is going on in the outside world. As for Marco, he is inevitably trying out some new supplier and we end up chatting about what is good and bad, how this Pecorino compares with the existing one and whether organic vegetables are really that much better than the ones his family grow in southern Italy. No prizes for guessing which win out.

Gather a newly laid egg and fry it in butter, pluck a stick of corn from a field of maize and plunge it into a pot of boiling salted water, or unhook a mackerel and, having cleaned it, fry it immediately... in each case, you will sit back in amazement, not just at the flavour, but at the texture, the smell, the sheer vitality. Shopping should mimic these experiences as closely as possible. I do not want to buy something shrink-wrapped, grown and flown. I do not care for something this tasteless, tired and insipid. Aeroplanes are meant for people, not for vegetables.

Perhaps it is my failure at planning, or could it be I cannot think further than my next meal? Whatever the reason, I somehow find it difficult to buy for more than one sitting, although I am indifferent as to whether that is for two of us or 20. Even taking into account the

I loathe throwing food out, it seems such a complete and utter waste, not just of the time that was spent shopping for it, but also of the time and effort that went into growing or producing it. Shopping regularly and locally may cost a little more, but I am convinced I waste less and win out in the end.

This book is born out of a love of eating well. I cook every day, but rarely for more than 30–40 minutes. My food is not complicated – in the winter it will be based around braises and stews, in the summer around grilled and barbecued food – and incorporates few ingredients. A lamb hot-pot for cooler days, a piece of grilled fish when the weather gets a little more summery, with a salad of couscous, perhaps, and a fresh salsa of chopped tomato, mustard seeds, parsley and olive oil.

I look for big flavours and lots of colour. The lamb hot-pot needs pickles: bright green gherkins, some piccalilli or maybe some raw beetroot grated and mixed with horseradish, chopped cornichons and oodles of parsley – the whole lot bound with fruity olive oil. I use herbs all the time, mainly parsley, but also basil, sage, rosemary, thyme and bay. Wrapped in a plastic bag, they keep for days at a time at the bottom of the fridge. Buy a decent chicken and you can marinate it in a mixture of herbs, olive oil and vinegar overnight to introduce a subtle but significantly different flavour.

needs of my five-year-old son take some effort, so I don't bother, tending to feed him on whatever we are eating, which seems to suit him well enough.

The truth is that none of us have time to shop. Whatever way you try, it is a time-consuming business, requiring thought, planning and a strategy. Ever noticed how you walk into a supermarket only to be faced by the joys of the fruit and vegetable section? You shop with your eyes here, and before you have passed row B the trolley is half-full. So on top of your glistening strawberries, perfectly straight leeks or bags of prewashed lettuce, you pile all the other essential clobber. Try things the other way round, once inside you canter to the other end of the store and work backwards, ending up at fruit and veg. See then how much you buy, and how much you end up throwing out on Wednesday.

Seasons drive my purchases, not just because that is how I want to eat, but also because I'm mean and want to spend my money carefully. I'd rather buy raspberries in the summer, not just because they taste better, but also because they cost a fraction of the price of those sold at Christmas. Our food is now globally sourced – this goes for organics as well as

more exotic ingredients – and not all of it is worth buying. I may be old-fashioned, but I want to eat what is in season locally, not in season on the other side of the world. 'Locally', however, does stretch as far south as the Mediterranean – the best aubergines I have ever eaten came from Sicily, bought in the market that afternoon and accompanied home on my flight. Local is relative and I am all for using the advantages of travel, but I draw the line at the other side of the world for so-called fresh produce.

On a recent trip to Trentino in Italy in the spring, everyone was eating white asparagus and blood oranges, the first tentative signs of summer. The sheer enthusiasm of everyone – little else was being eaten in restaurants – was so magnetic I dived into the nearest shop only to emerge with a bag of the same to take home. The menu: asparagus with chopped boiled egg to start, a bowl of pasta dressed with olive oil, garlic, chilli flakes and Parmesan, and a salad of blood oranges – their vivid red colour the most vibrant of desserts.

You do not need to be a great cook to eat well. After all, why on earth were restaurants invented and what are chefs for, if it is not to slave over a hot stove? Home cooking is something to be enjoyed, the eating too. And to those who say they have time for neither, I have to shrug my shoulders, as I have no answer save to say that for me it is the best part of the day. My desk is never clear, I'm far too unorganized for that, but I look forward to when I step into the kitchen as much as when I sit down at the table. I can relax, chat, gossip, argue and discuss anything over a plate of food and feel completely at ease. This book aims to show you how to achieve that end, with calmness and efficiency. You do not need to be a chef, you need only know what to buy and when.

introduction

'*There are banks of fruit and vegetables, freshly picked – depending on the season, baby violet artichokes, young broad beans, tiny green beans, peas, tomatoes, fennel and courgettes with their flowers still clinging; creamy white cauliflower the size of one's fist, giant sweet peppers, and asparagus – white, violet and green; figs, cherries, peaches, strawberries, raspberries and medlar; the endless tresses of garlic and wild mushrooms of all kinds... crates full of live snails and crabs... the odours of basil and* pissaladière... *a vibrant experience, the beauty of which is breathtaking.*'

RICHARD OLNEY, *Simple French Food*
(on the market at Toulon)

With a slow, firm twist-and-pull motion, the iron slides out to reveal a tube of gloriously pale yellow cheese. I break off a small piece and eat, a shower of complex tastes filling my mouth. This is Montgomery Cheddar, an enormous truckle of it. Then Randolph Hodgson, of Neal's Yard Dairy in London, moves on to another truckle of the same cheese and repeats the process. The difference is extraordinary, while the first had been good this is sensational. To start with, the texture is better, the cheese springing from the iron with a definite ridge, more body, its aroma is stronger and the flavour far more complex with elegant length, a taste that somehow drifts off into the distance.

Then came the revelation, both cheeses came from the same producer and had been made a day apart. One Randolph would have bought, the other not. He was on his way to America with both to explain to chefs there how important is the role of the cheese retailer. Just because the sign says it is a particular cheese is no indication of absolute quality, and that even applies to a farmhouse cheese like Montgomery's.

Buying fish in the central market in Tokyo I am faced with a similar dilemma, how to decide which fish to buy. The Japanese are obsessive about quality and you don't simply buy tuna – there are different grades, different prices – and gazing over hundreds of square metres it is hard not to be overawed. And so it is with meat, pasta, olive oil, spices, tea and coffee, how do you buy the best? This book is based on nearly 20 years of food buying, not just in the UK but throughout mainland Europe.

It is about buying seasonally, about avoiding industrial processing, about sourcing from producers who care about what they do. It is about spending money intelligently, not flippantly. It is about raising ingredients to their rightful place in the kitchen, seeing them – however minor – not as commodities but as elements that contribute colour, flavour, texture and aroma in an active, positive way.

Buy well and cooking can be kept to a minimum, allowing ingredients full rein. Robust, full colours and flavours come not from mass-produced uniform-looking ingredients, but from gnarled knobbly red peppers, peaches of different hues, sea-bass of different weights and beef that can look dried up and dull in colour when purchased because it has been properly hung for three weeks.

How you shop and what you buy are entirely up to you. This book is not dictating what you must do to live, rather it is trying to encourage you to think about what you eat and how you obtain those ingredients so they are the best. Books relating health to food are only stating the obvious – shop well, live well. This book is about turning shopping from a chore into one of the more pleasurable experiences of life, as pleasurable as cooking, I hope.

assessing quality

How to access taste and to evaluate what is the best are not easy tasks. As with wine, you are not searching for the holy grail – there is no 'best' claret, no perfect Riesling – but those ingredients that are good have a number of characteristics in common: structure, body, length, balance and acidity. Comparative tastings are amazingly instructive; I have done them for ingredients as diverse as canned tomatoes, carrots, even salt. My scoring is more or less as follows: out of 100, the ingredient in question automatically scores 50 for simply being there, even if it's the most dull of examples. One to 10 point(s) go(es) to colour: I am looking for a natural, intense healthy colouring, irrespective of what it is. One to 10 point(s) go(es) for aroma, which can be quite slight, but is always there – even a carrot should smell of a carrot. The flavour scores out of 20 and here I am looking for intensity, balance, cleanliness, depth and some sort of pleasant

aftertaste. The final 10 points are awarded on a 'what do I feel about this' approach. This scoring works only when doing a blind horizontal tasting, that is one ingredient – the source of which is unidentified – from several producers. Doing something like this, even occasionally, makes you realize how different your onions can be.

What emerges from such tastings are a number of common factors influencing ingredients. The variety – in the case of seeds – or breed – in the case of animals – has an enormous impact, something that has become increasingly obvious as farmers, forced by the market, have boosted yield by selecting certain strains bred for productivity rather than flavour in the case of both crops and animals. Husbandry,

craftsmanship and horticultural skill all have their role to play and, while I am not going to go as far as suggesting animals are talked to (or plants for that matter), there is no doubting, to my mind, the end quality of much small-scale production.

Delay from harvesting to consumption is also crucial. This can vary from the need for the shortest time, in the case of fish say, to correct ageing with beef, game or many cheeses. Although it is a crude generalization, the faster the time from field to plate, the better food tends to taste.

The best for me means flavour, texture, aroma. Best also means sustainable; it means production that has respect for the ingredient. Apples blasted with chemicals may not be quite on a par with the poor battery chicken in terms of

welfare, but I have no wish to eat either. A tomato, any tomato, will have colour and texture, even some flavour, so what do I mean by best? I mean a tomato whose texture is crunchy but giving, soft but not mushy. The colour should be a deep red, not translucent or washed out; it should have intensity but not be dull. The flavour should be strong: a tomato is not subtle, it should taste full, rounded, satisfying, rewarding; and it should linger somewhat, not leave you feeling you have tasted nothing but water.

In an age of vast consumer choice, we are bombarded with advertising campaigns and driven into making decisions not necessarily based on quality but often on lifestyle, aspiration, perception. How do you decide which olive oil to buy? And, when you do, what does that decision say about you? How do you access its quality? Decide you have made the correct decision? Know how to use that oil to best effect? A Tuscan oil can be overpoweringly peppery on fish, while a French oil can be distinctly oily on pasta. Do you need several, or is that being unnecessarily fashionable?

I am an obsessive shopper for food, indulging in it on most days and rarely using a supermarket. I want to buy the best because I want to eat the best – simply prepared, with unfussy flavours, using basic techniques. I cook every day because I enjoy doing so and, on average, spend half an hour in the kitchen every evening. It is not the cooking that is key, it is the shopping. Hence the reason for this book. The much overused phrase, 'you are what you eat' might seem a little tired now but, as with many such sayings, contains a great deal of truth.

I do not want to eat processed foods, but neither do I want to eat badly farmed beef, cruelly raised chicken, chemically induced vegetables. This book is about how to avoid these. It is also about how not to waste money on buying overpriced ingredients. Buying the best is not just about spending huge amounts of money, although it is frequently the case that you might spend a little more than you are used to. Good food does not come cheap, but consider the following.

A basic supermarket chicken takes around 40 days to grow, sits in a cage all that time and is fed by conveyor belt. It never sees daylight, has no human interaction and is killed and steam-cleaned on a processing line. It sells for around £2 per kilogram. The chicken I buy takes 120 days to

grow, spends most of its time outside doing what chickens like to do – grub around, dust-bathe and generally cluck about. Its diet is organic and cereal-based, and it is killed and dry-plucked by hand. It costs around £7 a kilogram. However, I might roast such a chicken for dinner one night, pick over the carcass the following day to make a salad for lunch, along with some toasted pine nuts, rocket leaves, black olives, a few poached eggs and cornichons, and then make stock for risotto the following evening from the carcass and some root vegetables. Try extending a battery chicken like that and you will have three tasteless, insipid meals.

Buying the best is not just about what to buy, but about how. In this book, I will show you what to look for and how to make an informed decision. If you shop in a supermarket and want to buy coffee, how do you decide which type? Most of us buy from habit or follow parents, friends, the attractive couple on television, but how do you know which is best for you?

We are presented with choice all the time, but rarely the ability to decide. Labels often cloud the issue, being seemingly reassuring but practically meaningless. What do terms like 'farm fresh', 'barn', 'naturally' actually mean? We are lulled into thinking about a

countryside that no longer exists. Large agro-companies are the reality for most – as focused on unit cost and profitability as any factory. The animals, vegetables and fish merely a means of production; it's just that we get to eat the production. Buy a pot of herbs and you imagine what? Some leafy greenhouse with pots scattered about? In reality, vast trays of herbs languish under hectares of glass, their growth computer-controlled through a watering system, their leaves untouched by pests because every week a host of bugs are let loose to gobble them up first. Sound nasty? Harnessing nature in place of chemicals sounds good to me.

What about flavour, however? A bunch of flat-leaf parsley bought in a Sicilian market was positively salty in its strength. This has something to do with the sun certainly, but also with the strain of seed, how and in what it is grown. If you want punch in your parsley, where do you go to buy it? Producing food on a small scale is no easy way to make a living and it is this more than anything else that tends to weed out the poor practitioners. Passion and interest are also important

from markets to super-markets

Supermarkets supposedly offer choice, value for money and convenience, but their products vary enormously, from the mediocre to the positively thrilling. Shop in a French supermarket and the cheese counter will be superb, as will most of the fresh vegetables. Most Italian villages have at least one, if not two, supermarkets which are really formalized delicatessens, with their tins of salted anchovies and capers, legs of ham and trays of fresh pasta overseen by an enthusiastic white-aproned man or woman. Spain follows the Italian model closely and most nations have the biggies – vast hypermarkets where you could easily spend most of your life, and some people do.

It is easy to knock supermarkets and yet for many of us they are convenient and quick, they generally offer good produce and, although you can criticize

and as anything becomes large-scale there is an inevitable tailing off of involvement, an implicit hands-off aspect. Why the urge to get bigger, to grow? Empire-building is an inherent human trait perhaps, but I am more interested in eating well than funding someone's expansion.

Does it all come down to money? In some senses yes, but this is not the same as saying you must always spend as much as possible to ensure quality. Buying olive oil for £15 a litre and comparing it with one at £5 a litre may well lead you to conclude that three times the price does not result in three times the quality. So it is with most ingredients.

For all of us there is a cost-benefit analysis – spend just a few pounds more on your bag of coffee and you might be amazed by the improvement, spend another few pounds and you may well be searching for what exactly justifies the added expense. Should your balsamic vinegar be three, six or 18 years old? This book should warn you off the so-called 'balsamic vinegar' produced by adding a caramel solution to ordinary wine vinegar, not because there is actually anything inherently wrong with it, but because it is not balsamic and, perhaps more importantly, because it has a shallow, bitter, unpleasant false taste.

them for their highly refrigerated, automated systems, they allow us to shop with confidence, having achieved a basic standard of which previous generations could only dream. They have also led the way, on occasion, in working with suppliers to improve quality. Marks & Spencer and the work it has done with soft fruit is just one example; Waitrose's work with potatoes is another. The structure of supermarkets, however, dictates that suppliers must be a certain size in order to guarantee supply and must conform to a specification covering colour, size, format and uniformity. There is implicitly little or no room for variation and eating quality can, as a consequence, lose out.

Supermarkets have greatly improved and increased their ranges of olive oils, for example, but while certainly good they lack much in the way of individual character. The same is true of herbs, sold in tiny overpriced containers or growing in pots, their flavour lacking punch. Vegetables and fruit are certainly better than in many street markets or corner stores, but compare them to ones bought at a farmers' market or farm shop – where they may well

have only been dug up hours previously – and you will notice a marked difference. You may also notice an improvement if eating organic vegetables, but then much depends on where and when they were sourced (see How organic is organic?, page 18). Is one chickpea much the same as another, one lentil as good as another? Not in my experience.

Buying in a supermarket, you are invariably dipping into a large company with sources all over the place. The Spanish chickpeas I buy from a specialist are far more meaty, sweet-tasting and tender than any I have managed to buy elsewhere. Supermarket fish is certainly better than it once was,

but much of it comes in frozen; while their meat, for me, is often rather bland and indifferent when I compare it to my own butcher's alternative. That said, I would be the first to admit that overall quality is much better than it was even five years ago. Supermarkets do what they do extremely well, but their aims are ensuring supply, upsetting nobody and delivering on their promise of price. When was the last time you saw a supermarket advertise a product on its eating quality rather than its price. They are pound-obsessive and keen to promote the idea of choice.

However, the perception of choice is often unrealized. You may be able to choose between

several brands of tinned tomatoes, for example, but the price points are similar and, in truth, there is not much to tell between them. There might be an own-label brand and an international brand, frequently both are made by the same company, the price driven not by the contents but by how the supermarket wants to 'manipulate' the shopper. Food is no longer sold but marketed, the consumer being manoeuvred into the position where they think they are making a decision. Try tasting several types of tinned tomatoes – a supermarket brand, a global brand and a couple of examples made in, say, Italy and Spain – and then tell me about choice. If choosing a chicken, you may well be able to go free-range (big deal) or organic or corn-fed, but you will not get told a great deal more information than this. Is this really choice?

I am not pretending that just because you use a specialist supplier you are guaranteed a better product, but chances are you will get one. Why is this? Supermarkets are supposedly driven by what the consumer wants and demands, yet this is patently untrue. In almost all cases, supermarkets are driven by their shareholders and this is not necessarily the best way to serve the customer. For years now they have gained ground through efficiency and British supermarketing has become a worldwide model for this. They also have immense purchasing power and marketing strength. Just look at the advertising campaigns focused on price and on making you believe that what they do is for you.

Compare this with a speciality shop – be it cheese, meat, vegetables, dry goods or a mixture. If they do not build a relationship with you and work hard to bring you the best, you will go elsewhere. Does it cost more? In actual money terms, almost certainly yes, but in overall terms? You haven't had to go to a supermarket, the cured ham being sliced in front of your eyes has, if you're lucky, been bought by the person slicing it and, more importantly, he or she probably knows quite a lot about it, how it was made, where it comes from, how to store it and what to serve it with.

Supermarkets certainly have their place, but they are not the paragons they like to think they are.

One area in which they excel is frozen produce, from ice-cream to vegetables – a few examples being peas and sweetcorn, both of which start to convert their sugars to starch as soon as they are picked, and frozen prawns, unless you are lucky enough to live in a place where prawns jump out of the sea.

The 10 best buys at a supermarket

Basic extra-virgin olive oil – usually from at least three countries.

Soft fruit – you can pick the best, linger and not be bullied; the choice is wide and the standard good, although not brilliant.

Dairy products, particularly butter, plain yoghurt and creams.

Chicken, not broilers, but organic, free-range and some branded versions.

Ice-cream – usually a wide range of good products on top of the rubbish.

Inexpensive wine.

Semi-dried fruit.

Frozen peas.

Root vegetables.

Citrus fruits.

how organic is organic?

The dash for all things organic is a recent phenomenon and one which I believe is too often done in the blind belief that it is always better. Better for what? For health, flavour, peace of mind. What is better about a carrot grown the other side of the Atlantic, flown so it has spent days out of the ground, the cracked earth on it a mere nod in the direction of the distant field it once came from?

What we mean by organic is in many ways a return to what happened in the past, something grown in a field, fed natural ingredients and harvested when nature dictated that it was ready.

I have no objection to a farmer using antibiotics, I just don't want them used uniformly and without thought for anything other than profit margins and ease – for the producer, that is, not the animal. We are scared about GM, but surely it is an extreme from of selective breeding, something we have been doing for centuries. What we are really scared about here is the unknown, the uncontrollable nature of something

(see right)

Certified organic bodies in the UK

Unless food has been grown or reared according to parameters laid down by the following bodies, it cannot really claim to be genuinely organic:

The Soil Association

British Organic Farmers and Growers

The Bio-Dynamic Agriculture Association

The UK Register of Organic Food

The Scottish Organic Producers Association

so potentially powerful and, quite rightly, we want more research and more controls than currently exist.

Organic food has, however, been at the root of something of a mini-revolution in this country. It is hard to avoid the rapid emergence of box schemes, organic shops and mail-order companies that even make sure their packaging is eco-friendly.

Yet, in the case of fruit and vegetables, much of the organic produce on sale comes from far away and is often grown in just as intensive a way as non-organic produce. Just because it says 'organic' does not necessarily make it better.

First of all the word is meaningless unless linked to a certification scheme (see right); secondly, however organic it actually is does not guarantee good taste.

The only way to decide if organic food tastes better than conventionally farmed food is to taste comparatively. You may feel better for having bought 'organic' beetroot, but did you know it was grown in a greenhouse in Holland and harvested five days ago? I do not want to be that separated from the source of what I eat. It relegates food to being a commodity and that is not what I want on my table.

how to shop

For most of us, shopping for food is just a chore to be fitted in around a busy schedule of work, leisure and household tasks. There is a temptation, therefore, to have one big splurge, fill up our ever-larger fridges and hope it will all last, typically, for about a week. Fridges are not, however,

the best keepers of fresh food and over a period of five to seven days most things slowly deteriorate. Using your fridge like a storecupboard for stock items, though, does make regular shopping for fresh ingredients much less of a tiresome chore.

I rarely shop with a list, yet I usually tend to have some idea of the kind of dish I want to cook. If it is a meat-based dish I have already thought, probably, whether to go for pork, beef or lamb, but I am easily persuaded by top-notch produce once in the shop. With fish the process is far less defined, what is available on the day usually dictating the dish that I cook.

I always eat salad, 352 days of the year, so I buy it constantly, the types of leaf and dressing contributing the necessary variety. I buy cheese by stating what else is being eaten and asking for a suitable partner. After that I am open to every idea, although I like a bit of bite in my cheese. Do I forget things? All the time, but half the fun of food shopping for me is working out how to overcome absences.

To give a list 10 things you can store may seem like a

contradiction in a shopping book, but it is these ingredients that are building blocks for so many dishes and, once you find a good source, they can be stocked up on infrequently as they keep well.

1 OLIVE OIL: I would never think of being without it – one bottle of expensive and strong extra-virgin oil for salads and drizzling over cooked food, and

one bottle that is not so strong or expensive, but still extra-virgin, for cooking, as it gives whatever you are cooking, be it meat or vegetables, a much more rounded, fuller flavour than the neutral vegetable oils.

2 SPICES: although, with a few exceptions, they must be bought whole and not ready-ground. It is a ritual for me to bin all my

spices on January 1 and then go out to buy fresh. Always grind spices as they are needed. A pestle and mortar are traditional, and none the worse for that, and a lovely piece of kitchen kit to have. If you use spices frequently, invest in a coffee grinder. If you have to double it up for use with coffee, use bread to finish the cleaning, as it is remarkably adept at picking up dirt.

3 VINEGARS: on the go at any one time in my kitchen will be a balsamic-style (six- or eight-year-old) sherry vinegar (from Valdespino) and Forum (a Spanish vinegar, the exact contents and method of manufacture of which the maker will not reveal, but it is somewhere between a really good wine vinegar and a balsamic).

4 DRIED CHILLIES: usually about six to eight varieties. I use chillies primarily for flavour and once you dip into the vast world of chillies you begin to see how broad is the spectrum.

5 DRIED PORCINI: usually bought in Italy by the carrier bag, where they cost vastly less, are easy to transport and keep without deteriorating. I tend to keep them in the freezer, just to make sure

that any bugs they may contain are killed off (I have, on occasion, lost my consignment to foreign pests, bought unwittingly in the same handful).

6 PASTA, PULSES AND GRAINS LIKE RICE, COUSCOUS, POLENTA, BULGUR WHEAT, PEARL BARLEY: all can make excellent dishes in their own right and also offer a starch alternative to, say, potatoes.

7 STOCK CUBES: I have no qualms about using these either. I do, however, insist on buying a top-quality brand like Star or Gallo.

8 FLOUR: both a strong version for bread and something more suitable for the baking of cakes. This area of the cupboard also includes cornflour, ideal for thickening stews and casseroles – although I am much more likely to reduce than thicken.

9 DRIED SCALLOPS: on the basis that I dislike fish stock and generally make a light chicken stock infused with these scallops. Why do I not make fish stock? Too often it tastes like glue. The Chinese don't make fish stock and something tells me it is with good reason.

10 TINS OF ITALIAN TOMATOES: having once blind-

tasted 10 different types of tinned tomato, I reached the scarcely surprising conclusion that the Italian brands are usually much better than any others.

The 10 things I always buy in bulk/ have in the fridge/freezer

BUTTER – can be perfectly well frozen.

YOGHURT – naturally long shelf-life in the fridge.

MILK – naturally long shelf-life in the fridge.

PARMESAN CHEESE – naturally long shelf-life in the fridge.

GOOSE FAT (as it makes the best roast potatoes) – will also keep out of the fridge, but goes rancid more quickly this way.

SALTED ANCHOVIES (make perfect hors d'oeuvre and they last for ever, or at least would if I didn't eat them all the time).

FROZEN PEAS – the one vegetable that benefits from freezing, together with sweetcorn, unless you are lucky enough to grow your own.

BREAD – freezes well.

CHICKEN STOCK – freezes well.

SLICED PANCETTA – freezes well.

Understanding E-numbers

What are they and what do they mean? They are a shorthand for long chemical strands, most of which I am unable to pronounce. However, the following applies:

E100–180 are colours
E200–283 are preservatives
E300–322 are antioxidants
E400–495 are emulsifiers or stabilizers

Quite a number of these, although by no means all (some are vitamins), are not particularly welcome in food; you must decide what is acceptable. Ingredients are listed on foods in order of volume present and E-numbers come at the end because, as a rule, a little goes along way. A combination of them suggests the formula has been built up to knit the dish together; why not just buy a piece of fish or a vegetable instead?

Healthy eating

Healthy food is not a subject on which I want to dwell. If what you eat has been freshly bought, prepared and eaten, and over the days contains the ideal balance of carbohydrates and proteins, vitamins and starches, raw foods and cooked foods, and not too much fat, you cannot really go wrong. Oh, and then there is exercise!

Those concerned about health issues are probably looking at the wrong book if what I say shocks them. Common sense still counts for a great deal in my view: fillet steak tonight, vegetable-based sauce for pasta the next and then maybe fish, or will it be chicken and a salad of raw, grated carrot with toasted sesame seeds and oil, mustard seeds marinated in lime juice and a generous seasoning of salt and pepper?

Dates on packaging

'Best before' is an indication that the eating quality of the food is likely to deteriorate after that date, but it does not imply that the product will then necessarily become unsafe.

If the term 'use by' is stated, it is a food safety instruction, the clear implication being that the food might become unsafe.

from shop to home

It does not take long for the ambient temperature in the back of your car to affect the food you have just bought, particularly on a summer's day. Food must be transported as quickly as possible. Even if you are good at packing it into the fridge on your return, during the trip to the swimming pool on the way home the temperature of the food may well have risen to quite a high level. Back in the fridge it cools down again, but the rise and fall will seriously hasten its deterioration. Move with speed, or bring a cool bag and a few ice-blocks and pack it in with the chilled goods. Don't be tempted to top it up with non-chilled items just to fill it up, as they will only serve to raise the overall temperature.

mail order and e-commerce

In some countries this has become quite an efficient and effective way to shop for foods as varied as fresh fish and chillies, cheese and olive oil. Sit in the comfort of your home, select – usually from a range of top-quality products – and pay by credit card. The only disadvantage being the need to be at home for delivery. Quantity can also be a drawback – it can help to team up with some neighbours to split a box.

An increasing number of specialist suppliers also now have extremely good websites. The following are a few personal favourites, but there are plenty more out there:

lobster.co.uk
simplyfood.co.uk
foodo.com
marchents.com
goodfooddirect.co.uk
eats.co.uk
fortnumandmason.com

acknowledgments

I am deeply grateful to my father, who initially thought up the idea for this book on one of our many walks and then set about discussing it with his usual unrestrained enthusiasm.

To Kyle, who saw immediately what I wanted to achieve and embarked on the project with her characteristic charm and energy.

To Kate Oldfield for her much-valued editing, interrupted only by the welcome arrival of her son, Kier.

To Lewis Esson, who took over the task of editing with such energy and devotion. I shall miss our daily telephone conversations and thank you for all your very valuable input.

To Jane Suthering, whose cooking for the photography looked just like it would in my own kitchen, thank you for being such a good interpreter.

To Paul Welti, whose design is both inspirational and timeless.

To Ray Main, whose photographs manage to capture so much life and activity while at the same time focusing on the food. It was both refreshing and inspiring to work with you.

To my agent, Jacqueline Korn who, with her usual devotion to detail and extensive experience has held my hand yet again, thank you.

To Rosie Stark, a friend, companion and confidante, whose reading of the manuscript opened up new areas of debate and forced some rethinking on important issues, your input was, as always, spot on.

Most of all to Sue, Tom and Ruby, who make it all worthwhile.

A number of excellent food retailers and wholesalers assisted in the production of this book by making themselves available for advice and photography; thanks to them for their help and also for their professionalism and pioneering spirit:

Algerian Coffee Stores Ltd
(020 7437 2480)
52 Old Compton Street,
London W1V 6PB

Carluccio's
(020 7240 1487)
28a Neal Street, London WC2H 9PS

The Fifth Floor, Harvey Nichols
(020 7235 5000)
Knightsbridge, London SW1X 7RJ

Fish! (020 7407 3801)
Cathedral St, London SE1 9AL

Fortnum & Mason
(020 7734 8040)
181 Piccadilly, London W1A 1ER

Harrods Food Halls
(020 7730 1234)
Knightsbridge, London SW1X 7XL

Mr Christian's Delicatessen
(020 7229 0501)
11 Blenheim Crescent,
London W11 2JA

Monmouth Coffee Co
(020 7379 3516)
27 Monmouth Street,
London WC2H 9DD

Neal's Yard Dairies
(020 7240 5700)
17 Shorts Gardens,
London WC2H 9AT

The Spice Shop
(020 7221 4448)
1 Blenheim Crescent,
London W11 2EE

various Portobello Market stallholders; various Chinatown stallholders and supermarkets, and Smithfield market.

fish  and shellfish

'Cooking a turbot or a mackerel requires little more skill, perhaps less, than boiling an egg.' MICHAEL RAFFAEL, *Fresh From the Sea*

'Clams were steamed in big pots full of clean seaweed, which gave them plenty of time to decide to open their shells. Those that refused escaped being eaten. Each of the others was taken from its shell, had its rubbery neck pulled off like a dirty undershirt, and was given a bath in hot broth. Then finally, the soothing dip in melted butter... it was like getting them ready for bed.'

JOHN THORNE with MATT LEWIS THORNE,
The Outlaw Cook

The choice of fish is enormous. How to decide? Will it be unctuous, succulent skate, to be served with glorious nutty-brown butter and capers; a grilled bream, preferably cooked over charcoal, served with a rough-and-ready olive-oil-rich salsa; a whole plaice, baked on the bone, its sweet chewy flesh to be enjoyed with a firm home-made tartare sauce; or perhaps some grilled tuna, cooked rare and served with an Oriental dressing laced with soy sauce, ginger and spring onion?

What seafood to order? The salty iodine freshness of a dozen or two oysters; mussels to be steamed with traditional but hard-to-beat white wine, garlic and parsley; a few scallops blasted to a caramelized succulence on a searingly hot pan and served with a pea and mint purée; or perhaps a whole steamed crab, served with a wibbling,

wobbling bowl of saffron-yellow mayonnaise whisked up at the last minute?

A large plate of shellfish must be one of the most glorious ways to start a meal. Majestically sitting on a bed of crushed ice, dark glistening seaweed and bright lemons offsetting the myriad colours of crab, lobster, langoustine, oysters, scallops, clams, mussels – the choice is almost unbearable. Home-made mayonnaise for scooping, some shallots and good vinegar, maybe, a bottle of Tabasco and some soda bread. Is there any need of a main course? Perhaps not, particularly if some kind person can rustle up some crispy, crunchy finger-licking fries – for who, in their right mind, would consider eating either seafood or chips with anything other than their fingers?

Smoked fish is no less abundant. The dusty pink of haddock is surely

part of its attraction; the rich, golden hue on smoked salmon, kippers and mackerel equally beguiling. Smoked cod's roe, rich and full-flavoured, simply spread on toast and served with crème fraîche and some home-pickled cucumber is a favourite way with this versatile food.

Caviar may be for the wealthy, but there are other fish roes to excite, from the humble lumpfish roe to the large, crunchy and salty salmon eggs and the creamy eggs of the herring in the recently developed Avruga. Salted cod sounds like an unnecessary way to preserve, given modern refrigeration, but the process renders this increasingly rare giant of the ocean into something elegant and beautiful – flaky, strongly flavoured and with a firm bite. Served with a stew of chickpeas and a generous sprinkling of parsley, lemon zest and garlic, it is a favourite winter treat.

So much for the enthusiasm, what about buying this wonder of the sea, river or lake? Most of the fish we buy is days old, an unfortunate fact determined by the length of time trawlers stay at sea, as well as by distribution. There is nothing to beat buying direct from a boat, but even then mishandling on board can render your purchase less than perfect.

where to buy fish and shellfish

The choice is extensive – fishmongers, direct from boats, at markets, from supermarkets – the variation in quality huge. The actual process of buying fish is, however, extremely simple. Fish generally keep better whole, which is why the cleaning and trimming is usually done after you have made your purchase. This is helpful, because it is far easier to tell the quality of a whole fish than that of one that has been filleted.

FISHMONGERS: these vary in quality from average to extremely good. The shop should be cold, with lots of water sloshing about, an abundance of ice and, above all else, it should feel good. A shop that is looked after is likely to sell good fish. If care and attention are not lavished on the shop, then they are unlikely to be on the product. Beware shops selling portioned rather than whole fish; the more you cut up a fish, the less chance there is of spotting shoddy examples.

SUPERMARKETS: you generally have several choices – a wet-fish counter, pre-packed and frozen fish. In most cases, the majority of supermarket fish on a wet counter has been previously frozen (and should say this on the labelling card). Contrary to popular belief, frozen fish can be superior to a lot of fresh fish. Not, of course, if the fresh fish is in fantastic condition and hours old, but as mentioned above this is not necessarily the case.

If buying supermarket pre-packs, there are two types. In some instances fish is filleted, wrapped in cling-film and packed; in others, the fish, nearly always filleted, is sealed inside a 'controlled atmosphere' package in which the ratio of oxygen, carbon dioxide and nitrogen is 'altered' to prolong the life of the fish (this method is also used for meat). This keeps the fish 'fresh' for longer, but raises the question of what freshness really is. There seems little wrong with the method of packaging, but arguably the customer should be told on the label.

STRAIGHT FROM THE BOAT: in theory, this should be the freshest fish you can buy, but it is also the trickiest to judge. That large turbot or brill could well have been bathed in intense sunlight for the last hour, or the red mullet kicked about in the bottom of the boat. Use the guidelines overleaf, however, and you should not go far wrong.

SMOKERIES: these tend to operate to a high standard, buying very good fish to start with. The smoke flavour can vary enormously, from very delicate to quite overpowering and you should try and taste before you buy. Remember, if they feel confident about what they are selling they should be enthusiastic about this.

MAIL ORDER: this has increasingly become a sensible, if expensive, way of buying fish. You usually have to order a significant quantity, so much that you need to team up with other people, or freeze it. If you live away from the coast, it is certainly worth considering.

what to look for when you buy fish and shellfish

The eyes on any fresh fish will be bright and full; sunken, dull eyes are warning signs. The skin colour, too, should be bright and vivid; as a fish deteriorates, the colour dims. The fish should have a covering of slime (although stale fish also have a slime covering, but it is sticky, smelly and unpleasant). Be prepared to walk away if what you are intending to buy doesn't match up – there is nothing you can do to improve stale fish.

SALTWATER FISH: above all else the smell should be fresh, of the sea, with a pleasant iodine aroma. There is nothing fishy about fish, or at least there shouldn't be. All the above criteria also need to be met. Historically, there has been some debate about skate, which needs a day or two before being in the right state for cooking, supposedly evidenced by a smell of ammonia. But buying something smelling of ammonia seems utterly daft; the idea that this powerful aroma will disappear in the cooking even more so. Skate is tough just after it is killed, the tenderizing and building up of ammonia occurring over a period of about seven days. For tender skate you want fish a day or two old, but smelling sweetly of fish, which is exactly what you should get in any decent fishmonger.

FRESHWATER FISH: carp, pike, perch and eel are the freshwater fish we used to eat in substantial quantities. These days, we seem to limit ourselves to farmed trout, most of which, in my experience, tastes muddy, even when smoked – the result, in large part, of consumer demand for a cheap fish. You look for the same characteristics in freshwater fish as you do in saltwater fish. I am occasionally given river-caught brown trout by a fisherman friend and they are sensational: moist and succulent, with that riverbank cleanness to the taste. Baked or roasted, with white wine, shallots and cream, they offer sensational eating.

EXOTIC FISH: things like pomfret, parrot fish and hoki are all becoming increasingly popular, particularly with the supermarkets, as they like consistency and reliability. Flown thousands of miles, these fish are likely to be joined by others as the overfished Atlantic goes into decline. In my opinion, they rarely offer good eating, invariably being rather tasteless.

SHELLFISH: a lot is frozen, which misses the point – half, if not all, of the joy of shellfish is in the salty sweetness that is such an inherent part of the eating. Prawns, langoustines and shrimps invariably fall into this category

Lobsters and crabs, on the other hand, are a different matter. Buy them live, if you can; cooking them is remarkably easy. If you buy them cooked, they have probably been prepared in large numbers, the cooking, by implication, being crude rather than precise. How to buy? The lobster market is awash with Canadian and American imports that are not a patch on those from the UK and northern France (both coastlines are also the best sources for crabs) which, unfortunately, are also more expensive.

The best season for crabs is April to June, although they are good through to December. Lobsters are at their prime from April through to September and then on to December. In both cases avoid them from January through to March. Hen crabs yield more white meat than dark, the reverse is true of cock crabs.

To cook, prepare a large pan of boiling salted water and don't skimp on the salt (175g/6 oz per 4 litres/7 pints of water). Plunge the poor creatures in live (actually the RSPCA-recommended way!), slam on the lid and return to the boil: cook for 15 minutes for a medium-sized (1-kg/2-lb) crab or lobster.

and there is not a huge amount you can do. It is far better, however, to buy frozen raw shellfish and cook it yourself. Secondly, do not buy cooked shellfish and then try to grill it, as the result will taste and feel like cardboard. Avoid packaged frozen shellfish, unless you know your supplier. Often inside these hard-to-view containers lurk shellfish with the doubtful benefit of an ice overcoat. This added weight – it can be as much as half the gross weight – quickly disappears as they thaw.

The best way to buy clams, mussels, scallops and oysters in the shell is live, when their shells should be bright, uncracked and tightly closed. If they're open, a light tap should have them snapping shut; if they don't do so, watch out as they probably dead and already unfit to eat.

The exception to this is the scallop, which will often have been forced open so the muscle controlling the shell is severed. If you find scallops sold out of their shells (the more usual option), they should be an off-white, pearly colour – snow-white scallops have usually been injected with water. Scallops are either farmed in nets suspended under the water, or caught by divers or dredged. The best are diver-caught; dredged scallops are to be avoided, full of grit and sand, the dredging also damages the sea bed.

Clams come in various shapes and varieties: *palourdes*, *praires*, *verni* and, my favourite, the *olive de mer* or *coquina* in Spain, which are to be found furiously spitting in tapas bars in Andalucia. As a general rule, the smaller clams are the sweeter they seem to be.

29

In all cases, look for a fresh and sweet aroma, little if any damage to pincers, tails and legs, and shells should look smooth and shiny with little damage; there should be no mud or silt. There should be no sloshing when you shake them.

If you are buying cooked crabs or lobsters, look for examples that feel heavy in the hand; anything surprisingly light may well have been moulting. The shells should be intact. If you think they might be old, smell them; freshly cooked shellfish smells of very little – ammonia is the warning sign.

Squid, cuttlefish and octopus should all have a shellfish sweetness to them. When you buy, make sure what you are getting looks bright and full; dull and tired examples are to be avoided. Squid is a cephalopod of extremes, requiring long slow cooking or almost none at all: a brief grilling, or a long stewing.

SMOKED FISH: some smoked fish is dyed with a colouring, which is easy to tell as it has a vivid, almost luminous, result. Properly smoked fish has a gentle, subtle hue, a bright surface, firm texture and gentle smoky aroma. It is common for smokeries to use frozen fish – indeed one of London's best smokers uses frozen wild salmon – but the freezing has to be done properly. If the flesh on smoked fish is flabby, the fish may well have not been frozen properly, or was in a poor state when it was.

Smoked salmon is nowadays considered luxurious, but there are both decidedly good and decidedly not-so-good examples. Was the fish wild or farmed? How was it smoked and over what? This information should be on the packet, or conveyed by the person who did the smoking. The ingredients should be salmon and salt, only. What makes good smoked salmon? The texture should be firm, but not tough, there should be a richness rather than any oiliness and the smoke element should not overpower the flavour of the fish.

SALTED FISH: salt cod, caviar, other roes, anchovies and sardines are all cured in some form of salt and then packed. The salting gives them an almost indefinite shelf-life. It is extremely hard to tell the good from the bad until you are eating it; so brands, suppliers and price are the key guides.

Spain and Italy are good sources of anchovies, sardines and bottarga (the salted and dried roes of tuna and grey mullet); Spain and Portugal are particularly good on salt cod, but ironically most of the cod salted comes from Iceland and the UK.

CAVIAR: this is a bit of hot potato at present, with concern about over-fishing of the sturgeon. If you can afford it, buy it (lucky you); if not, go for salmon eggs or keta, which is completely different but rather delicious. We are likely to see more farmed caviar in the future – at the mouth of the Gironde in France, for example, they are farming sturgeon for caviar, the reintroduction of an activity that ceased some years ago.

Whether you opt for beluga, sevruga or oscietra is a tricky question; the increasing price is partly driven by rarity. I generally feel so lucky to be eating any of them I hesitate to offer an opinion. A new roe on the market, Avruga, comes from the herring. It is not a patch on the real thing, but curious, rather silky with a smoky flavour.

frozen versus fresh

There is nothing inherently wrong with frozen fish. Like so many food practices, success lies in how it is done. From the consumer's point of view, it also depends on what else is on offer. If the choice is between an unappetizing fishmonger and frozen, I'd go for frozen.

When fish is frozen it tends to lose its sweetness and some of its flavour. If the freezing is done carefully, however, this should be minimized. Bear in mind that well-frozen fish is often chilled at sea, hours after it has been landed, and

should not be shunned. Your best guide is probably price. There is no such thing as cheap fish. Anything expensive is likely to be so because it was purchased on the market at quite a high price, and this should reflect its quality.

farmed versus wild

Farmed salmon we all know about, but such is the pressure on fish stocks that turbot, bream, bass, halibut and even cod are being farmed. How can you tell? In a good supermarket the label should tell you; other tell-tale signs to look for are uniformity of size, colour and shape. An advantage of farmed fish is control of harvesting and portion sizes are incredibly popular with restaurants.

What should we think about farmed fish? It's a complex issue and, indeed, industry, with large corporations involved and surprisingly low margins for extensive start-up costs. Money is at the root. If we, the consumers, insist on cheap fish, what we will get is pretty nasty. There is nothing inherently wrong with farmed fish, but how it is done is crucial. Habitat, diet and breeding all have an influence on the final

31

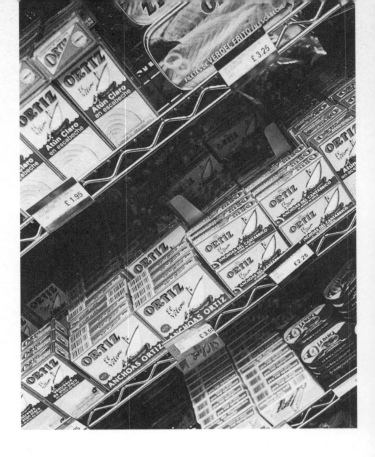

taste and flavour. What appears to be emerging is a two-tier structure much as that which has appeared in the salmon and poultry industry – pay adequate money and you will get good fish.

seasons

Crack a crab in May, linger over a lemon sole in March and tuck into turbot all the way from August through to February – fish and shellfish, like fruit and vegetables, have seasons and, while availability is no longer the guiding issue, quality is. We all know about oysters and 'r's in the month, but there are months when it's a bad idea to eat brill (May to August) and halibut (May and June). Either you will be sold fish that is not in prime condition, or it will have come from far away and be expensive. The list in the directory (page 40) is meant as a guide.

tinned and bottled fish and shellfish

Anchovies, sardines and tuna are all sold in tins and bottles, either in oil, brine or salt (never buy those in tomato sauce), and any comparative tasting should show you that what is grabbed off the supermarket shelves is a world away from what you can obtain in a good delicatessen. No Italian delicatessen is without its tin of salted anchovies, and with good reason, for they are a delight. Look for Spanish and Italian brands and don't balk at the price; tinned fish is only as good as fish that goes into the tin.

storing fish and shellfish

The best way to store fish and shellfish is on ice, where the temperature is a more-or-less-ideal 0°C (32°F) and the ice keeps the atmosphere moist. Once home, the fridge is very much second-best, 5°C (41°F) and dry, and should not be entertained for more than a few hours. Wrap the fish or shellfish in cling-film and place on a plate or shallow bowl. Scatter with ice cubes and put in the fridge. If storing fish, it is much better to buy them whole than filleted.

If you are keeping fish for more than a day, it might be worth considering freezing or salting it as soon as you get home; even 24 hours can make a huge difference.

If contemplating freezing, consider buying the fish ungutted, and then do the job yourself when the fish has defrosted.

Shellfish, both live and cooked, need to be bought as fresh as possible and used as soon as possible. If you delay, all the sweetness goes, rather defeating the purpose. Crabs and lobsters will keep for a day or two if lively when bought. Put them in the bottom of the fridge gently covered with a damp cloth or seaweed.

prawns

This most ubiquitous of shellfish presents the consumer with considerable problems.

Buying fresh prawns is like looking for a needle in a haystack, as they simply don't exist. There are two main sources: either those fished at sea, cooked at sea and frozen at sea, or those farmed. The latter, in turn, are generally frozen. The quality varies widely from both sources, with the so-called 'cheaper' offerings tending to have an extra overcoat of ice. With the farmed versions, feed, stocking density and husbandry all play their part in delivering a good prawn and on the whole you get what you pay for.

My own preference is to buy good frozen prawns, rather than defrosted specimens sitting on the fishmonger's ice. A good prawn should smell and taste sweetly of the sea and the texture of the meat should be dense and quite firm; anything remotely woolly suggests staleness.

oysters

Such is the popularity of this once everyday food that they deserve somewhat special treatment. Additionally, there is still a great deal of misunderstanding about oysters. Natives (*Ostrea edulis*) versus Pacifics (*Crassostrea gigas*), size one verses size three, whether there is an 'r' in the month – there is a great deal of rubbish talked about oysters, a lot of fuss made by those that eat them and by those who make funny faces and refuse to.

I like an oyster or three, but only as a precursor to other things, and I can see no point in eating them if you don't really fancy the idea. As for whether to swallow or chew, I simply cannot see the point in not savouring what you eat and as all the necessary information on taste is gathered by the tongue, there is a strong argument for some chewing.

Native oysters breed during the summer months, when the flesh tends to go milky and limp, and there is some discoloration evident as the young are hatched. There is no danger in consuming them in this state, but they hardly make the best eating – a reason, if one is needed, to follow the old adage about only eating oysters when there is an 'r' in the month.

Tabasco sauce and cayenne are popular accompaniments to raw oysters, but many find them far too strong, knocking the taste of the sea and the inherent subtle sweetness sideways. Chopped shallots and vinegar (try a Japanese rice vinegar, which is delicate) are also traditional.

Lemon juice is hard to beat, although horseradish and tomato ketchup in the Acme Oyster House in New Orleans is rather delicious ($6 a dozen).

A popular way in Bordeaux is to serve them with some hot spicy sausages, which you can then eat alternating between oysters and sausage.

SHELLFISH AND FOOD POISONING

As for the danger element of eating oysters, like mussels and other bivalves, the oyster filter-feeds on small organisms and other material in the water. These can be bacteria related to viruses as well as necessary nutrition. Some oysters are purified before they are sold in a process called depuration that involves washing them in tanks of cleaned sea water under ultraviolet light. The depuration over about 48 hours is designed to remove the bacteria, but the virus can still remain. It is thought that food poisoning from oysters can often be attributed to a lurking virus and, unfortunately, there is no way of telling simply by examining an oyster, There is therefore an inherent risk.

Why, if you do get ill, are the results so violent? If a Norwalk virus is present – thought to be the most common – symptoms are violent vomiting, an attempt to rid the body of the virus as speedily as possible. It may be small comfort, but recovery is normally very quick afterwards.

The law requires anyone selling shellfish to maintain evidence of where and when it was bought by them. If you are ill from shellfish, notify the restaurant or fishmonger as soon as possible, and also consider informing your local Environmental Health Office.

OPENING OYSTERS

To open an oyster, you need to sever the muscle that holds the two shells together. You will need an oyster knife (short and blunt) and a tea towel to protect your hand. Hold the oyster with the fat rounded shell downwards to catch the juice. Insert the oyster knife to the right of the hinge at the back of the oyster (on the left if you are left-handed) and work the knife towards the upper side of the hinge. Twist gently and the oyster should open. Scrape the oyster so it is free from its shell but still in place and lay on a bed of crushed ice, removing any visible grit. Several practice runs are usually necessary – an excuse, if one is needed, to eat a few. Try to save as much of the liquor as possible.

preparing fish and shellfish

GENERAL FISH: whatever fish you buy from a fishmonger or wet-fish counter in a supermarket should then be cleaned, the head removed or left on depending on preference and either filleted or left whole. Fish retains its freshness longer if

the guts are left intact. As for the head, it makes no difference to the cooking, being purely aesthetic, apart from some fish, like cod and monkfish, the cheeks of which are regarded as delicacies. As a rule, fish cooked on the bone tends to be sweeter and more succulent, but serving can be problematic.

If you are given whole fish, or buy from a boat, the cleaning is easy and not nearly as unpleasant as people fear. Slit open the stomach and remove the innards,

which generally come away in one piece. You now want to get rid of all the near-black blood that adheres to the bones. A stiff brush, some granular salt and lots of water are what is needed.

TO FILLET A FLAT FISH: run a sharp, flexible knife along the backbone and then slide it outwards, keeping close to the bones. Repeat on the other side, giving you 4 fillets.

TO REMOVE THE SKIN OF FLAT FISH: make an incision just above the tail and then pull back and tear off the skin. Getting a grip can be difficult. Salting your fingers helps, pliers can be useful, but I find the best is a J-cloth.

TO BONE WHOLE FISH: clean and remove the head and then place the fish on a board, stomach side down, and press gently on the backbone, from behind the head towards the tail. The backbone should come away easily.

SHELLFISH: their killing is the subject of some debate and involves spikes and orifices, neither of which I have a great deal of time for. As quickly and efficiently

as you can, hurl them into a large saucepan of boiling water – this is what happens in any restaurant kitchen in which I have ever worked. Timings (once the water has come back to a rolling, not fierce, boil) are 15 minutes for a 1-kg (2-lb) example, a further 5 minutes for each 500 g (1 lb) over that, although very large crabs and lobsters are to be avoided as they can be tough and stringy.

Mussels, clams, scallops and winkles, cockles and whelks, if you can be bothered, can all be eaten raw, but – in the case of mussels, scallops and clams – are more usually cooked. I could eat mussels and chips for ever, provided the mussels are *à la marinière* and the chips thin, French-style, salty and crisp. Clams with pasta never fail to please and scallops are undoubtedly one of the ocean's treats.

Clams naturally grow in sand and, in my experience, are inevitably full of it. I wash them well and then just steam them open in a dry covered pan. Remove the top shell and then proceed, recovering as much juice as possible from the pan without any grit. Tip-top clams can be eaten raw, much like

oysters, and opening them is also similar.

If you are lucky enough to get scallops in their shells, open them exactly like an oyster, then discard the dark stomach section and remove the gristly sinew that joins the body to the shell. If you eat scallops prepared in lazy kitchens, this is the part you end up rolling round your mouth wondering what on earth it is. Whether you cook scallops with or without their corals (the pink roes) is a matter

of personal taste, but bear in mind that they cook much faster than the scallop itself.

A chef trick with prawns that have been frozen is, once they are thawed, to swirl them in a bowlful of heavily salted water. This 'sweetening' process removes any off-flavours (the water turns a very unappealing grey) and improves their own flavour remarkably. Whether or not you remove the shells and/or heads of prawns generally depends on how you are cooking them, but they do undoubtedly retain greater flavour if cooked in their shells (also remember that the shells add great taste to a fish stock). If you are shelling larger prawns, it is then worthwhile 'deveining' them, i.e. removing the dark intestinal tract that runs in a line along their middles, with the tip of a knife.

To prepare squid and cuttlefish, slide your fingers inside the sac and detach the body section from the sac. The quill-like bone and head are discarded; cut the tentacles off just below the eye and reserve. Wash thoroughly and proceed. The process with cuttlefish is similar, although you also need to extract the cuttle bone.

Preparing octopus is a bit of an epic journey. You need to cut off the tentacles in front of the eyes as for squid, then cut the head part from the body sac at the round openings in the body, discarding the head. Turn the body inside out, pulling away and discarding the insides. The bone-like lengths of cartilage need to be removed from the body and discarded. Transfer the octopus to a saucepan of salted water, bring to the boil and simmer gently for 45 minutes.

smoking fish and shellfish at home

A form of smoking that lies somewhere between hot- and cold-smoking is easily achievable by the home cook. This adds a smoky 'veneer' to the outside of the food and is popular in some types of Chinese cooking.

Combine a handful of green oak sawdust (i.e. not dried, or it may catch fire) and a handful of black tea leaves. Line a wok with foil, spread out the sawdust mixture and place over a moderate heat. Cover the wok and leave for about 10 minutes, or until it starts to smoke.

Place whatever you are smoking on a rack over the smoke, replace the lid and leave for 10–15 minutes, turning once. You need to ensure the smoke does not become too intense or tarry, a function of the heat.

The food will be raw and still require cooking, but will now be tinged with a smoky flavour.

basic methods of cooking fish and shellfish

While there is a host of classic recipes, my own preference is for simplicity when it comes to fish. Lightly grilled, steamed or sautéed, it can be sea bass, tuna, cod or sole. To serve, spring greens, combined with ginger, soy sauce, lemon grass and sesame oil, perhaps, for the sea bass; a powerful salsa verde of green herbs, chopped anchovies and gherkins and good fruity olive oil for the tuna; the cod might have sun-dried tomatoes, some steamed new potatoes and more olive oil. And the sole? Something classic like lots of butter and capers.

BOILING: generally only used for soups and stews, this has the advantage of extracting the most flavour. However, care must be taken to ensure the fish is not overcooked. Fish bones, if they are

cooked too long (more than 20 minutes), tend towards glue in flavour and texture.

FRYING: gently in clarified butter or olive oil is great for fillets and extremely quick. Deep-frying in batter is ideal if you like fish and chips, otherwise fish like anchovies and whitebait are done in seconds.

POACHING: often in a court-bouillon, water with added flavourings and lemon juice, wine or vinegar, but it's hard to beat well-salted water. It should be done at no more than a gentle simmer.

STEAMING: much used in China, this works best when the fish is flavoured with aromatics like

ginger, coriander, spring onion, soy sauce, sesame oil and chilli. Put the fish on a lightly oiled plate in a steamer and cook until done.

BAKING OR ROASTING: this is one of the most versatile ways of cooking fish. In a really hot oven you can crisp up the skin on certain fish like cod and sea bass. In a cooler oven, bake them with a whole range of herbs and vegetables, with a little stock, a little butter or olive oil – the variations really are endless.

BAKING IN FOIL: this is useful if you lack a fish kettle, as it is a good alternative and helps to keep the fish warm if you are catering for numbers. Beware overcooking,

however, and if taking directly from the fridge you need to add 5 minutes to your cooking time (the foil seals in the cold).

GRILLING: use either a char-grill or barbecue, or a conventional grill. The following apply whichever you are using. For whole fish, cut three slashes in each side through to the backbone, rub with oil and season with salt and pepper. This ensures the centre is cooked when the outside is. It also helps to stop the fish curling up.

For flat fish, lightly oil the skin and season well before grilling. For steaks, lightly oil them and season.

Fillets can really only be done under a conventional grill. Brush with oil, season well and, if you have left the skin on, do this side last so that, if your grill is hot enough, the skin will crisp up.

To tell when fish is cooked, take a sharp knife and gently dig into the deepest part of the fish; it should be just opaque and, if being cooked on the bone, should just come away. Beware overcooking and remember that, just like meat, fish should rest in a warm place for a few minutes, when it will go on cooking.

FISH STOCK

Many fish soups suggest using fish stock. It is worth learning from the Chinese on this one – they never use fish stock, relying instead on a light chicken stock. It is less glutinous, provides more body and complements the sweet sea taste of fish. The exception is stock made from roasted shellfish bones which normally tastes intensely and deliciously sweet.

WHOLESALE FISH MARKETS

These are fascinating places, as much for the human interaction as for the fish. Northern France, Spain, Italy, the west coast of Scotland, Japan, Singapore, India are all places where I have visited fish markets and all, without exception, have been fascinating, particularly Tokyo.

This is the largest market in the world for selling tuna. Fish is not simply sold, but graded, down to different body parts of the different species of tuna, the fatty belly being much prized. From sole and plaice to sea urchin and tuna, from cockles the size of feet to salmon roe at £5 a half-kilo tub. The sole was two feet long, the monkfish were still flapping – indeed about half the fish were still alive. Some were even sold in water in a plastic bag blown up with compressed air so it remained that way.

I watched two men filleting a tuna, not an easy task given its size, but they made it look that way. With enormous metre-long knives and saws, they reduced this monster of the sea to four exquisite fillets – later, the stallholder said, to be cut up for customers. He had 12 enormous fillets in his fridge, all at different prices, and I started on the process of trying to understand why. Quality, he kept saying, it is all to do with quality. I stared at the fillets none the wiser; they all looked the same. Two stalls down the same process was being repeated, this time with frozen tuna and an enormous bandsaw – not nearly as attractive. The Japanese do not have quite the same aversion to frozen fish as some of us Westerners might have. Tuna, or *maguro* in Japanese, comes in four grades for the sushi chef: *akami*, *chutoro*, *toro* and *otoro*. The differences are a reflection of quality and overall mouth-feel.

Breakfast down by Tokyo's fish market is one of two things, sushi or noodles. If you are in any doubt as to what sushi is all about, this must be one of the best places to buy it. Tokyo is the home of sushi; it was invented here and the most problematic ingredient, the fish, really doesn't get much fresher than this.

directory

UK seasons for fish:

BRILL - January to March

CLAMS - all year

COD - September to February

CRAB - April to June

DOVER SOLE - July to February

GREY MULLET - July to February

HADDOCK - May to February

HAKE - June to February

HALIBUT - July to April

HERRING - June to February

JOHN DORY - January to March

LANGOUSTINES - all year

LEMON SOLE - January to April

LOBSTER - April to September

MACKEREL - November to June

MONKFISH - all year

MUSSELS - September to December, but now farmed, so all year

OYSTERS - September to April

PLAICE - July to January

PRAWNS - all year

RED MULLET - July to September

SALMON - April to August

SARDINES - June to August

SCALLOPS - December to March

SEA BASS - July to December, but now also farmed, so all year

SEA BREAM - June to December

SEA TROUT - March to July

SKATE - September to February

SQUID - May to October

TUNA - all year

TURBOT - August to February

Mail-ordering fish is becoming an increasingly popular route, particularly for those inland. Try Brown and Forest (01458 251520) for smoked eel and salmon; potted Morecambe bay shrimps from Bob Baxter (01524 410910); oysters from Seasalter Shellfish (01227 272003), Loch Fyne Oysters (01499 600264) and Butley Orford Oysterage (01394 450277). Merchand le Franc (0870 900 2900) do fresh fish as well as caviar, and Clark Trading (0800 731 6430) do caviar but not fresh fish; H Forman and Son (020 8985 0378) for smoked salmon.

I buy most of my fish from Steve Hatt (020 7226 3963), Cecil and Co (020 7700 5738), Harrods (020 7730 1234) or Fish! (020 7407 3801) – the last two happily deliver.

fish and shellfish recipes

cracked crab

serves 4

4 small-to-medium-sized crabs
salt
Mayonnaise (see page 198)
salt and pepper
good bread, to serve

*For me there is no finer shellfish...
even lobster fails to excite me as
much as crab... a delicious, heady,
sweet and meaty beast that is
supper in itself. Home-made
mayonnaise is a must, and perhaps
some saladings. Chips add to the
feast, but they are not really
necessary, good bread is sufficient.*

1 If you are cooking your own
crab, bring a large pan of well
salted water to a rolling boil, drop
the crabs in and bring back to the
boil. About 15 minutes is sufficient
for a medium-sized crab; 20 if
they are particularly large. Remove
and allow to cool.

2 Crack the crabs: grip both sides
of the body and, with the crab
vertical, bring it down sharply on a
hard surface; the body should
come away from the shell. Remove
the unappetizing lady's fingers (the
green-tinged, okra-shaped strands
at the front) and scoop out the
brown meat from the shell.
Remove the claws and legs and
crack open sufficiently to allow
you to prise them open with your
fingers. Cut the main body part in
half with a sharp knife and, using
the handle of a teaspoon or
something similarly narrow, scoop
out the copious white meat
contained therein.

3 Serve each crab on a plate with
the mayonnaise, salt and pepper,
and some good bread. Finger
bowls and nice linen napkins are
de rigueur.

poached hake,
fennel and broad bean salad with aïoli

serves 4

2 heads of fennel
4 tablespoons olive oil
salt and pepper
400 g (14 oz) frozen broad beans
1 hake, cleaned and trimmed, about
   1 kg (2¹/₄ lb)

FOR THE AÏOLI:
2 fat garlic cloves, bashed
2 egg yolks
300 ml (¹/₂ pint) sunflower oil)
juice of 1 lemon

The Portuguese eat hake all the time, but we seem to ignore it – which is a shame, as it is a wonderfully succulent fish and surprisingly inexpensive. It takes to strong flavours amazingly well, particularly that of garlic. By all means use fresh broad beans if you can get them, but frozen broad beans and peas are both extremely good.

1   Cut the fennel into thin slices. In a saucepan, combine these with the olive oil and some salt and pepper. Simmer over a gentle heat, covered, until tender. Blanch the broad beans in boiling salted water for 2 minutes and remove the grey skins. Add the beans to the fennel, cover and set aside.

2   Make the aïoli: finely chop the garlic and mash together with a little sea salt to form a paste – the easiest way to do this is to use the side of a large-bladed knife, rocking it back and forth. Place the egg yolks in a bowl and incorporate the garlic paste. Add the oil, drop by drop initially, until the mixture emulsifies and forms a thick heavy paste. At this point you can increase the stream of oil to a steady trickle. About halfway through adding the oil, add a little of the lemon juice to loosen the mixture. Once all the oil is incorporated, adjust the seasoning and add more lemon juice if appropriate.

3   Poach the hake in lots of gently simmering well-salted water until cooked (the flesh flakes readily when forked), which will take about 10–12 minutes, but test towards the end.

4   Gently reheat the fennel and broad bean salad while you are carving up the fish. Serve the fish with the salad and a generous scoop of the aïoli.

mixed ceviche

serves 4

225 g (8 oz) salmon fillets

225 g (8 oz) John Dory, brill or
   turbot fillets

225 g (8 oz) mackerel fillets

juice and zest of 4 limes

juice and zest of 2 lemons

juice of 1 orange

1 tablespoon white wine vinegar

300 g (10 1/2 oz) unpeeled potatoes
   (preferably a waxy salad variety,
   like Charlotte, pink fir apple or la
   ratte), sliced into 5-mm (1/4 -inch)
   thick discs

salt and pepper

about 5 tablespoons extra-virgin
   olive oil

bunch of chives, finely chopped

4 handfuls of mixed salad leaves

Popular in South America, ceviche
(also spelt seviche*) is a way of
preparing fish so it is 'cooked', or
cured, in lime or lemon juice, or a
mixture of the two, and seasoned
with salt and rather more pepper or
chilli. What follows is a suggestion
rather than a strict recipe. Serve it
with slices of tomato, roasted red
peppers, hard-boiled eggs, crispy
salad leaves and bread for mopping
up the juices.*

1 Well ahead, ideally the day
before: cut the fish into strips
about 2 cm (3/4 inch) thick and
place in a bowl. Sprinkle with the
juice and zest from the limes,
lemons and orange, together with
the vinegar. Cover and refrigerate
for 6 hours, or preferably
overnight.

2 Blanch the potatoes in boiling
salted water until just tender, drain
and refresh in cold water, but try
to keep them slightly warm.

3 Pile the potato slices in the
centre of 4 plates. Drizzle over a
little olive oil and season with salt
and pepper.

4 Strain the fish, reserving the
citrus juices, and scatter the pieces
around the potatoes. Sprinkle over
the chives and top with the salad
leaves.

5 Combine a dessertspoon of the
reserved citrus juices with 3
tablespoons of olive oil, season
with salt and pepper and pour
over the salad leaves to serve.

char-grilled black bream
and Mediterranean vegetables with parsley pesto

serves 4

2 red peppers
2 aubergines
2 courgettes
1 red onion
olive oil, for brushing
4 bream, cleaned but scales left
    on, each about 275 g (10 oz)
1 lemon , to serve

FOR THE PARSLEY PESTO:
4 tablespoons chopped parsley
2 garlic cloves, finely chopped
1 tablespoon pine nuts
115 ml (4 fl oz) olive oil
3 tablespoons grated Parmesan
2 tablespoons grated Pecorino

1 Put the peppers on a barbecue or grill and cook until well blackened all over. Transfer to a bowl (keeping the grill or barbecue on), cover with cling-film and set aside.

2 Trim and slice the aubergine, courgettes and red onion into 1-cm (1/2-inch) slices. Coat lightly with olive oil and grill until golden brown. Transfer to a bowl (again keeping the grill or barbecue on) and set aside.

3 Make the parsley pesto: combine the parsley with the garlic and pine nuts in a food processor or blender. Blitz, drizzling in the olive oil as you do until you have a thick paste. Transfer to a bowl and stir in the cheeses. You may need more oil if the mixture is too thick.

4 Grill the fish for 5 to 7 minutes on each side, until cooked through.

5 Serve the fish with the vegetables, a drizzle of pesto and a lemon quarter.

grilled John Dory, minted couscous and harissa

serves 4

1 teaspoon harissa
2 tomatoes, finely chopped
100 g (3 1/2 oz) green olives, stoned
4 John Dory
olive oil, for brushing

FOR THE MINTED COUSCOUS:
250 g (9 oz) precooked couscous
juice of 1/2 lemon
 4 tablespoons extra-virgin olive oil
salt and pepper
1/2 cucumber, skinned, deseeded
    and finely chopped
6 radishes, finely chopped
1 courgette, finely chopped
3 tablespoons finely chopped mint

If the only fish you can get are larger than single-portion specimens, buy 2 and cut them across through the backbone to make 2 portions.

1 First make the minted couscous: combine the couscous with an equal volume of boiling water and set aside for 5 minutes. Fluff up with a fork and add lemon juice, olive oil and salt and pepper to taste. Stir in the cucumber, radishes, courgette and mint and set aside.

2 In a another bowl, combine the harissa with the tomatoes and olives, season with salt and pepper and set aside. Preheat a hot grill.

3 Trim the fish of their heads and the spikes around the sides. Lightly coat the fish with olive oil and season them inside and out with salt and pepper. Grill for 4 to 5 minutes on each side.

4 Serve the fish with the couscous and harissa.

escalopes of salmon
with cream sauce and herb salad

serves 4

1 tablespoon finely chopped shallots
1 tablespoon finely diced button
    mushrooms
2 glasses of dry vermouth
2 tablespoons chicken stock
100 ml (3½ fl oz) double cream
4 salmon escalopes, each about
    250 g (9 oz)
olive oil, for brushing
salt and pepper
handful of parsley
handful of chives
handful of dill
big handful of sorrel

Sorrel is essential in this recipe, an adaptation of a classic dish from the Loire, where any freshwater fish is teamed with sorrel. The lemony tang of the sorrel is made for salmon, and what better way to celebrate summer. If you can get hold of sea trout, it is even better.

1 Combine the shallots, mushrooms and vermouth in a small saucepan and boil to reduce until almost all the liquid has evaporated. Add the chicken stock, boil for 1 minute and then add the cream. Continue cooking over a gentle heat until syrupy and then set aside. This can be done in advance.

2 Preheat a hot grill. Lightly brush the salmon with olive oil, pat with kitchen paper to remove the excess and season well with salt and pepper. Grill for 3 minutes on each side, or until cooked, and keep warm.

3 Roughly chop the herbs and toss them together, seasoning them well. Distribute on 4 hot plates. Place the salmon on top, reheat the cream sauce and pour over each serving.

Variations:
Other ways with grilled salmon include combining it in a warmed baguette with sun-dried tomatoes, salad, capers, the best extra-virgin olive oil you have, and a squeeze of lemon juice. Alternatively, toss some just-cooked hot salmon, gently flaked, into a salad of salted cucumber, skinned and deseeded tomatoes, basil, mint, olive oil and a few tablespoons of yoghurt.

Parmesan-crusted sardines,

summer salad and fresh tomato relish

serves 4–6

1 kg (2¼ lb) sardines
salt and pepper
5 tablespoons breadcrumbs
3 dessertspoons grated Parmesan
    cheese
small saucer of milk
plain flour, for coating
2 eggs, lightly beaten
1–2 lemon(s), quartered, to serve
oil, for frying

FOR THE FRESH TOMATO RELISH:
1 teaspoon black mustard seeds
juice of 1 lime
4 tomatoes, deseeded and diced
1 avocado, stoned and diced
about 3–4 tablespoons extra-virgin
    olive oil

FOR THE SUMMER SALAD:
4 handfuls of mixed summer salad
    leaves
1 small shallot, finely chopped
2 dessertspoons pine nuts
bunch of parsley, separated into
    small sprigs
4 tablespoons extra-virgin olive oil

1 Combine the mustard seeds and lime juice for the tomato relish and set aside.

2 Insert a sharp knife behind the head of each fish, cut down to the backbone and then work the blade towards the tail along the backbone to release a fillet. Turn the fish over and repeat. Cut the thin flesh off the bottom of the belly.

3 Wash each fillet carefully, pat dry and season with salt and pepper. Combine the breadcrumbs and Parmesan in a shallow bowl. Dip each of the fillets in the milk, then in the flour and then in the egg. Roll them in the breadcrumbs and Parmesan, gently pressing so each fillet picks up as much of the mixture as possible.

4 Make the fresh tomato relish: combine the tomatoes and avocado with the mustard seed mixture and enough olive oil to bind. Season with salt and pepper.

5 Make the summer salad: combine the salad leaves with the shallot, pine nuts, parsley, salt and pepper and the olive oil. Toss well to coat.

6 Shallow-fry the sardines in hot oil until they are crisp and serve on top of the salad leaves, with a dollop of the tomato relish and a lemon quarter.

grilled tuna fish *with salsa verde*

Swordfish steaks also work well with this treatment.

serves 4

4 tuna steaks, each about
    200 g (7 oz)
olive oil, for brushing
1 lemon, quartered, to serve

FOR THE SALSA VERDE:
1 garlic clove
salt and pepper
bunch of flat-leaf parsley, chopped
1 spring onion, finely chopped
2 anchovy fillets, finely chopped
1 teaspoon Dijon mustard
1 dessertspoon capers
about 4 tablespoons olive oil

1 Preheat a hot grill.

2 Make the salsa verde: finely chop the garlic and crush it with a little salt. Work all the ingredients except the oil in a mortar with a pestle until they form a rough paste. Whisk in the olive oil (you may need a little more) until the sauce has a thick consistency. Adjust the seasoning.

3 Lightly brush the tuna with olive oil, season well with salt and pepper and grill for 2 minutes each side.

4 Serve each tuna steak with a generous spoonful of the salsa and a lemon quarter.

Variations:

Other things to do with tuna steaks: cook an extra steak and make it into a salad niçoise; using fresh tuna is the difference between heaven and hell.

Sear the steaks and serve with a rice noodle salad: cook the noodles according to the packet instructions, drain and toss with lots of roughly chopped coriander, sliced spring onions, toasted sesame seeds, grated zest and juice of 1 lime, a dessertspoon of toasted sesame seed oil, 2 tablespoons of vegetable oil, a dash each of soy sauce and Tabasco sauce (rather more soy than Tabasco, chilli lovers can always add more).

Serve grilled tuna with a rough guacamole: rather than mash everything up, make a salsa of roughly chopped, deseeded tomatoes, chopped avocado and cucumber, Tabasco sauce, the juice and zest of 1 lime, chopped coriander with vegetable oil to combine. Serve with some lemon juice and olive oil.

meat, poultry and game

'*Long ago in Burgundy, when we ate the Sunday roast of beef or lamb, Madame Bonamour always put a big spoonful of this hot juice into the salad just before she stirred it. We liked it, especially if the bowl held escarole and what we rather indelicately called* pisse-en-lit.'

M. F. K. FISHER, *The Art of Eating*

'*A chicken should taste like chicken and be so good in itself that it is an absolute delight to eat as a perfectly plain, buttery roast, sauté, or grill.*'

SIMONE BECK, LOUISETTE BERTHOLLE and JULIA CHILD, *Mastering the Art of French Cooking*

meat

My grandmother taught me about meat. Her roast beef was incredible, always perfectly cooked, rare in the middle, and invariably served with good, sticky gravy and the crispiest roast potatoes. Her meat came from a butcher in nearby Sligo, who was expensive, but she never shopped elsewhere. For a woman as frugal as she – even paper bags were saved – it seems extraordinary that she would be seemingly extravagant in her purchase of food. If you want good meat, she once said to me, then be prepared to pay for it.

Do not be under any illusions, meat is often not what it seems. More than 50 per cent of all beef, for example, comes from old dairy-herd cattle, beasts designed to produce milk and lots of it, not to turn into the most succulent *côte de boeuf*. The market pays for weight and a whole cocktail of chemicals assists in this matter. A salami can contain a concoction of meats from various sources, as well as a host of other ingredients, when all you think you are buying is pork. Ham may say 'no added water', but legally it can have up to 10 per cent of its weight added

These are ingredients that range in quality from the sublime to the frankly ridiculous. Feast on a slow-growing breed of chicken that has led an outdoor 'farmyard' life and compare it with something raised at speed in a cage on pellets – there simply is no comparison. The same goes for genuine Aberdeen Angus beef, raised on lush pasture in Scotland and matured for a good three weeks after slaughter as opposed to one of the inferior breeds raised partially on an intensive feed and hung for only 10 days after slaughter. The former has a full-bodied, rounded taste and texture that cannot be equalled. Game that is wild – a great deal of it is not – is an uncertain

commodity, but then that is part of its appeal. The sedentary farmed specimen, however, fed pellets in a risk-free enclosure, cannot be compared with a bird that has flown for its life. Sad, perhaps, that it didn't make it, but then that's supper for you.

There has been more control, regulation and legislation in the supply of meat, poultry and game than in any other area of food, yet little of that information is passed on to us poor consumers. A good supplier is worth their weight (have you ever met a skinny butcher?) in gold. Stick by them and encourage as well as criticize; they are generally fonts of knowledge.

in water before the label has to tell you. Select an Aberdeen Angus steak in a UK restaurant and the beast from which it comes may well never have been in Scotland, let alone Aberdeenshire, and certainly may not have come from Aberdeen Angus stock – but the restaurant is not breaking the law. The public think of farms; the industry of 'production units', with the animals simply 'a commodity'.

However, the situation is improving and, ironically, a lot of that is due to the various food scares to have hit the industry in recent years, particularly in the UK, but also in Belgium and France. Concern over welfare, a growing suspicion over animal foodstuffs and the use of chemicals, research into stress in animals prior to slaughter, better slaughtering techniques and a better understanding of the need for maturing have all led to better meat. Additionally, a recognition that meat should not be eaten too often has led to a less-but-better approach, coupled with a growing awareness that the cheap-meat post-war policy has created a distorted market. Even when buying expensive meat, its price in real terms has fallen since the war.

Fast modern production may strip the animal in question of any dignity; it has also removed fat, for which read texture and flavour, and encouraged the idea of young and immature meat, which means it can taste of little.

The backlash against lean industrially produced meat is palpable, however. All over Europe the inexorable rise of the supermarket is being stunted by local markets, small producers with websites and a mail-order service. In Spain and France, local markets persist; in the Britain they are re-emerging, together with mail-order suppliers, as small but strong and appealing alternatives.

what makes good meat?

Meat cannot be better than feed and breed, husbandry and slaughter, maturation and butchery. How do you make sure all of these characteristics are correctly controlled? You cannot, which is why you have to pay somebody to do that for you. That somebody is a good butcher and every time you buy a piece of meat you buy his (or occasionally her) knowledge and expertise.

Provenance

Whether you buy from a supermarket or an independent butcher, provenance is the first

51

characteristic to look for. Ideally, the label should specify the farmer, but in the case of lamb bought in May, for example, the answer might be from the West Country. If the information on offer is evasive, the buying policy is almost certainly centred on price, in which case the meat might have come from anywhere. In order for a butcher to know about his meat, he should ultimately know the person who has raised it. Attitude is all when it comes to animals.

With beef you want meat from beef-suckler herds – that is, those designed to produce beef, not ex-dairy animals. With lamb, you want to know is it upland, lowland or marshland (see below), and, particularly with pork, the animal should be an older breed, or at least one that has not been designed to produce fatless meat.

Husbandry

Feed is crucial, but also general living conditions, as well as weather – beef cattle from Scotland tend to have a marbling of fat as insulation, whereas cattle from warm southern mainland Europe tend to be devoid of fat, and consequently lean, less succulent and lighter in flavour.

One of the inherent flaws in the meat industry is that the final price paid for a carcass has to do with three attributes: weight, muscle and fat conformation… as yet nothing to do with the eating quality is taken into consideration – so even specimens perfect in all three judged attributes can taste of nothing. If the meat is sold on to the market there is no inherent reason why a farmer should take any interest in improving the quality of the meat he is rearing, beyond a certain base level.

If, on the other hand, he joins one of the many schemes aimed at marketing the meat as being superior, the extra revenue received will usually feed through to him and, in most cases, he has to satisfy certain criteria set down by the scheme. Having said this,

there are certain schemes – and the supermarkets are particularly guilty of involvement in this – in existence that specify very little. You need to read the fine print carefully.

Handling

Animals used to be slaughtered close to where they had been raised, but due to a number of factors, including European standardization and economics, the number of slaughterhouses has decreased substantially and their size increased. This means longer journey times for the animals and the need to handle larger numbers. How that handling is done affects the eating quality of the meat, as stress tends to toughen the muscles. Abattoirs are hardly pleasant places, but the differences

between a good one and a bad one are immense. Once the beast has been slaughtered, its handling again affects the final flavour and texture. How the meat is chilled, over what period and with what intensity will all influence its eating quality.

At this stage, meat is delivered to the butcher and they then decide how long it will be hung, in what conditions and also how the carcass will be divided. There are many ways to butcher a carcass. The UK traditionally cut across the muscle, mainland Europe along the muscle, and the general move has been to follow mainland Europe. Keeping the muscle intact where possible means that there is less wastage and it seems to produce more tender meat.

how to spot a good butcher

The state of the shop says a great deal about the general attitude of the butcher. It should look and smell clean, with a tidy display of meat and a respectful attitude to the stock. Meat being thrown about doesn't bode well. Independent butchers have had to diversify, so look at what else is on offer... Organic eggs? Good

cheese? A variety of different condiments, perhaps? They will also tend to make their own sausages and make up marinades for chicken breasts, pork chops and beef steaks. Cooked dishes may also be part of their range. This may be a combination of the traditional French roles of *charcuterie* and *boucherie*, but things have changed. Economics may drive the change, but how it is engineered relies on the attitude of the butcher. If he knows how to hang beef properly, he probably knows how to make a decent sausage.

marbling

Good meat should have a marbling of fat running evenly through it; these small veinings of fat, when heated, will baste and

flavour the meat. Spreading dripping on bread may seem old-fashioned and be out of favour, but the flavour is unparalleled. Meat should be neither too light nor too dark in colour, although well-hung beef and, certainly, mutton start to become quite intense in flavour. Excessive moisture is to be avoided, as is flabbiness. As for smell, like fresh fish, good meat has almost no smell at all.

why meat is hung or aged

During ageing, the natural enzymes in the meat turn from their normal job of digesting proteins so they can be absorbed by the cells to attacking the cells themselves. Flavour changes are

attributed to the processing of the proteins, which separate out into amino acids that are thought to have a stronger flavour. Some of the activity also starts to break the meat down, making it more tender.

how much to spend?

If you are looking for inexpensive meat, the supermarket is easily the best source. Their buying power is immense and an independent butcher trying to compete is on a hiding to nothing. What you get, however, is the end-product of a streamlined, fairly automated system, with little room for variation. Go to an independent butcher and the beef carcass may have been hung for a day or two longer than usual because the butcher decided it needed it. The pork chop on sale may have a slab of extra fat round the side, but the butcher felt it was worth putting up with this because the marbling through the meat was so good.

If you want steak every time you eat beef, be prepared to pay for it. Alternatively, go for a cheaper cut every now and then; skirt, or *onglet* as it is called in France, offers superb eating and costs a fraction of the price of

steak. Lamb shanks require slow cooking, but they are full of flavour and cost very little; the same can be said of ham hocks. As a general rule, meat from those parts of the animal that work the hardest (such as legs, shoulders and feet) tend to require slower cooking, but the effort required is repaid in the lower cost. Cuts from where there is little activity, along the back of the animal in particular, tend to require shorter cooking. Meat is muscle, and

where the muscle has worked hard it needs slow careful cooking.

General rules apply for all meats: the more expensive, tender cuts require brief cooking, while the cheaper, coarser cuts need long braising and stewing. If you are roasting, it is better to do so on the bone; it lends a sweetness and succulence. It is crucial that after frying, grilling or roasting the meat is allowed to rest in a warm place. This produces a juicier result and allows the muscle structure to relax

to ensure more tender eating. A large joint of beef might need 20–30 minutes, a steak or chop 5–10 minutes resting. Even barbecued food benefits from being left for 5 minutes.

storing meat

If you are buying meat from a supermarket in sealed plastic containers, simply transfer it to the fridge when you get home. If you have bought loose-packed meat, remove it from the packaging and pat it dry, place on a plate, cover loosely with cling-film or foil and transfer to the fridge. It is important that no juices from the meat fall on to other ingredients, which is why it is better to keep raw meat at the bottom of the fridge. How long you keep it depends on what it is. Offal, mince and sausages should ideally be used on the day of purchase, other meats will keep for two to three days.

how to tell if meat is done

Recipes will specify a time, but this is really only a guide, a help to planning. Regardless of whether you are roasting a large joint or grilling a steak, gently prod the meat with your fingers. You want it to give slightly, but then bounce back.

A French chef once made me do the following: with your fingers, touch your cheek (underdone), touch your forehead (overdone), touch the end of your nose (perfectly done, for which read rare or pink). It can take a few prods and bit of experience, but I've cooked meat on this basis ever since and been perfectly happy with the result every time.

beef

It is impossible to discuss beef and not refer to BSE, yet rather than get tied up in the scientific, medical and political aspects, I would like to focus on the positive. For all the augments raised (few of which are genuinely over), what has emerged is a meat industry transformed from secrecy, some distinctly shady practices and a complete lack of traceability, to one which is now much more tightiy regulated, has traceability and in which many of the less savoury aspects have either been eliminated, or made a great deal more difficult.

I ate beef throughout the crisis, fed my family on it and had not one sleepless night. However, my beef comes via a butcher in whom I have complete trust, from a farm he knows and it is genuine Aberdeen Angus. I reckoned the risk was minimal and far less significant than that posed by eating battery chicken.

A well-hung side of beef is not a pretty sight, which is one reason, I suspect, why supermarkets don't like well-matured beef. The carcass loses moisture as it hangs, the meat drying out and becoming dark in colour. The fat, too, is creamy white rather than pale white – even yellow if it is grass-fed; unappetizing unless you know that it is likely to convert into the most delicious succulent meat when cooked. It is far better to have the bright red and moist-looking immature meat which is what we tend to think of when we think of beef.

Supermarket and high-street practice is to hang beef for between seven and 10 days, although some supermarkets have it on the shelf within an even shorter timespan. Around 21 days is fairly optimal, but it depends a little on the carcass and the weather.

What is the difference between 'beef' as labelled in a supermarket and so-called 'superior' or 'premium-grade' beef? In general 'beef' is likely to be ex-dairy herd Holstein or Friesian, breeds prized for their milk-producing ability, not for their eatability. This meat

is also likely to have been matured for less time. As for the superior grades, it is as well to look at exactly what is being claimed. Many of these schemes are initiated by the supermarkets themselves and either self-policed, or administered by a third party. The supermarket, however, is often paying the said agency, so it is quite a cosy relationship. The meat may be perfectly edible, but not many of these schemes actually offer anything in terms of superior eating quality. And, if the supermarket is paying, chances are you're paying the supermarket.

What to look for when you buy beef

A distinct and generous marbling of fat that should be off-white rather than pure white. The colour of the meat should be a dull red, nothing too vibrant. It should be moist but not shiny, and it should look plump and healthy, not tired or sunken.

veal

You cannot have milk without veal, a fact that is conveniently overlooked by too many people. If you want the females for milking, you have to address the fact that males inevitably form a significant proportion of births. If the males are not raised for meat, they are slaughtered for nothing, which is incredibly wasteful. A lot of this is to do with our perception that rearing veal is cruel.

What is outrageous is the demand for pale tasteless veal, which, in turn, drives the crated system we have all come to abhor – animals kept in restricted cages, fed a non-roughage diet and promptly slaughtered. There is a growing production of what is often called 'pink' veal, a reflection of the colour the meat picks up from its diet of mother's milk, grass and hay.

Veal should be seen in the same way as lamb, a baby version of the meat; perhaps 'calf' would be a better term. The calf is kept with its mother to suckle as it would do normally and also has access, as it grows, to other natural foodstuffs like hay. It is generally slaughtered at about the same time that it naturally starts to drift away from the mother. The analogy with lamb is fairly obvious, although in the UK the general public seems curiously resistant to this concept.

What to look for when you buy veal

Look for some marbling, although because of the age of the beast this is unlikely to be developed. A moist clammy surface is to be avoided and is, unfortunately, all too common. Veal varies hugely in colour from very light pink through to something quite dark. Diet influences the colour of veal enormously, as does husbandry and age. Pale veal is a function of fashion and not really to be encouraged; a good pink colouring suggests a healthy diet and lifestyle.

lamb

While hardly the most intelligent of animals, sheep have resolutely refused to be farmed intensively. In addition, it is more effective and cheaper to leave them out of doors most of the year, so they tend to lead a fairly free-range life, particularly those raised on uplands, where the use of fertilizers is kept to a minimum. Sheep tend to reflect their diet, so those grazed on marshland, for example, tend to pick up a salty tang, while those that graze on wild grasses and moorland gain a sweetness.

Sheep give birth once a year and, although some manipulation goes on to try and breed them out of season, the vast bulk follow the weather: starting in the spring we get lamb from the south-west and, as the year progresses, from further north, reaching Scotland towards the end of the summer. There is little incentive for farmers to grow lamb beyond one year, when it begins to develop a stronger flavour (and later becomes mutton), as the price consumers are prepared to pay does not outweigh the cost of keeping them. Far easier to sell them as lambs.

Rare-breed lamb, Romney Marsh or Soay, for example, is making a small impact on the market. Lamb is naturally quite highly flavoured anyway, so I am not entirely sure the breed is as significant as the diet. Many older breeds were developed as they could live in difficult highland or lowland conditions, developing meat which is darker and stronger. I prefer pink delicate lamb, but it is all a matter of taste.

What to look for when you buy lamb

The meat should have a good pink hue, with an off-white fat covering. There is a trend towards reduced fat covering and, undoubtedly, some lamb can have too much fat, but a great deal of it melts in the cooking and can be left behind in

the pan, its role of keeping the meat moist fully accomplished.

What about imported lamb?

In the UK this means New Zealand lamb, a product much favoured by catering butchers for its uniformity of size, even cooking and reliable – if slightly under-developed – flavour.

pork

Of all the meat we eat, it is the humble pig that has suffered the most from intensive farming and, as a consequence, so have we. Pork can be sweet and succulent, full-flavoured and with a delicious rounded texture. No wonder so many class it as a desert-island meat. Where would we be without pancetta, sausages, salami, pâtés

and ham, let alone roast pork and crackling? The fat was successfully bred out of the pig in the mistaken belief that this was what we wanted. We don't, we like fat. From it we get flavour and succulence – lip-smackingly juicy succulence – and the pig gets to have a good time too. It was born to root about and exercise, and in return its meat has started to taste again.

What is free-range pork?

Well, it all depends on the farmer... The idea is that the pigs live outdoors with shelter provided in mini-Nissen huts that get moved around so the pig has fresh ground to explore. Often the piglets are weaned from the mother and moved indoors to start their fattening process, returning to the outdoors later on. In reality, some farmers do this better than others, and the consumer has no way of telling other than through experience. In practice, however, those that operate this system well and produce pork that eats well, are more likely to be able to charge a premium, so there is an incentive. As a general rule, free-range or outdoor pork has a

whole lot more flavour and texture than standard pork.

What about organic pork?

This is the business. Not only do the animals have to live and eat organically, there are stringent regulations relating to its diet and husbandry. Banned are all the nasty practices associated with intensively reared pigs. These animals live a life as near to the one they should do and, not surprisingly, produce the kind of meat we all claim to remember from our youth. This is roast pork with serious crackling, loin of pork that tastes gamy and has succulence and texture; this is the pork to make into good old-fashioned coarse terrines; this is the pork that produces bacon which doesn't leach liquid into the frying pan.

It is hard to talk about organic pork without also talking about older breeds, like Gloucestershire Old Spot, Saddleback and Tamworth, for example. These breeds are slower-growing, have more fat, are more suited to outdoor living and, in general, offer a more flavoured, succulent and complex meat.

What to look for when you buy pork

There needs to be a good distribution of marbling in the meat, given modern pork's tendency to dryness. Don't buy anything too white either. Watery, clammy surfaces are to be avoided. Good pork should be quite fatty; it is only modern breeding that has encouraged fat away, something we should try to avoid wherever possible.

How to tell a good sausage

A sausage is only as good as the meat used to make it. I may be a purist, but I have never been keen on flavourings in sausages along the lines of mint or pesto; I'd rather add this element as a mint salsa or pesto dressing. If the sausage is made with good – that is free-range or organic – pork, it will say so. After that, you have to taste and see.

Ask what the other ingredients are. In a processed or industrial sausage, the items will be listed on the side; if water is listed early, you are unlikely to be overly impressed – and if this is followed by polyphosphates, even less so. The latter go in to keep the added water in there.

wild boar

Wild boar is rarely anything of the sort, but a cross-breed of something resembling wild boar and ordinary domesticated pig. I'm not a big fan – I'd rather eat good pork any day – but if you are tempted, the same suggestions as for buying pork or beef also apply here.

offal

Some people love offal – I'm one; others think it is some kind of joke. My list includes most things – sweetbreads, tongue, brain, kidney, liver; I adore them all. Yet you must be sure of your source, as the traces of drugs found in offal are far greater than in muscle meat. Buy it fresh; it should have good colouring and look bright and inviting, not tired and dull. You will probably need to order the likes of sweetbreads and brain, but kidney and liver are usually widely available.

meat products

If you want to be sure about your mince, get the butcher to mince it in front of you. Into the top should go beef steak or, in the case of lamb, a prime cut like leg or shoulder meat cubed; out the bottom comes minced steak or minced lamb. It is an easy area in which to adulterate meat.

With hamburger the same is true; far better to see them being made. In reality, this is unlikely to be the case, so ask. A good hamburger is only minced steak with some seasoning, a little egg to bind, perhaps, and finely chopped onion (the easiest thing in the world to make yourself at home with your hands).

ham and bacon

Both ham and bacon are cured pork, the ham being the hind leg, the bacon being from the back and belly. The curing is either dry, where salt and seasonings are rubbed on to the surface of the meat; or wet, where the meat is immersed in a brine solution. Both processes extract moisture from the meat and the salt helps to preserve it.

Unfortunately, the process that has been used for centuries has been much complicated with modern practices that involve retaining moisture in the meat (more weight equals more money) and using other methods of preserving. There are only two added ingredients necessary – salt and time.

Which ham should I buy?

Buy, if you can, from a specialist certified organic small-scale producer, or ensure your butcher does. Buy cooked ham cut directly off the bone; it is most likely to have been traditionally cured.

Which bacon should I go for in a supermarket?

Look for a bacon that is dry-cured, as it's the closest you will get to old-fashioned bacon and your only chance of achieving something mouth-watering and crispy. You are more likely to find this in good old-fashioned butcher shops, particularly organic ones.

salami

Salami is a mixture of lean and fat meat, cured and chopped to varying degrees of fineness and stuffed into natural casings. The making of salami is both an art and a science. The salt, being the preserving agent, must be accurately judged; the combination of lean and fat meat and how it is chopped provides the texture that can change from one salami to the other.

If you want good salami look for one made in Italy, Spain or France. Just because it says Milano doesn't necessarily mean it comes from that wonderful city. Something which is irregular both in size and in the distribution of lean and fat should look irregular; if it has string, it will have embedded itself slightly in the meat as it dries. It goes without saying that natural casings don't come in squares or oblongs. And be prepared to pay, as good salami is never cheap. By way of sourcing, delicatessens run by enthusiastic owners are easily the best, and ask them to let you taste... a slice of salami costs nothing. If the salami is all wrapped up, ask them to cut one open.

raw hams
Dry-cured and air-dried, these hams are not cooked but eaten raw, usually in wafer-thin slices.

The likes of Parma, Serrano, Bayonne and Speck all have their followers, and with good reason. They are all registered and controlled to ensure a certain standard is maintained. Parma is probably the best-known. My own favourites are San Daniele and Veneto (and Pata Negra from Spain). There are many other hams made throughout Italy; although most are considered to be somewhat more crude, both in flavour and texture, all are excellent.

Next on my own list are the Spanish Serranos, the best of which is, for me, the Jabugo. Others are either classified or in the process of being classified and include Teruel and Guijuelo. These are all of very high quality and worth trying.

Others quality hams to look out for are the French Bayonne and Ardennes, which are both equally good but, in my view, too often cut too thick, and the German Black Forest and Westphalian hams.

poultry

Roast chicken is undoubtedly one of my favourite meals. Golden crispy skin, full-flavoured and succulent meat, the juices from the roasting providing all the gravy that is needed. A little tarragon to add some bite, or maybe some fresh thyme. As a child I would eat white meat, then brown and then attack the bones. These days I do just the same, rolling up my sleeves in anticipation. Some French bread to mop up things at the end and finally the licking of sticky fingers – who cares if it's Sunday lunch, when food is this good there is no need to stand on ceremony.

It's a fine feast, roast chicken, or it can be. It does depend rather a lot on the chicken in question: golden crispy skin, juicy flesh and real bite, a Sunday lunch without compare. Certainly, provided you buy well. Breed, husbandry and diet all play their part. And all cost money – something big business tries its hardest to keep under control. Attempt to fashion a feast from a mass-market bird and not even a three-Michelin-starred chef will succeed. Buy well, however,

and with a lemon, some olive oil or butter and salt and pepper a real feast will be on the table in an hour.

If chicken is first on my list of favourite poultry, guinea fowl follows closely behind, its slight gamy flavour and firm bite welcome characteristics. Widely available in France, it has now made its way on to most supermarket shelves, but still tends to be intensively reared, unless it says otherwise on the label. It has

a slight tendency to dryness and when being roasted, needs constant basting; pot-roasting and poaching are the better routes.

why don't battery birds taste of anything?

Do not underestimate the degree of abuse levelled at the average supermarket chicken. I know people in the meat business who will not touch chicken; it's beef, lamb or pork every time. Chronic overcrowding in enormous warehouses and no daylight, while automatic feeders dispense high-protein feed laced with antibiotics and other disease-preventing drugs, makes for a pretty miserable life for the bird and tasteless meat for the consumer.

That's all right, I hear you say, I buy free-range chickens every time. Sadly, life is not quite that simple. Certain criteria have to be met in order to describe a chicken as free-range. Unfortunately, really free outside access, a grain-based diet and farmyard-style life are not among them. Nor is the breed specified and it is perfectly within the regulations to supply the fast-growing breeds used for straight-forward (or not so straightforward) 'farm' and 'fresh' chickens – meaning fresh from the battery farm – and call them free-range.

Economics reveal a great deal. The cost of the chick is minimal; even the slow-growing breeds are inexpensive. Feed, however, represents the greatest cost and, after that, correcting infection if it occurs, as well as the cost of housing. As a result, the pressure is on to increase the weight of

the chick in the shortest possible time, while handling it as little as possible and giving it the minimum house-room.

All intensively raised poultry runs the risk of being infected with salmonella and campylobacter – another good reason to buy birds that are raised less intensively, and that means looking for something more on the label than simply free-range, as they can also harbour both bugs. As I said above, poultry farming is often a nasty business, so the more information you are given the less likely there is something to hide.

In the UK, I would encourage you to buy certified organic poultry, as not just the feed but the welfare of the bird too is likely to be better.

husbandry, breed and feed

In France, chicken is held in high regard and consequently its production is closely monitored. Much effort has gone into creating brands that use slow-developing birds that are fed a rich grain diet and allowed a more attractive life. Those with names like Bresse, Les Landes and Label Rouge really do taste, have substantial texture and

offer far superior eating. Label Rouge, for example, operates much like the Appellation Contrôlée system for wine, with the breed, feed and time-scale stipulated and farms registered. No wonder that the majority of top London restaurants all source their poultry from France. There are changes afoot in the UK, too, with labels like Label Anglais looking at slower-growing breeds. There is a price differential, which can be as much as a factor of two, but the difference is incredible.

A meat and poultry buyer told me about his visit to a farm producing Poulet de Bresse chickens: 'The birds were almost part of the family, children just hanging around in the trees and fields surrounding the farm buildings. A week before slaughter they were brought into sheds thick with fresh straw and soft music. I just couldn't believe it.'

The most difficult area in which to offer advice comes when you are buying a non-recognized label. Even within categories like 'traditional free-range' or, indeed, 'organic free-range' there can be substantial variation. Paul Grout, meat and poultry buyer at Harvey Nichols in London, offers the

following advice: 'For all the regulations and specifications, the overriding, and often overlooked factor is the relationship between retailer and producer. We are as cost-conscious as the next retailer and customer, but I know that to have a quality chicken costs money, so I am looking for a supplier who produces a bird that majors on flavour and texture, rather than growth ability, and has lived and eaten well.'

In the same way that Mr Grout has to establish a relationship with that supplier, so too does the consumer have to establish some relationship with his or her retailer. Hard to do with a supermarket, but an easy and

pleasant task if you use a butcher. For example, quail at Harvey Nichols come from France, are twice the size of British farmed ones and cost more than twice as much. No doubt some of the cost reflects the fact you are buying your quail in Knightsbridge rather than an out-of-town supermarket, but there is simply no comparison in terms of taste and texture.

What to look for when you buy poultry

CHICKEN: look for 'organic free-range', 'free-range total freedom', or Label Anglais. Otherwise the French chickens, like black and red leg, Les Landes, Bresse and Label

Rouge as above, Janze and Bresse, Cou nu, Rock Cornish. Questions to ask: the breed, lifespan, diet and access to open air. A broiler (the trade term for a battery-reared chicken) takes about 40 days to mature; poulet Les Landes typically takes several months. A poussin is a young or spring chicken and is a perfect size for one person, ideal for catering. Unfortunately they are all intensively reared and rarely taste of anything.

DUCK: much of the domestic (as opposed to wild) duck on sale is raised in intensive systems where diet and general access are as restricted as they are with broiler chickens. It will come as no surprise, then, when what you buy tastes of very little. Look for information – if possible accredited – on the label stating the diet and living conditions.

The mass-market ducks, like Aylesbury or Peking, are quick to mature and again taste of little. A Barbary duck takes nearly twice as long to grow and carries considerably less fat, but this is not necessarily a sign of good eating. The feed is often less than satisfactory. Gressingham and Trelough ducks are modern breeds, gamier in flavour and smaller than an Aylesbury.

Most of what we buy in the shops is not duck at all, but duckling. The change comes about when the bird is 2 months old, when it reaches its second-feather stage. Ducks can get really big, up to 3 kilos is not uncommon. The criticism often levelled at duck is that it is fatty and there is not very much meat. True, it does have a lot of fat, but most of this melts in the cooking and helps to keep the meat moist and full of flavour. As to cost, most of the meat is in the breasts, but if you buy two birds you can feed four from the breast meat, feed two again with a stew

made from the legs and wings, plus you have the added benefit of great stock from the carcasses and if you collect the fat it makes the most fantastic roast potatoes.

GUINEA FOWL: now widely available, again the French birds tend to be superior in taste and texture, but much of the guinea fowl on sale is as intensively reared as battery chicken.

QUAIL: look for French birds, which are larger and are likely to have been fed a superior diet. Ask too about diet, husbandry and rearing time. A quail should take 2 months to mature; many of the quails sold actually live for only five weeks, never see daylight and eat pellets of 'enhanced' feed. This is the case for nearly all UK quail.

SQUAB: this is the bird that used to occupy the dovecotes of large country houses – pigeons, reared specifically for the table on a diet of grain. They are the best of poultry and game combined. Simply roasted (and frequently basted) in a hot oven for 20 minutes and then allowed to rest for 15, they need nothing more than a few sautéed potatoes and

a watercress salad. They are available, but you will need to order them from a good butcher.

TURKEY: although semi-wild in character, turkeys can be bred in much the same way as broiler chickens, densely packed, with medicated feed and little or no outside access. The market for turkeys has developed along the various breeds and breeders. Good examples to look out for include Bronze and Norfolk Black.

GOOSE: a tricky customer, the goose. It refuses to be intensively farmed, becoming frightened and hostile if it is herded and enclosed and, wisely, refuses to have its breeding cycle interfered with. It is in season from October through to January.

By default, it lives a relatively natural existence, but diet and husbandry remain variables to watch for. In part because of its high price (and low meat content), most of the goose available is of a fairly high standard. Keep the fat for even better roast potatoes than those cooked in duck fat, or to make your own confit.

a carcass can stretch, but that is not much use to you if you need to put supper on the table in an hour. You can, of course, always buy a whole bird and portion it yourself in a fairly short time, keeping the carcass and slower–cooking pieces for later.

Where to buy poultry

Brand names on chicken have become increasingly important and you will see equivalent brands in better supermarkets and good butchers. Price is a fair guide: expect to pay twice as much for an older-breed bird as for the basic broiler, rising to three times as much for certain brands. The money will be well spent, providing chicken like it used to taste. Good quail is very hard to find; if you give your butcher notice, he might be able to source French quail. Guinea fowl often comes under the same brand names as chicken. For turkey, duck and goose I would generally favour a butcher over a supermarket and, in the UK, consider mail order (see page 72).

Storage

Unwrap birds, pat dry, place on a clean plate, cover loosely with cling-film and store at the bottom of the fridge, taking care there is nothing underneath on to which juices from the bird might leak. If you buy in sealed packets from the supermarket, you can store them in these. Portion packs are a convenient, time-saving – albeit expensive – way of buying poultry. Generally, however, the chicken used is the basic broiler (although some free-range is available). Most butchers too will sell chicken and duck breasts. In both cases, however, you do pay more (typically 30–40 per cent) than if you are buying a whole bird. In many instances the convenience outweighs the cost. It is all very well listening to stories of how far

Chicken stock – the most useful stock of all

The Chinese use chicken stock all the time, even with fish. Why? Because, provided your chicken is a good one, the stock has a powerful flavour, but one that works with – rather than dominates – other ingredients. Chicken stock is extremely easy to make: put the carcass in a pan and add a roughly chopped onion (no need to peel), a sliced carrot, a chopped celery stalk, a bay leaf, a few sprigs of parsley and thyme, half a dozen black peppercorns. Add water to cover, bring to the boil, skim, turn down the heat and simmer gently for 2–3 hours. Strain, cool and chill the stock. Boil up and re-chill every other day or freeze.

Chicken wings

Butchers are frequently left with wings from trimmed chickens which nobody wants. I adore wings, as the meat is deliciously succulent and, although there is a lot of finger work, a plate of chicken wings that have been marinated (use the marinade on page 85) and roasted makes one of the best mid-week suppers I know, accompanied by a few bottles of ice-cold beer and some kettle crisps.

game

Of the widely available game, partridge is the most versatile and delicious; for me, its sweet moist flesh is one of the highlights of the season. Closely following that is pheasant, and my favourite way with this bird remains the classic Normandy pot-roast with leeks, apples, cream and Calvados, but the same approach in red wine with porcini comes a close second. Mallard, or wild duck (there are others, like teal and widgeon), is in third place. If you have a good game dealer,

woodcock is unforgettable, but not to everybody's taste I realize. Hare, particularly done the Italian way as a rich thick sauce for egg-rich and wide-cut pappardelle, is a winter delight. I don't care for venison, which I find too unpredictable and even when reliable too dry – I'd rather eat beef any day. If you can get good rabbit, it is succulent, delicate and gamy all at the same time.

how wild is the game you are buying?

Whichever of the above you wish to buy, game is one of the hardest ingredients to source. Modern game rearing can involve quite a lot of intervention, so husbandry, feed and breed can be important, with many different combinations leading to widely differing results. You can buy game that tastes of little more than chicken, and game that is strong enough to put the reluctant adventurer off for life.

While some game is at least partly wild, its habitat can vary enormously. Heather and wild grasses perhaps, but also fields of corn laced with pesticides and chemicals. Defining 'wild' causes problems, and increasing amounts

of game are reared in pretty controlled environments where they are allocated feed rather than allowed to hunt for it, or with a mixture of the two.

Game is not uniform in quality. Shooting can often be messy and people miss. They don't use bullets either, but cartridges that contain lead shot – worth considering as you gaze at a row of uniformly beautiful, plastic-wrapped, undamaged partridges. How wild are they? Increasingly not at all. What is emerging is a two-tier market, with farmed or highly managed unhung (or hardly hung) game and a more traditional supply of wild, shot and properly hung game. You tell by looking at it: the former will come neatly wrapped, looking unblemished and uniform; the latter comes every which way, contains shot and can often be partly damaged. Labelling should make it easier for the consumer to tell what it is they are buying, but often game is not even labelled.

hanging game

Hanging game, as with hanging meat, is quite an art. Much depends on the weather and on personal choice. Most birds, like pheasant, grouse and partridge, can be hung for few days or a couple of weeks. The aim is to tenderize the meat and strengthen flavour. You can go too far but, in principle, some hanging is a good idea.

An unhung pheasant, for example, can make for tough and very dull eating. The old school are keen on very 'high' game, which, understandably, is not to everyone's taste. In reality, however, you need to ask for your game to be hung to achieve this state; it is not normally sold like this. If you are given a freshly shot pheasant or grouse, they should be hung from the neck for about a week in a cool, well-ventilated room. If the weather is warm, however, a day or too is probably sufficient. The best way to tell is to smell it; once it starts to give off a slightly sweet, gamy aroma, it is time to get plucking.

Almost all game birds and furred game are hung with the insides intact; this contributes to the overall flavour. The art of hanging is knowing when to stop. Initially, there is a tenderizing as the enzymes in the meat change; as the process continues you get bacterial decomposition, which will eventually leave the meat tasting high. The degree is up to the hangman (or woman).

What to look for when you buy game

It's all very well reading books which tell you to look at beaks, feet and wing-tips, but most of the game we buy is already missing those items and wrapped in plastic. A good game dealer is by far the best route. If buying from supermarkets, you will find there is little or no significant hanging of game, so it tends to be relatively lacking in flavour. Some people do prefer it that way, however.

If you are lucky enough to be able to buy – or are given – game in feather (or fur), you can tell a lot about a bird from its beak, feet and wing feathers (and an animal from its fur and feet, etc.). As more of the creature is removed, it becomes increasingly difficult to tell age and quality, and you need to rely on your dealer. General things to look for in birds include an even colouring and plump and healthy-looking flesh, with no clamminess or moisture. If your intended purchase is wrapped in cling-film, ask for it to be unwrapped. Avoid excessive broken skin, as this is likely to be due to clumsy plucking, but can also suggest a generally sloppy approach. Whether game smells or not is partly dependent on what it is and whether it has been hung, but even well-hung game smells sweet as opposed to rank – and wet-fur aromas are not for me, I'm afraid.

Where to buy game

Supermarkets if you want easy access and mild flavours; otherwise a game dealer, who will be happy to advise and supply to order. Experiment: if you like your game well hung, they will be happy to do it for you. If there is a shoot nearby, it is usually possible to buy direct.

Storage

As for meat and poultry, pat dry, put on a plate and wrap loosely in cling-film.

Preparation

Feathered game is rarely seen in cities, but often in the country the gift of a brace or two of pheasant or partridge brings a smile to some and a look of horror to others. Plucking game is neither difficult nor time consuming, although it

does make a bit of a mess – with feathers flying everywhere. It is best to do it outside, pulling the feathers towards the head; they should come away easily. Make an incision at the base of the throat, reach in and remove the innards – they come out quite cleanly – then cut off the head and feet. Wash, truss and cook – it really is that simple.

Of crucial import is the determination of the age of the birds in question. The main telltale signs are the beak and the feet. In young birds, both are fairly immature and you will find the beak, in particular, soft. No head or feet? Then be suspicious and casserole or braise slowly.

Roasting game

All game lacks fat, so the trick is to keep basting. If I'm roasting a partridge, for example (which takes about 20 minutes), I baste it at least three times, sometimes four. Bacon is often used to cover the breasts but, to my mind, it tends to impart too strong a flavour. Much better to use back fat, or the wrappers from butter. Use a hot oven (220°/425°/Gas 7 or even 230°/450°/Gas 8). Resting is, as ever, vitally important.

Some people roast the birds on a croûte (slice of bread). My own preference is to roast them by themselves; that way you get the gravy. If you want to serve them on a croûte, allow them to rest on one prepared earlier and the juices from the resting bird will then soak into the bread.

Best flavours to accompany game

The traditional ones like watercress, bread sauce, game chips (kettle chips if I'm at home), lentils, cabbage, jellies of autumn fruit, dried fruit and winter roots (parsnips in particular).

some points on various types of game

DUCK: choose from mallard (the most common), widgeon or teal. Mallard can be quite intensively reared, or 'managed', and then released, making it rather fatty and tasteless. These species are all dabbling ducks, feeding on vegetation under the water's surface, so their diet can include mud and this will affect the flavour.

GROUSE: wait until September, as the price will fall and quality improve, and it means the birds will have been hung – an advantage that seems forgotten by those who rush off on 12 August with such gusto. Grouse dines almost exclusively on heather and the meat is strong, with a rich pâté texture. Allow one bird per person.

HARE: there is increasing concern over the scarcity of hare. It cannot be farmed, so it must be wild and its diet is therefore uncertain. In my experience, however, hare is only tricky if you insist on roasting it. When cooked as in the recipe

on page 165, it is certain to be tender and tasty.

PARTRIDGE: the grey-legged variety is favoured over the cruder and larger red-legged or French. Allow one grey per person; a red can feed two, but only just. One of the sweetest-tasting and most approachable of game birds.

PHEASANT: the hen is favoured over the cock and hanging is to be recommended, if not actively encouraged. Pheasant can be particularly dry, so care should be taken when roasting.

RABBIT: farmed rabbits can be, and usually are, raised in the same way as chicken. There is little control – beyond your supplier's judgement – as to the breed, feed and lifestyle. Wild rabbits are unpredictable, part of the challenge being to tell how old they are. In France, where rabbit is highly valued, the farmed rabbits on sale can be extremely good.

SNIPE: pale in colour, their flesh is delicate and rich. One bird per person may suffice as a starter, but for a main course you need to allow two or even three. Like woodcock, they are traditionally roasted with their insides, which melt away to form the sauce.

VENISON: wild venison is quite an unpredictable meat, ranging from utterly delicious to inedible, and I've had my fair share of both. If you want consistency, farmed venison is the better idea. In general, the animals are allowed free rein outdoors, being brought indoors in winter months and fed on root vegetables and hay. British Farm Venison is of a high standard, but watch out for imports, from both New Zealand and eastern Europe, where quality is not as assured. The lack of fat in venison meat means it is tricky to cook, benefiting from marinating and probably best suited to use in stews and pies.

WOODCOCK: these are traditionally cooked complete with their entrails because they are night-feeding and, therefore, 'clean' when shot the following day. They are not to everyone's taste, I realize, but for me they are the ultimate game bird.

WOOD PIGEON: extremely cheap, but quite tricky to cook, these benefit from stuffing and continual basting as the meat tends to dry out. If cooking the breasts only, it is better to poach them in stock rather than roast them.

directory

meat

Top beef breeds to look out for:
Aberdeen Angus: to be called Aberdeen Angus, the steer can be cross-bred with other breeds, but only up to 50 per cent. In practice, this mean the cow must be sired by a pure-bred Aberdeen Angus.

Other top breeds:
Highland and Shorthorn, Hereford, Galloway, Devon Red, Lincoln Red and Sussex Red.

Interesting breeds of lamb to look out for:
Romney Marsh (although cross-breeds of this animal are prolific in New Zealand), Scottish Blackface, Shetland, Soay and Welsh Mountain.

regulations for poultry

'FREE-RANGE': usually a rapidly growing breed, the birds must have access usually to external vegetation-covered runs for at least half their lives. During the final fattening stage, 70 per cent of the feed must be cereal-based, although proteins and growth-promoters can be added.

'TRADITIONAL FREE-RANGE': slower-growing breeds, with twice the outside access of free-range birds and, consequently, older when slaughtered. Husbandry tends to be of a higher standard than with 'free-range'. Diet is not specified in the regulations but, at this stage, the farmer is beginning to supply a high-value product so there is more of a commercial incentive to provide a 'good' diet.

'FREE-RANGE TOTAL FREEDOM': birds given continuous daytime access to an unlimited area. In practice, accommodation tends to be in small hen-houses, often ones that can be moved about. The label carries a premium, so feed quality is likely – although not required – to be cereal-based.

'CORN-FED': if you imagine your purchase to have lived its life constantly gorging on maize, think again. Corn-fed comes in both free-range and conventionally reared guises, but neither system requires an exclusive maize diet. As for the colour, beta carotene is just one of the colorants used.

'ORGANIC': chickens must conform to a strict set of guidelines covering not simply diet, but also breed, diet, husbandry and flock size. To ensure that these criteria have been met, select birds that have been certified by an authorized body as below.

certified organic bodies in the UK

THE SOIL ASSOCIATION
BRITISH ORGANIC FARMERS
    AND GROWERS
THE BIO-DYNAMIC
    AGRICULTURE
    ASSOCIATION
SCOTTISH ORGANIC
    PRODUCERS ASSOCIATION
THE UK REGISTER OF
    ORGANIC FOOD

the law and the future selling of game in the UK

Efforts are being made to change the law forbidding the sale of game during the closed season in the UK. This, it is argued, is to allow the sale of frozen birds, as nobody wants to kill birds in the breeding season. It makes some sense, but I for one have no wish to eat game all year round. I adore its seasonality: grouse on the glorious 12 August, perhaps, but far better about a month later and so much more enjoyable for all the waiting.

the UK game season:

GROUSE: 12 August to 10 December

MALLARD: 1 September to February

PARTRIDGE: 1 September to 1 February (best Oct and Nov)

PHEASANT :1 October to 1 February (best Nov and Dec)

WOODCOCK: 1 October to 31 January (begins 1 September in Scotland)

HARE cannot be sold between March and July

WILD RABBIT has no closed season, but is best between August and April.

sources for meat, poultry and game

In London: Allen's 020 7499 5831, F. Godfrey 020 7226 2425, Harrods 020 7730 1234, Blagden's 020 7935 8321;
Elsewhere: Heritage Fine Foods, Barrow Gurney, nr Bristol, 01275 474707, which does mail order.

A number of particularly good butchers are loosely allied in the Q-guild: their customer enquiry line is 01383 432622.

There is now also a website listing organic butchers and farm outlets: www.organicbutchers.co.uk

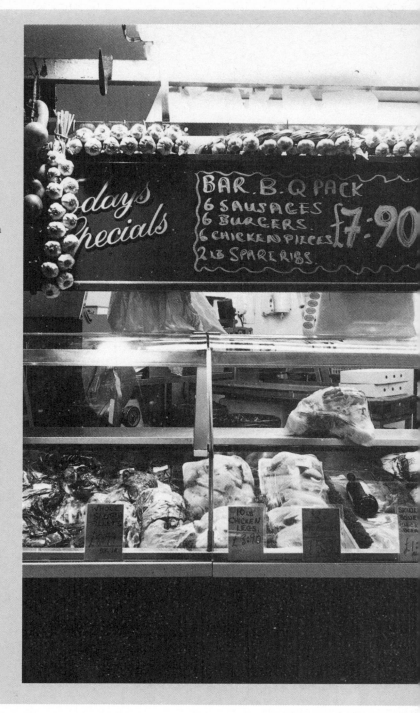

meat, poultry and game *recipes*

grilled onglet,

béarnaise sauce and caramelized shallots

serves 6–8

800 g (1³/₄ lb) onglet (thin skirt of
  beef)
olive oil for brushing

FOR THE CARAMELIZED SHALLOTS:
4 tablespoons olive oil
1 kg (2¹/₄ lb) banana shallots
salt and pepper
1 tablespoon sugar

FOR THE BÉARNAISE SAUCE:
250 ml (9 fl oz) white wine vinegar
2 tablespoons dried tarragon
55 g (1³/₄ oz) finely chopped shallots
¹/₂ teaspoon cracked black
  peppercorns
1 bay leaf
200 g (7 oz) butter
2 egg yolks
bunch of fresh tarragon, roughly
  chopped
bunch of fresh chervil, roughly
  chopped

Called onglet *or* bavette *in France, here this beef cut is probably most usually called 'thin' or 'thick skirt'. It is also known as 'the butcher's cut', as it is a choice piece of beef that butchers were inclined to keep for themselves. The secret of cooking this cut is either to do it briefly, as in this recipe, or to give it long, slow cooking. The thick* bavette *cut is more suited to long stewing, the thin* onglet *to quick grilling or frying. The* bavette *can be successfully substituted for stewing beef – just cook it more slowly and for longer.*

1 Make the caramelized shallots: heat the olive oil in a frying pan over a moderate heat. Add the shallots, season well with salt and pepper and sauté, turning frequently, for 10 minutes, or until lightly coloured.

2 Sprinkle the sugar over the shallots, lower the heat and carry

fillet steak,
balsamic and rocket salad

on cooking, stirring often, for 20 minutes more, until well coloured.

3 While the shallots cook, preheat a hot grill and make the béarnaise sauce: combine the vinegar, dried tarragon, chopped shallots, peppercorns and bay leaf in a stainless-steel saucepan. Bring to the boil and reduce until there is almost no liquid left, just about a dessertspoonful.

4 Melt the butter in another pan. Combine the egg yolks with the strained reduction in a third heavy-based saucepan. Set over the lowest heat. Add the melted butter in a steady thin stream, as you would do oil to egg yolks when making mayonnaise, stirring all the time until it thickens. If it gets too thick, thin with a little hot water. Remove from the heat, stir in the chopped fresh herbs and adjust the seasoning. Keep warm.

5 While making the reduction, coat the beef with olive oil and season generously with salt and pepper. When the grill is good and hot – but not before – grill for 5 minutes on each side.

6 Set the beef aside to rest in a warm place, loosely covered with foil, for at least 10 minutes before serving, cut across into slices. Serve with the béarnaise sauce and caramelized shallots.

serves 4

500 g (1 lb 2 oz) piece of beef fillet
salt and pepper
olive oil, for frying
balsamic vinegar, to dress

FOR THE ROCKET SALAD:
4 really generous handfuls of rocket
about 3 tablespoons extra-virgin
   olive oil

In summer I serve this cold; in winter at room temperature. It is a perfect main course if you have eaten a pasta dish and, perhaps, some antipasti before that. Don't skimp on the rocket, you needs its sharp pepperiness to cut the meat. Some people like to scatter shavings of Parmesan on top, but I think it is too strong for the meat.

1 Generously season the fillet with salt and pepper.

2 Heat a frying pan and, when hot, lightly coat the base with oil. Press the fillet into the frying pan and sauté for 6 minutes. Turn it over and cook for another 6 minutes. Remove and keep warm, allowing it to rest, covered loosely with foil, for at least 10 minutes.

3 Arrange the rocket on a large flat plate. Drizzle over the extra-virgin olive oil and season with salt.

4 Cut the fillet into thin slices and arrange these on top of the rocket. Drizzle over the balsamic vinegar and serve.

baked best end of veal
with wilted summer leaves

serves 4

trimmed bone-in best end of veal,
 weighing about 2 kg (4¹/₂ lb)
2 tablespoons olive oil
salt and pepper
150 ml (¹/₄ pint) rich veal stock (or a
 rich chicken stock)
150 ml (¹/₄ pint) dry white wine
1 tablespoon finely chopped shallot
150 ml (¹/₄ pint) whipping cream
bunch of dill
bunch of parsley
small bunch of tarragon
bunch of chives
225 g (8 oz) butter, chilled and cut
 into cubes
450 g (1 lb) sorrel, roughly chopped

You need a garden or an enlightened grocery for this dish. The 450 g (1 lb) of sorrel just about fills a carrier bag, but its lemon tartness is reduced to a silky smoothness.

1 Preheat the oven to 150°C/300°F/Gas 2. Coat the meat in olive oil and season well with salt and pepper. Place in a roasting tin and bake in the oven for 2 hours, adding a third of the stock every 30 minutes. Allow it to rest, covered in a warm place, for 15–20 minutes.

2 Remove the meat from the roasting pan and keep warm. Add 200 ml (7 fl oz) of water to the pan, increase the heat and simmer, scraping up the residue, until reduced to a syrupy consistency.

3 Combine the wine and shallot in a saucepan and simmer until almost completely reduced to a spoonful. Add the cream and simmer until it turns syrupy. Allow to cool slightly and then combine in a liquidizer with the dill, parsley, tarragon and chives, and blend to a green sauce.

4 Pour into a small saucepan and, over a gentle heat, whisk in the butter, a cube at a time. Remove from the heat, pour into a bowl, add the sorrel and toss.

5 Carve the meat and serve with a little of the reduced gravy and the sorrel sauce.

braised lamb shanks
with winter couscous salad

serves 4

4 lamb shanks
4 tablespoons olive oil
4 cloves
4 cardamom pods
6-cm (2^1/2 -inch) piece of cinnamon
    stick
2 onions, finely chopped
1 teaspoon sweet paprika
1 teaspoon hot paprika
2 teaspoons ground cumin
3 garlic cloves, finely chopped
1 teaspoon tomato purée
one 400-g (14-oz) tin of chopped
    tomatoes
1 litre (1^3/4 pints) chicken stock

FOR THE WINTER COUSCOUS
SALAD:

2 carrots, very finely diced
1 celery stalk, strings removed and
    very finely diced
1 parsnip, very finely diced
2 turnips, very finely diced
salt and pepper
200 g (7 oz) couscous
2 tablespoons extra-virgin olive oil
juice of ^{1}/2 lemon

1 In a saucepan large enough to hold the shanks, heat the olive oil and brown the shanks all over. Remove the shanks and set aside.
2 Add the whole spices to the hot oil and, after 30 seconds, add the onions and gently sauté for 10 minutes without colouring. Add the paprikas and cumin and cook for a further 2 minutes. Add the garlic and, 30 seconds later, the tomato purée. Sauté, stirring all the time, for 2 minutes and then add the tinned tomatoes with their liquid, the stock and the shanks.
3 Gently bring to the boil, lower the heat and simmer for 1^1/2 hours, or until the meat is tender.
4 Make the winter couscous salad: blanch the diced vegetables in boiling salted water until just tender. Drain, reserving the water. Bring 200 ml (7 fl oz) of it to the boil and combine with the couscous in a heatproof bowl, stir and cover with a tea towel. Leave for 5 minutes and then fluff up with a fork. Stir in the vegetables, olive oil and lemon juice. Season to taste with salt and pepper.

5 When the shanks are cooked, remove them from the pan and keep warm. Using kitchen paper, skim off as much fat from the liquid left in pan as you can and then boil to reduce by one-third.
6 Serve the reduced sauce with the shanks and the couscous.

braised sausages
with cauliflower and mustard

serves 4

500 g (1 lb 2 oz) best pork sausages
4 tablespoons olive oil
2 onions, halved and thinly sliced into
  half-moon shapes
1 garlic clove, finely chopped
1 teaspoon fennel seeds
1 small cauliflower, broken into florets
200 ml (7 fl oz) chicken stock
1 dessertspoon Dijon or English
  mustard
salt and pepper

*This is a version of a dish eaten in a
small bar called Bacco in Milan. We
were en route to the airport and in
need of lunch on the right side of
town, the sort of occasion made for
mobile phones. A call to a designer
friend resident in the city and we
were eating within 20 minutes.*

1 Gently sauté the sausages in
the olive oil until they are lightly
coloured.
2 Add the onion and continue to
cook for a further 10 minutes,
taking care the onion doesn't burn.
3 Add the garlic and fennel seeds,
stir to coat in the oil and then stir
in the cauliflower, stock and
mustard. Season well with salt
and pepper, cover and simmer for
10–15 minutes, or until the
cauliflower is tender.

club sandwich

serves 1

3 slices of bread
2 slices of streaky bacon or
   pancetta
knob of butter
1 skinless chicken breast fillet
handful of lettuce leaves (shredded
   iceberg is traditional, but I'm not
   a fan if there are other types
   around)
1/2 teaspoon finely chopped shallot
1 tablespoon mayonnaise (preferably
   home-made)
salt and pepper
1 tomato, cored and sliced
sprinkling of olive oil
few drops of white wine vinegar, or
   balsamic vinegar for a modern
   twist
a little chopped parsley

*This is much imitated and so often
disappointing when ordered in cafés
and sandwich bars. It is my
favourite Sunday brunch dish, hard
to beat when eaten with a peppery
bloody Mary at about noon.*

1   Toast the bread and grill the
bacon or pancetta until crispy.
Butter the toast. Slice the chicken
breast into 4 or 5 thin slices. Mix
the lettuce with the shallot and
mayonnaise and season well.

2   Start with a layer of half the
tomato slices on the bottom slice
of toast, drizzle over a little olive
oil and vinegar and season with
salt and pepper. Then make layers
of half the lettuce mixture, and
half each of the bacon, chicken
and parsley. Season again with salt
and pepper before topping with
the second slice of toast. Repeat
with the remaining ingredients to
make a second deck, finishing with
the last slice of toast.

warm pigeon salad

serves 4

4 oven-ready pigeons
2 tablespoons olive oil
salt and pepper

FOR THE STOCK:

2 carrots, roughly chopped
1 onion, quartered
2 garlic cloves, smashed
2 tablespoons olive oil

FOR THE SALAD:

2 tablespoons chopped shallots
2 tablespoons olive oil
1 garlic clove, finely chopped
4 beetroots, quartered
1 dessertspoon sherry vinegar
100 ml (3½ fl oz) port
4 handfuls of salad leaves
1 dessertspoon finely chopped
   chives

*This is the only way I have found of
cooking wood pigeon successfully; its
meat is so lacking in fat, it dries out
if roasted or braised. It offers
inexpensive eating, however, and is
available all year round. If you
haven't got the time or inclination to
make stock from the carcasses, use
chicken stock.*

1 Preheat the oven to
220°C/425°F/Gas 7. Remove the
breasts from the pigeons by
carving down along the backbone
on either side. Rub with olive oil,
season with pepper and set aside.
2 Make the stock: roughly break
up the carcasses and place in a
roasting tray with the carrots,
onion and garlic. Drizzle over the
olive oil, season and roast in the
preheated oven for 30 minutes.
3 Place the contents of the
roasting pan in a casserole dish or
saucepan, cover with boiling water
and simmer, uncovered, for 40
minutes. Strain into a clean
saucepan and bring back to the
boil.
4 Prepare the salad: lightly sauté
the shallots in the olive oil for 5
minutes without colouring them.
Add the garlic and, 1 minute later,
the beetroot. Toss to coat in oil
and then deglaze the pan with the
sherry vinegar. Add the port and
simmer for 5 minutes.
5 Lightly poach the pigeon
breasts in the simmering stock for
5 minutes, remove and keep warm.
6 Arrange the salad on 4 plates
and spoon over the beetroot
mixture. Slice the pigeon breasts
across at an angle and arrange on
top of the salad. Sprinkle over the
chives and serve.

braised quail with
sun-dried tomatoes and pine nuts

serves 4

8 quail
salt and pepper
2 garlic cloves, finely chopped
1 tablespoon chopped fresh thyme
2 tablespoons olive oil
600 ml (1 pint) chicken stock
150 ml (1/4 pint) dry white wine
generous handful of sun-dried
    tomatoes in oil, drained
2 tablespoons pine nuts
55 g (2 oz) butter, chilled and cut into
    cubes

If you can, buy French quail. These may well be larger, in which case you need only 4. Finger bowls are a necessity; you can't give this sort of food to a genteel elderly aunt, as there comes a point where you simply have to dispense with cutlery.

1 Preheat the oven to 200°C/400°F/Gas 6. Season the quail and toss in a bowl with the garlic, thyme and a little of the olive oil. Transfer to a casserole and place in the oven. Roast for 30 minutes, turning and basting at least three, or even four, times – remember, quail is essentially a dry meat and you need to keep basting if you want the end result to be moist. Remove and allow to rest for at least 10 minutes.

2 Meanwhile, simmer the stock and wine together in a pan over a moderate heat until reduced by half.

3 Roughly chop the tomatoes and heat the pine nuts in a dry frying pan until just coloured. Combine.

4 Deglaze the casserole with the reduced wine and stock, and simmer for 2 or 3 minutes, scraping up all the bits at the bottom. Whisk in the butter, a cube at a time.

5 Serve the quails with a neat dollop of the tomato and pine nut mixture and a little of the sauce.

crispy peking duck

serves 4-6

1 oven-ready duck, weighing about
    2–2.5 kg (4¹/₂–5¹/₂ lb)
3 tablespoons honey
300 ml (¹/₂ pint) hot water
12 spring onions
1 large cucumber, cut into
    matchstick pieces
about 200 ml (7 fl oz) hoisin sauce
20–30 Chinese pancakes

This is remarkably easy to do – no wonder Chinese restaurants are so keen to sell this dish – and relatively easy to prepare in advance. If the duck is a good duck, this dish is raised from the good to the superb. Peking duck is more usually accompanied by plum sauce, but hoisin (a dark, spicy vegetable-based sauce) makes for a welcome change – the plum often being too sweet for me. Chinese pancakes are a very simple combination of flour, water and a little vegetable oil. Making your own is not difficult, but rather time-consuming. More than half the fun of this dish is in the eating; it's a great first course to break the ice, given that most of the eating is done with your fingers.

1 Well ahead, ideally the day before you want to serve, place the duck in a colander, pour over a kettleful of boiling water and, when drained, transfer the duck to a large bowl.

2 Combine the honey and the hot water and pour this over the duck. Turn the duck in the mixture several times; you really need to make sure it is well covered (a pastry brush is useful for the nooks and crannies).

3 Hang the duck in a well-ventilated place, using an 'S' hook or string, and leave for 12–24 hours, or until the skin is parchment-dry.

4 Preheat the oven to 180°C/350°F/Gas 4. Place the duck, breast side up, on a wire rack in a roasting tin with some hot water underneath. Roast for 20 minutes, or until the skin is golden brown. Turn the duck over and roast for a further 30 minutes. Turn over again and roast for a final 20 minutes. Adjust the heat up or down a little towards the end of the cooking, depending on how dark or light the skin has become. Remove from the oven and allow to rest, covered loosely, in a warm place for 10 minutes.

5 Thinly slice the white part of the spring onion and the cucumber lengthwise into matchstick strips and place on plates with some hoisin sauce. Heat the pancakes according to the instructions on the packet. Carve the breasts off the duck, then shred the meat with two forks.

6 To eat, spread a little sauce on a pancake, arrange some duck, cucumber and spring onion on top, roll up and devour.

roast mallard

with Puy lentils and salsa verde

serves 4

2 mallard
salt and pepper
1 onion, finely chopped
2 celery stalks, strings removed and
    finely chopped
4 tablespoons olive oil
2 garlic cloves, finely chopped
bunch of parsley, finely chopped
    (stalks reserved)
1 teaspoon tomato purée
400 g (14 oz) Puy lentils
1 litre (1³/4 pints) light chicken stock
one 400-g (14-oz) tin of chopped
    tomatoes
1 bay leaf

FOR THE SALSA VERDE:
bunch of parsley, finely chopped
bunch of mint, finely chopped
1 tablespoon finely chopped
    gherkins
1 dessertspoon capers, well rinsed
1 dessertspoon Dijon mustard

1 Preheat the oven to 180°C/350°F/Gas 4. Season the bird inside and out with salt and pepper and roast for 1 hour. Remove from the oven and allow to rest in a warm place for at least 15 minutes.

2 Sauté the onion and celery in half the olive oil in a large flameproof casserole for 10 minutes. Add the garlic and the chopped parsley and continue frying for 2 minutes more. Add the tomato purée and cook for a further 2 minutes, stirring all the time. Add the lentils, turn to coat well in the oil and vegetable mixture and then add the stock, tomatoes with their liquid, bay leaf and the parsley stalks tied together with string. Bring to the boil, lower the heat, cover and simmer for 30 minutes, or until the lentils are tender, but still with some bite. Remove the parsley stalks and bay leaf and season with salt and pepper.

3 Make the salsa verde by combining all the ingredients with just enough of the remaining olive oil to bind the sauce together. Season well with salt and pepper.

4 Carve the breasts and the legs from the bird, and serve on the lentils, drizzling a spoonful of the salsa over the top.

marinated chicken,

French beans and sautéed rosemary potatoes

serves 4

1 chicken, jointed into 8 pieces
450 g (1 lb) French beans

FOR THE MARINADE:
2 tablespoons olive oil
2 tablespoons balsamic vinegar
bunch of thyme, chopped
2 tablespoons chopped shallots
4 unpeeled garlic cloves, smashed
  and roughly chopped
salt and pepper

FOR THE SAUTÉED ROSEMARY
POTATOES:
1 kg (2¼ lb) potatoes
6 tablespoons olive oil
2 sprigs of rosemary, chopped

There are three advantages to cooking chicken like this: first, there is no carving at the table; second, you can vary the marinade ingredients to provide variety; and third, the cooking time is much less than that required for a whole chicken.

1 Well ahead, ideally the day before, put the chicken in a large bowl with the marinade ingredients and a generous grinding of black pepper. Toss so everything is well coated, cover and set aside for at least a few hours, preferably overnight.

2 Preheat the oven to 220°C/425°F/Gas 7. Cut the potatoes into 1-cm (½-inch) dice (I leave the skins on, but you may wish to remove them). Parboil in boiling salted water for 5 minutes, drain and refresh briefly in cold water. Drain them well.

3 Toss the chicken so it is well coated in the marinade, season with plenty of salt and place at the top of the oven. Turn gently twice while it is cooking (which should take about 30 minutes). Remove from the oven and allow to rest in a warm place for 15 minutes.

4 About halfway through the chicken cooking time, put the olive oil for the potatoes in a heavy sauté or frying pan and toss the potato in this. Season with salt and pepper and sauté over a moderate heat for about 20 minutes. Add the rosemary and garlic, and cook for 2 minutes more.

5 While the chicken is resting, cook the beans in plenty of boiling salted water for 4 minutes, or until just tender.

6 Serve the chicken with the potatoes and beans.

grilled chicken breast *with*

pearl barley 'risotto' and lemon and thyme butter

serves 4

600 ml (1 pint) chicken stock
1 onion, finely chopped
100 g (3¹/2 oz) butter
100 g (3¹/2 oz) pearl barley
4 chicken breast fillets

FOR THE LEMON AND THYME
BUTTER:

100 g (3¹/2 oz) butter
1 generous teaspoon fresh thyme
   leaves
1 lemon
salt and pepper

This favourite way with chicken is quick and easy, leaving you with bags of time to read the paper, chat to friends or just put your feet up.

1 First make the lemon and thyme butter: combine the butter with the thyme leaves, the zest and juice from the lemon and seasoning to taste. Roll up in some foil and chill.
2 Bring the stock to the boil.
3 In a large heavy-based pan, lightly soften the onion in the butter for 10 minutes without

colouring. Add the pearl barley, stir to coat well in the butter and cook for 5 minutes, again without colouring. Add the boiling stock, cover and simmer for 30–40 minutes, or until tender. Season well with salt and pepper.
4 Season the chicken breasts well. Fry, grill or barbecue them for about 7 minutes on each side. Allow to rest for 5 minutes.
5 Slice the chicken breasts and serve on top of the pearly barley, with a slice or two of the lemon and thyme butter.

pot-roasted guinea fowl *with*

paprika, preserved lemons, balsamic and pilaf

serves 8

2 large guinea fowl
2 tablespoons olive oil
salt and pepper
1 teaspoon sweet paprika
1 teaspoon hot paprika
2 heads of garlic, broken into cloves
   but unpeeled
2 tablespoons chopped preserved
   lemons
5 tablespoons balsamic vinegar
1 litre (1³/4 pints) chicken stock

North-African preserved lemons are often available from good delicatessens. To make your own, cut a cross vertically through each lemon and stuff it with sea salt. Push them into preserving jars, top with more lemon juice, seal and set aside for at least 10 days. You use the skin, not the flesh, which should be discarded.

1 Preheat the oven to 220°C/425°F/Gas 7. Rub the guinea fowl well with olive oil and

season with salt and pepper and the paprikas. Place in an open casserole dish, add the garlic cloves, preserved lemon, balsamic vinegar and 400 ml (14 fl oz) water and place in the oven for 30 minutes, basting frequently.
2 Bring the chicken stock to the boil and add to the casserole, lower the oven setting to 180°C/350°F/Gas 4 and cook for 45 minutes more, or until the guinea fowl is done (the juices run clear).

FOR THE PILAF:

1 kg (2¼ lb) basmati rice
6 tablespoons vegetable oil
2 cinnamon sticks (each about
 5 cm / 2 inches long)
6 cardamom pods, lightly crushed
4 cloves
2 teaspoons cumin seeds
salt

3 Strain off the chicken stock, leaving the guinea fowl, preserved lemon and garlic in the casserole. Cover and keep warm. Reduce the stock by at least half and adjust its seasoning. Keep that warm.

4 Make the pilaf: rinse the rice in plenty of water and drain. Boil a kettleful of water. Heat the vegetable oil in a large pan and, when hot, lightly sauté the whole spices for 1 minute. Add the drained rice and turn to coat well in the hot oil for 2 minutes. Add 2 litres (3½ pints) of the boiling water and season with salt. Stir so none of the rice is sticking, reduce the heat, cover and simmer for 15 minutes, or until tender. You need to stir the rice two or three times at the beginning and, if things look like drying out, add a little more boiling water (not too much, though, or the rice will be soggy). When it is cooked, fluff up with a fork, cover and set aside.

5 Roughly carve up the guinea fowl, arrange the pieces on a large warmed plate along with the reduced stock gravy, the preserved lemons and the garlic, and serve with the pilaf.

pheasant *with red wine porcini and soft polenta*

serves 4

4 tablespoons olive oil

salt and pepper

2 pheasants

3 tablespoons finely chopped
    shallots

15 g (1/2 oz) dried porcini, soaked in
    hot water

125 g (4 1/2 oz) pancetta, cut into
    lardons

1/2 teaspoon tomato purée

1 garlic clove, finely chopped

1 bottle (750 ml / 27 fl oz) of red wine

500 ml (18 fl oz) chicken stock

1 packet of polenta

1 Preheat the oven to
180°C/350°F/Gas 4. Heat the olive
oil in a large heatproof casserole.
Season the pheasants and brown
them evenly in the oil. Remove
from the casserole.

2 In the same pan, sauté the
shallots gently for 5 minutes
without colouring them. Add the
porcini (reserving the liquor),
pancetta and the tomato purée.
Sauté gently for 5 more minutes.
Add the garlic and, 1 minute later,
the wine. Bring to the boil and
simmer gently for 5 minutes.

3 Return the pheasants to the pan
and place in the oven, uncovered,
for 40 minutes, or until cooked
(the juices run clear). Remove the
pheasants and keep them warm.

4 Add the stock to the casserole,
along with liquor from the
mushrooms, and reduce by two-
thirds. Adjust the seasoning.

5 Cook the polenta according to
the instructions on the packet and
season well.

6 Carve the pheasant and serve
with the red wine porcini sauce
and the polenta.

roast partridge *with braised Savoy cabbage*

serves 4

4 tablespoons olive oil

4 partridges, barded with fat back
    and tied with string

salt and pepper

2 carrots, finely diced

1 celery stalk, finely diced

4 tablespoons finely chopped
    shallots

225 g (8 oz) pancetta, cut into
    lardons

1 large Savoy cabbage, cored and
    thinly sliced

300 ml (1/2 pint) chicken stock

*Sweet, succulent and gamy without
being overpowering, partridge is a
delight as much for those who know
their game as for those coming to it
for the first time.*

1 Preheat the oven to
230°C/350°F/Gas 8. Heat the olive
oil in a flameproof casserole and
lightly colour the partridges in it.

2 Season with salt and pepper
and roast for 8 minutes on each
side. Remove from the casserole
and set aside.

3 Add the carrots, celery, shallots
and pancetta to the casserole and

sauté gently for 5 minutes. Add
the cabbage and stir to coat well.
Cover and simmer for 5 minutes.

4 Stir the cabbage again and
place the partridge on top. Pour
over the chicken stock, bring to
the boil, cover and replace in the
oven for 15 minutes.

5 Remove the partridges from the
casserole and keep warm. Allow
the cabbage to simmer for 10
minutes more uncovered on the
stove top.

6 Carve the partridge and serve
with the cabbage. Some creamy
mash is a good accompaniment.

dairy produce and eggs

3

'Cheese is milk that has grown up.
Everyone feels a tinge of revulsion when
strong, bearded men are caught in the act
of milk drinking; we feel that this food,
ordained for the mouths of babes and
sucklings, is not for them. But with cheese
it is otherwise; it is pre-eminently the
food of man – the older it grows the more
manly it becomes, and in the last stages
of senility it almost requires a room to
itself, like the jokes consecrated to the
smoking-room.'

EDWARD BUNYARD, *The Epicure's Companion*

Good butter explodes with flavour, a spread for bread of an ancient kind, no need for jam. Good eggs wibble and wobble, the white thick and viscous, the yolk yellow and firm. Good milk is complex and deep, rich and creamy, and so should cheese made from it be. Yet in so many instances what we drink is white and tasteless, what we poach is pale and slimy, and what we spread on our bread is devoid of flavour. We see these everyday ingredients as commodities, standard and uniform, and yet nothing could be further from the truth. An egg is only as good as the hen that laid it and the food the hen ate, how it lived, what it did – all these factors influence the final taste. The same is true of milk and, in turn, the cheese made from it.

milk

As it is in meat, the fat is the source of much of the flavour of milk. The best and tastiest milk comes from breeds of cow, like the Jersey and Guernsey, in which the milk has a relatively high fat content (see page 102). If you are lucky, the carton or bottle might tell you; alternatively, the brand name may promise a percentage of milk from a certain breed.

Next look for milk from a small dairy producer, as they are more likely to feed their cattle a more varied diet, using pasture containing herbs, clovers and wild grasses – translating into the milk as more complex and rounded flavours. They are also unlikely to need to supplement diet with the protein-enhancers that are so common in large dairy herds.

As the consumer, you should be concerned about husbandry, stock size, diet and medical treatment (see pages 51–3). Look for this information on the carton or bottle; the more you are told the greater the chance that the milk you buy will taste of something. In practice, not all this information is readily available, but these days a reliable producer will endeavour to supply some of it. If you want to know more, ring them up and ask – and be wary of vague language.

Milky puddings to shout about: rice pudding (with raisins, sultanas, pine nuts and spices), bread and butter pudding (made with panettone), crème caramel and brûlée.

Storing milk

Milk can be frozen, but once defrosted its shelf-life is quite short, typically one to two days. Homogenization of milk (redistributing the fat particles evenly through the milk) gives it a longer shelf-life and prevents old-fashioned 'top of the milk' forming… rather a shame really.

Pasteurization

This now ubiquitous process involves heating milk to 72°C (160°F) for 15 seconds, then cooling it rapidly to a around 10°C (50°F) to kill off any harmful bacteria. The process can, however, also destroy natural antibiotic qualities the milk may possess, as well as the many beneficial bacteria that contribute complexity, length, structure and balance to its flavour. See also page 98. Pasteurization was introduced as a means of ensuring that milk from various sources reached a certain, relatively low, level of cleanliness, and it undoubtedly had a huge influence in removing the scourge of TB. Yet if raw milk is clean, pasteurization is not necessary.

cream

Cream is the fattier part of full-cream milk (which, as it is – surprisingly – lighter than water, rises to the top) that has been skimmed off and sold separately. As it is the fat part of the milk it has a much better flavour and also contains most of the milk's nutrients. It is marketed in various forms: single, whipping, double, extra-double (for which read 'really thick'), clotted, crème fraîche, soured cream and smetana. As with butters (see overleaf), Continental types of cream, like crème fraîche, are given added lactic cultures to help them develop a gentle acidity and greater flavour. Apart from these souring agents, the principal distinction between types of cream is

fat level. (See the Directory on page 102 for more detail on types of cream and their properties.)

What to buy depends partly on what you intend to use the cream for and partly on quality. As with milk, look for a small producer who is likely to give some information on the farm, on as to which cows are used and what they are fed. A good cream should be rich, full-flavoured and almost meaty in texture. We have become remarkably used to bland cream, but a cream of distinction should leave you quite invigorated.

yoghurt

An ancient food, yoghurt is milk curdled by benevolent bacteria. Often overlooked in favour of

cream, yoghurt can be stirred into stews and casseroles to give an added richness and sharpness; it can also be used for sauces, dips and dressings. It is useful for marinating meat, its lactic acids acting as tenderizers. Yoghurt curdles if it is boiled, so needs to be stirred into hot food just before serving, or it can be stabilized by mixing it with a little cornflour.

When buying yoghurt, look for small organic producers. Yoghurt comes in various styles (see the Directory) and is increasingly low in fat, which is fine for eating but usually hopeless for use in cooking. The fat content (about 10 per cent) of Greek-style cows' milk, being an inherently important characteristic. It is this fat that effectively neutralizes the acidic quality, giving Greek-style yoghurt its full, rich, creamy character.

The best yoghurt matches its acidity with a full flavour, coming from good milk (which can be from cow, sheep or goat).

'Live' yoghurt
To some extent all yoghurt is live in that the bacteria added in the first place, *Lactobacillus bulgaricus* and *Streptococcus thermophilis* will

still be active. In many yoghurts, however, there are growth inhibitors present that effectively lengthen the shelf-life of the yoghurt. In 'live' yoghurt these inhibitors are absent, the yoghurt having a shorter shelf-life.

Making your own yoghurt

Stir a heaped tablespoon of live yoghurt into about 600 ml (1 pint) tepid milk and pour into a vacuum flask. Leave overnight, transfer to a suitable container and store in the fridge

fromage frais, quark and other white items in pots

These are essentially fresh cheeses with a culture that provides them with an interesting flavour and texture (smooth is achieved by whisking). In their pure form, they are perfectly healthy and will taste as good as the products in them, namely milk and often a fruit flavouring. If the list of ingredients is long and contains anything other than milk, cream, fruit and sugar, it is likely to be highly processed.

butter

For many people, butter is just something spread on bread, often before adding another ingredient – cheese or perhaps jam or marmalade – but almost everyone notices when the butter used is changed.

This is a foodstuff that has had the character progressively stripped out of it until all that remains is something flat and fatty (around 82 per cent to be accurate, the remaining 18 per cent being made up of water and milk solids, and it's these solids that make butter burn at a lowish temperature). As with milk, the higher the fat content of butter, the better its flavour and richer the colour.

There are two main types of butter, sweet-cream butter (popular in the UK, America and New Zealand) and lactic butter (popular in mainland Europe). The former is made by churning pasteurized cream, then generally adding salt; the latter, usually unsalted, is made from cream to which a culture of benevolent bacteria has been added – think of the difference between fresh cream and crème fraîche. There was a time when nearly all butter was naturally lactic butter, the cream ageing naturally and developing its own lactic cultures before being churned.

Both types of butter can be good, although there is more inherent character in lactic butter. Like crème fraîche, the cultures produce a more complex, deeper flavour. Butter can only be as good as the cream from which it is made; and this, in turn, depends on the breed of cow, the season, the type of grassland on which the cattle fed, how gently or fiercely (i.e. how industrially) the milk and butter are treated, how fresh it is and how much salt is used. How much of this information is on the packet of most commercial butters?

In practice, most sweet-cream butter is now made from cream heavily heat-treated, with salt then added to reintroduce some flavour. The lactic route tends to require less salt, the flavour being derived from the cultured cream. In a sweet-cream butter you are looking for inherent flavours that are fresh, clean and bright; its colour deep, with a golden hue. A lactic butter tends to have a smoother mouth-feel and, although rich, is cut by its natural acidity, so you are left with a flavour that is deep and long.

how and where to buy butter

In supermarkets look for butter made in France or Italy. The Isigny, Lescure, President and Echiré brands are notable. The best route is to buy what you normally buy, plus a few other brands, take them home, taste them and compare. At least that way you are sure of what you are spending your money on. A few delicatessens and small specialist shops will have good butter, often one type and possibly local; again taste and compare.

storage

Although you would hardly believe it looking at the sell-by dates on most packets, butter is as perishable as cheese, so buy little and frequently. It can, however, be frozen without significant damage to its flavour and this is probably the most sensible route. Have a small quantity to hand, but keep it in the fridge, covered. Left out on the table it deteriorates quickly into a tasteless mass of fat.

farmhouse butter

This is generally an artisan product, made by hand, and often quite strong-tasting (the fat content tends to be high). We have grown remarkably unused to the idea of flavours coming from butter. This is not to say all farmhouse butter is wonderful, it certainly isn't, but I'll buy some if I see it in a market. In Britain the best farmhouse butters tend to come from Devon, Cornwall and the Channel Islands; in France they are usually from Normandy.

whey butter

Made as a by-product of cheese-making by separating the cream from the whey and churning it, whey butter is an extreme form of lactic butter. Its flavour is strong, too much for some. Its cheese origins are evident and it is often packed with sweet flavour.

Spreadable butter

This has been either whipped or manipulated after it has been made to incorporate air, or it is butter made from milk where the cows' feed has been altered with that aim in mind. Good butter is not that convenient, I'm afraid.

Salted v unsalted

Salted butter can have up to 2 per cent salt. This is not an indication of quality, although an excellent butter can contain this much salt. The crucial question is why the salt is there. If it is to contribute flavour because most of the inherent taste has been knocked out (as with most commercial butters) be suspicious; if, on the other hand, the salt has been added to draw out inherent butter flavours, you are probably on to a winner.

Beurre noisette, or nut butter

This is butter that has been cooked to a golden-brown hue, the object being to draw on an inherent almond flavour in butter, and is used to dress plainly cooked food like grilled fish. Too often this delicious sauce is over-zealously concocted by chefs who, in effect, burn the butter. The pan must be caressed over the heat, the butter allowed to swill in the pan so it gently takes on the nut colour.

butter substitutes

All such products have been manipulated and added to, making them spreadable. They contain either less fat, or different fat. Far better to forgo the butter on occasion and enjoy the real thing less frequently.

cheese

At first glance, cheese-making is a very simple and straightforward affair. Take milk, warm it and introduce a starter culture to sour it. When the correct acidity has been reached, coagulate the milk by adding rennet (a digestive enzyme) so that the milk curdles and separates to produce curds and whey. Then cut the curds. The degree to which this is done affects the texture of the final cheese; fresh cheese, like chèvre for example, is hardly cut at all, while hard cheese, like nutty Beaufort or pungent Parmesan, is finely cut.

The next stage is to place the curds in moulds, allow them to drain and either dry-salt them or dip them in brine before ageing.

With a cheese like Parmesan, this ageing will be for years, while with a soft goats' cheese, the process is much more simple and the ageing far shorter, but essentially all cheese is made the same way.

Simple in theory certainly, but enormous skill is required in practice, with experience counting for much. Just when to remove the curd from the whey, how much acidity to allow – these things require skill and judgement. And any cheesemaker worth his or her salt will admit they get it more right on some days than others.

Crucial ingredient number one is the milk. Although you could be forgiven for thinking otherwise, milk is not a standard product and varies enormously through the seasons and being heavily influenced by what the cows, sheep or goats eat (see page 90).

Cheese is commonly divided into the following groups according to the processes used in their manufacture: hard cheeses, like Parmesan and Pecorino; semi-hard cheeses like Cheddar, Cantal and Emmental; white-rind cheeses, such as Chaource and Brie; goats'-milk cheeses like Crottin and Valençay; orange-rind cheeses like Munster and Reblochon; blue cheeses like Roquefort and Stilton; and fresh cheeses, like ricotta, feta and mascarpone. Any assessment of quality by means of physical characteristics will obviously vary from type to type.

cows'-, sheep's- and goats'-milk cheeses

The lion's share of cheese is made from cows' milk. Compared with sheep's or goats' milk, it is quite bland in flavour. As a result, the fresh cheeses made from it – mascarpone and fromage frais for example – are somewhat lacking in character. Made into semi-hard cheese, like Cantal, say, it begins to develop some complexity that is further enhanced if the curd is slightly cooked, as it is with cheeses like Provolone and Gruyère. Even with these cheeses, however, there is a characteristic full, round, rich flavour. Sheep's-milk cheeses have a pleasant weight to their flavour, a gaminess that is quite pronounced, and tend to be hard or semi-hard, Italian Pecorino for example, or Spanish Manchego, both of which have a good salty tang. Goats' milk has a pleasant, well-focused sharpness, yet the cheeses can vary from fresh and creamy to tangy and quite powerful; as the cheese dries out the flavour becomes more intense.

what to look for when you buy

A good cheese will look bright, alive and vibrant. Its aroma should be fruity, slightly acidic, pleasing and well rounded; if it displays a sharpness or overpowering character – ammonia being the most common – then warning bells should be sounding. The taste should reinforce the aroma, taking it forward so the aromas you picked up on then exhibit themselves as flavours. The taste should be rounded, the structure whole rather than disparate and there should be a cleanness to the

flavour. There should also be some length, a sense of the cheese after you have eaten it. In a fresh chèvre, this will not be as powerful or developed as with, say, Gruyère, but it should still be present.

While it is useful to talk about the grassiness of Vacherin, the spicy-apply flavour of Livarot, or the nutty-buttery flavour of Gouda, it is more revealing to assess the broader categories of depth and length, complexity and structure. After all, a Gouda can taste nutty and buttery, but be distinctly unexciting – boring even. A cheese must express character within certain constraints and this is more likely to come from a small producer than a large one, somebody who has access to their own milk, or is buying from neighbours.

Parmesan in Italy, Roquefort in France and Stilton in Britain can be made only in a certain area, in a certain way and with specific types of milk. These relatively tight controls operate to try and ensure the character of the cheese is maintained within a given band. Papillon Roquefort tastes richer and creamier than Carles Roquefort, which has a drier, sharper character, but they are both unmistakably Roquefort.

the maturing of cheese

Not every cheese made will be the same – a welcome relief – and the job of selecting the best should be down to somebody who is not the cheesemaker. Cheese is a living thing crowded with lots of wonderful bacteria that need looking after. In France, perhaps the greatest cheese country, this is the job of the *affineur*.

When a Vacherin arrives at my local cheese shop it has a pale milky crust. About two weeks later, after several baths and (I suspect) soothing words from *affineur* Eric Demelle, it will develop a mellow straw-coloured hue. The texture is transformed from spongy and rubbery to that of thick double cream. Allow it to come to room temperature and you are in for one of the most sublime experiences I know, the flavour nutty and fruity, with immense highs and lows of tangy acidity followed by a gentle rounded creaminess.

Like so many craftsmen, Eric is somewhat cagey about what he actually does. His equipment involves a number of suspicious-looking bottles (wines of various types, the odd marc or two), a bucket of salt (actually a delicate *fleurs du sel*, see page 205) and crème fraîche. Quite how the latter is used he will not say. The cheese is turned and washed – sometimes in wine, sometimes in brine, sometimes in water – to develop the character while at the same time maintaining a balancing acidity.

But so much cheese never reaches anything like this desired condition. An unaged Vacherin, even an artisan one, is about as exciting as processed cheese; Caerphilly, a cheese that is frequently dull and boring, can taste as complex and exciting as Comté, but only if given the correct *affinage*.

The ageing of cheese, fresh cheese excepted, starts as soon as it has been made and in many instances this is all the maturing that will be done. When the cheesemaker feels he has aged it long enough, it is sold to a wholesaler, who sells it on to a delicatessen, where it is put in the chill cabinet and sold to the public. What leaves the cheesemaker is, therefore, generally very much what you eat.

If you are lucky, though, the wholesaler may well do some ageing, and if you are very lucky,

so will the retailer. In both latter cases, the aim should be the continued development of the inherent characteristics of the cheese.

where to buy cheese

If you want good cheese, you must find a retailer who does their own ageing, or somebody who buys from one. How to tell? Look at the condition of the cheese and at the range. Anyone who really cares about cheese will realize that a small selection, well handled, is far better and easier to sell than a huge range. As to condition, a lot of the tell-tale signs might seem slight, but they illustrate an attitude of mind.

If you find a really good shop, it will have a purpose-built *cave* – which, in many cases, is the shop itself – that is air-conditioned to provide cold moist air. In these circumstances the cheese will be unwrapped and should look bright and vibrant, with no grease or sweat. In many instances, however, shops are too small, or the quantity of cheese sold too little, and the cheese will be kept in a chill cabinet. The characteristics of the cheese should be the same, but it should also be wrapped in

cling-film. In the latter case, the retailer is really a holding operation. Their chill-cabinet may operate at a slightly warmer, albeit constant, temperature than your fridge at home, but it is far too cold and dry for any ageing to occur.

Everything – chill-cabinets in particular – should be clean and tidy, labels clear and informative. 'Mature Cheddar' tells the buyer nothing. The name of the cheese, where it is made and by whom, and perhaps a few words on its character – 'nutty, rounded with a long aftertaste', or 'sharp, apply and fruity' for example – are far more informative.

Ask about individual cheeses, for a careful buyer knows something about what they buy. It may be that the chill-cabinet holds a few mass-produced cheeses – everyone has to make a living and some customers might want the bland flavour – but interrogating the owner of a chill-cabinet usually draws out indifference rather than enthusiasm.

Tasting is pivotal, and any good cheese retailer will encourage you with a sample, which, after all, is the only way you can really ultimately make an informed

both good and bad retailers of cheese. You may think that buying from the producer will save you money (and it may well), but remember that the cheese they sell to you they would, in most cases, have sold to a cheesemonger, who should then age it properly. If you are going to take it home and eat it, that's fine if it's chèvre, but not so fine if it's St Marcellin.

what to look for on the label

The producer and the *affineur* (or maturer) are important. This doesn't mean you need to know the name of every producer of St Nectaire, but the styles of each one do differ within the set parameters of the cheese.

Likewise, the various AOC (Appellation d'Origine Contrôlée) and equivalent schemes of countries like France, Spain and Italy should inspire confidence. The same can be said for terms like 'farmhouse', '*artisanale*' or '*fermier*' (French for farmhouse) when taken in context – a retailer with uniformly processed-looking cheese shouting '*fermier*' all over the place is likely to be somewhat odd... as indeed will be their cheeses.

decision. And it's hardly difficult, or expensive, with cheese – a sliver is all that is required.

Paradoxically, appearance is first on the list when you are tasting. Avoid anything which looks tired; both the rind and the inside should look alive and bright, with no blemishes or greasy marks (a sign of allowing the cheese to get too warm). The aroma should be sweet and earthy, but not stinky, and there should be no overpowering whiff of ammonia, a sign of a well-over-aged cheese (preferable for some). The taste should be rich and full-bodied, its individual characteristics showing complexity and length. Not every artisan cheese is a gastronomic

wonder, but they should all show character, complexity and variety.

If you are buying cheese in an unhelpful environment like a supermarket and are concerned about quality, go for a blue cheese. Blue cheeses develop and age well at much lower temperatures than many other cheeses and so are more likely to exhibit some complexity. Above all else, however, look for a cheese that is vibrant and bright.

the price of cheese

Good cheese is not cheap, but don't think that just by spending money you will automatically obtain good cheese. There are

Fresh cheese

From the simplicity of fromage frais to the delicate subtlety of ricotta or the richness of mascarpone, fresh cheese is wonderfully versatile. A fresh cheese is essentially one that is not matured, but eaten shortly after it is made, so no rind develops. You don't expect the depth and length of flavour of older harder cheeses, but you should look for some complexity and a full rich creaminess, usually offset with salty tangy flavours. Balance is important, with nothing too dominant, which is what makes these cheese so versatile. They go as well with herbs, garlic and spices as they do with honey, sugar and jam. The latter make a superb way to finish up a meal; the former a focal point, along with a salad, for a quick and easy lunch. How to select? The cheese should be soft and delicate, the flavour mild and gentle, the taste clean and uncluttered. These cheeses are highly perishable and should be stored in the fridge and eaten as soon after purchase as is possible.

pasteurization and cheese

I would always favour a cheese made with raw milk (see page 90), for all the extra characteristics it is likely to exhibit. Pasteurization does not, however, by itself make milk safe. Semi-soft rind cheeses like Brie and Camembert may carry a slight risk of listeriosis for example, and it is therefore suggested that pregnant women, the young, elderly and those with impaired immune systems avoid them. Pasteurization, however, does not kill listeriosis and nor can it eliminate the risk of e-coli either. In a hard cheese it is largely the acidity – not pasteurization – that enables it to age safely, so the question of pasteurization becomes less relevant. Less than one tenth of 1 per cent of food poisoning cases in Britain involve cheese. Compare that with 10 per cent that are traced back to fruit and vegetables.

cheese size

Although small truckles of cheese look attractive and make very good presents, the rule of thumb is buy from the largest truckle the cheese comes in. Goats' cheese, for example, is made in small sizes and that is the way to buy it, not in extended wrapped logs. Beaufort, on the other hand, comes in truckles the size of a car wheel.

The reasoning is as follows: the maturing of a large cheese takes longer, water loss is less and the ratio of skin to interior is as it should be. Larger cheese therefore tend to have a greater complexity; if they are made in smaller sizes this is not developed fully. I tested this out one Christmas on Stilton and eight people in a blind tasting of 12 went for the cheese from the large-sized truckle.

flavoured cheeses

I'm an unashamed dyed-in-the-wool traditionalist. If you want another flavour with cheese, put it on the plate not in the cheese.

Cheeses can legitimately be wrapped in leaves, stored in wood, or aged in a cave to give them a hint of another flavour, but ingredients like chives and garlic, apricots and Christmas cake – even the smoking process – to my mind are only masking something... or trying to create an artificial market. If the cheese is good, get on and eat it just as it is.

the seasonality of cheeses

Because of seasonal differences in what the cattle eat (lush spring pasture as opposed to winter hay) and climatic conditions as the cheese ripens, there are distinct differences in the flavour and texture of cheese at different times of the year. In general, though, hard cheeses are less affected by time of year than soft-rinded cheeses. Munster, with its strong ash-tainted aroma and sharp, apply flavour, is best in the summer and autumn months, although the commercial version is available all year. Goats' cheese, traditionally in season from late spring through to the end of autumn, will have all the added complexity of summery herb flavours that are simply not present in winter. Vacherin, in season from late autumn through to the following spring, has nothing like the creamy, buttery depth in the middle of summer.

storing cheeses

Ideally the storage temperature should be consistent at around 8–10°C (46–50°F), with a humid environment. At home, however, you have little choice other than to use your fridge, which probably maintains a temperature between 2 and 5°C (36 and 41°F). If you are lucky enough to have a cellar, you may be able to use that. Measure the temperature and if it maintains a steady temperature of around 6°C (43°F) you are in luck, but check with your cheesemonger for specific cheeses.

Waxed paper is the best for wrapping cheese; after that, cling-film, which is hardly romantic but is the best means of keeping the cheese sealed and, therefore, moist. Buy little and often; it helps expose you to variety and means you don't have to store too much. Don't re-use cling-film; re-wrap the cheese in fresh clean plastic each time you return it to the fridge.

To enjoy a cheese's full flavour, you should remove it from the fridge at least an hour before you intend eating it, so it can come to room temperature.

Freezing cheese

Heresy for some, practical for others... I know a woman who ages cheese in her kitchen for her guest-house in Northern Ireland and then freezes it well wrapped in freezer foil or film. Each evening she thus manages to have perfectly matured cheese to serve to her guests. The results were impressive, particularly given that the closest cheese shop was about 50 miles away. This is not perhaps a practice for everyone, but in a situation such as the one described the options are obviously limited.

Making up a cheeseboard

Serve a dozen cheeses if you must, but it is hard to find that many in good condition all at the same time. Far better to serve a few – even just one perhaps – in perfect condition. Somehow a big disc of Chaource, for example, looks particularly impressive, certainly more so than a mousetrap-sized piece. What to serve with the cheese? Keep it simple and plain; the cheese should be the star. To follow? For me it is always a green salad dressed with extra-special extra-virgin olive oil, salt, pepper and a splash of very good vinegar.

Cooking with cheese

Cheeses made with a cooked curd tend to melt well; examples are Emmental, Gruyère, Comté and Beaufort. How do you tell a cooked cheese? They have a characteristically shiny, hard surface. If you melt cheese in a sauce, you should not allow it to boil, or the cheese will become granular. If you want shavings of cheese, Parmesan for example, a swivel vegetable peeler gives just the right thickness and sexy curve when shaved over salads.

My favourite cheeses

PARMESAN (the one I always have in the fridge) – rich, salty with a fresh, tangy aftertaste.
VACHERIN MONT D'OR – smooth and buttery, hinting of the spruce bark used to wrap it.
BEAUFORT – nutty and buttery.
ST MARCELLIN – fresh, bright and mellow.
CHAOURCE – soft, full and chalky.
ST NECTAIRE – all straw and earth with sweet herbal flavours.
CAERPHILLY – smooth, rich and round when aged, relatively dull when not.

MUNSTER – all buttery and spicy, with an elegant sharpness.
EPOISSES – either fresh and herbal in the summer, or marinated and aged to complexity in the winter.
ROQUEFORT – still king for me, with its rich elegance perfectly matched with its tangy, sharp focus.

eggs

Although you can certainly tell a bad or over-aged egg while it is still in the shell (see Storing eggs, opposite), there is only one way to tell a good egg and that is to crack it open. The white should be thick and viscous, the yolk a deep yellow and dense. It should sit on top of the white, the whole egg maintaining its shape. Depending on diet and time of year the yolk may change colour, becoming paler perhaps.

what to buy

White- or brown-shelled, both are good, the colour difference being dependent on the breed of the hen rather than anything else. Ideally, you want eggs from hens that eat a varied diet, are free to run about, sit in the sun and generally have a nice time. In practice, these hens lay their eggs all over the place and are 'uneconomic'. Most of us are looking for an egg laid by a hen that gets as close to this 'ideal' as possible. About 20 per cent of eggs sold make some attempt to approximate these conditions (see page 104).

The battery hen is not a happy bird. Without dwelling on its unpleasant life, it has no outside access, lives – if that is what you call it – and dies in a cage and produces flabby, horrible eggs. 'Free-range' is not hugely better; the hens have notional access to the outside but the regulations do not in any way guarantee that each hen actually gets any fresh air or specify what sort of access – a concrete yard or dust and vegetation. There is no stipulation on breed or diet. Almost all is left up to the individual producer, and consequently there are both good and bad free-range eggs.

what to do with really good-quality eggs

Simple is best, dishes like eggs Benedict; eggs Florentine; omelettes, tortillas and frittatas; oeufs en meurette (a poached egg with a rich red wine sauce, bacon and onions); scrambled, poached, fried and baked.

storing eggs

The air pocket inside an egg expands as it ages, so while a fresh egg will sink in water, an old one will float – if it's very old, it literally shoots to the surface. Eggs should be stored in a cool, moist environment. For most of us that means a fridge, but keep them in the door and covered; despite their impenetrable appearance, egg shells are porous and will readily absorb other flavours. Eggs thus stored should be left to come to room temperature for 30–40 minutes before being cooked.

Eggs' ability to absorb other flavours can be used to good effect: they take on the flavour of truffles if stored with them and they can be rubbed with garlic and then hard-boiled for a salad, although take care not to mix these up with your breakfast eggs.

To poach an egg: have the water at a rolling boil (and with really fresh eggs you don't need to worry about adding vinegar or lemon juice – if the egg is fresh it will poach neatly, if it is stale no amount of acid will help). With a spoon, stir the water so it rolls from top to bottom, slide in the egg and try to keep the motion of the water going as this will encourage the egg to set in a neat globe.

Why do eggs crack when you boil them? Usually this is because of the shock of hitting hot water. It helps if the egg is at room temperature. It also helps if it is fresh: as the egg becomes stale, the air pocket inside the shell expands, exerting more pressure on the shell, making it more susceptible to breakage. Pricking the shell and membrane to allow the expanding air to escape will obviously help.

telling the good eggs from the bad

A great deal is in the wording on the packaging – or lack of it. If the eggs are organic, the pack should have an endorsement from one of the organic bodies (see page 19). There should be an address, advice on whether the eggs come from one flock or several, information on feed, breed and lifestyle. The better a producer is, the more they will want to tell you about their product; partly, it has to be said, to justify the higher price, but also because they have a pride in what they are selling.

where to buy eggs

If you are seeking out smaller producers, specialist shops like delicatessens, butchers and whole-food stores are good hunting grounds. Farmers' markets are also good sources of fresh farm eggs. Most supermarkets now sell organic free-range eggs, which are likely to be the best choice there.

directory

milk

Cattle breeds to look out for: Jersey, Guernsey, Ayrshire.

FULL-FAT: fat content of 3–5 per cent
SEMI-SKIMMED: fat content of between 1.5 and 1.8 per cent
SKIMMED: fat content of between 0.1 and 0.3 per cent

British supermarkets now have large sections of organic milk and, while it is often produced on a large scale, it will have more flavour and body than conventional milk. Look out for cartons and bottles from small producers. The latter are also likely to be found in delicatessens.

In the UK, typical breeds for good milk include Jersey and Guernsey, where the milk is produced on a small scale and handled not by a central dairy but by the farm where the milk is produced. Most milk is produced from Friesian, Holstein and crosses of these two breeds, because they are high-yielding and their male calves can be sold on into the beef industry.

Why are Jersey and Guernsey milks the best? These breeds, and the likes of Ayrshire, have a fat content which is higher (typically over 4 or 5 per cent compared with less than 4 per cent for Friesian and Holstein) and this is the source of much of the flavour. Worried about your fat intake? That 1 per cent will make little difference and what benefit you gain in lowered fat, you lose in lack of flavour, the finished product becoming rather watery.

cream

In the UK cream comes as follows:
SINGLE CREAM: the low fat level, a minimum of 18 per cent, means you cannot whip it and it is generally used for pouring over desserts or into coffee.
WHIPPING CREAM: its higher fat content means it can be whipped and will hold its shape. The slightly lower fat content than double cream, however, means that it is often used by chefs in preference to double cream as it gives the luxury without quite the same level of fat.
DOUBLE CREAM: with a minimum of 48 per cent fat, it is usually thick (spoonable rather than pourable). This does not necessarily denote quality – it is perfectly possible to have an indifferent or average double cream. The flavour should, however, be complex and long, well rounded and balanced (if this can be said of an ingredient so rich in calories and cholesterol).

Double cream can also be whipped, but is more likely than whipping cream to turn to butter, so take care not to over-beat. It is essential in the making of crème brûlée and ice-creams.
EXTRA-THICK CREAM: generally double cream homogenized to give it a slightly more rigid texture.
CLOTTED CREAM: something of a speciality of Devon, Cornwall and parts of Somerset, this is essentially a double cream made from rich milk. It is never liquid, instead being spooned over scones and desserts in place of butter.
SOURED CREAM: not cream that has been left to sour, but one in which a culture or souring agent is added, often to single cream, which coagulates the cream and gives it a slightly sour flavour.
CRÈME FRAÎCHE: fresh cream to which a culture is added to give it a gentle acidity, but without the sourness present in soured cream.
SMETANA: a milk substitute for soured cream, being a combination of skimmed milk, some cream and a culture. Its main benefit is a lower fat content than soured cream. It is popular in Eastern Europe, where it is added to dishes like goulash. Both soured cream and smetana should be stirred into hot foods just before serving as they separate when boiled.

butter
What to buy
Farmhouse butters in the UK:
Berkeley Farm Dairy 01793
812228; Elm's Dairy 01749
890371; Domini Quality Foods
01359 221240.
Whey butters in the UK:
Appleby's 01948 840387;
Duckett's 01934 712218; Keen's
01963 32286; Montgomery's
01963 440243; Quicke's 01392
851222.

Supermarket and specialist shop
butters in the UK: President, Beurre
d'Isigny. Look out, too, for butters
from Charentes-Poitou and Deux
Sèvres, which have AOC status.

cheese
Good cheese shops all do mail
order: La Fromagerie 020 7359
7440; Harrods 020 7730 1234,
Neal's Yard Dairy 020 7240 5700;
Ian Mellis 0131 266215.

Best-sellers at La Fromagerie
● Montgomery's Cheddar (beguiling, approachable, slightly granular
with deep soft tones)
● Keen's Cheddar (smooth,
supple and powerful)
● Brie de Meaux (unpasteurized;
protected by an *appellation
contrôlée*; the best is reputed to
come from the Grand and Petit
Morin. Good from May to
October)
● Colston Bassett Stilton (warm,

smooth with elegance and length)
● Camembert (farmhouse)
● Selection of mini sheep's-milk
cheeses from the Pyrenees (spicy,
tangy and fruity)
● King Richard III Wensleydale
(moist and crumbly with a rich
sweet flavour and soft, mellow
overtones)
● Berkswell (hard sheep's-milk
cheese with close texture and
complex developed flavours)
● Appleby's Cheshire (when
young, mild and mellow flavours
which age into a rich piquancy)
● Taleggio (farmhouse-made with
complex, smooth well-focused flavours and a soft,
smooth texture)

Best-sellers at Neal's Yard Dairy
● Montgomery's Cheddar (see
above)
● Colston Bassett Stilton (see
above)
● Cookham's Lancashire (a
crumbly open texture, the flavours

are flowery and summery)
● Appleby's Cheshire (see above)
● Appleby's Double Gloucester
(open texture with a mild mellow
flavour both sweet and salty)
● Todd Trethowan's Caerphilly
(creamy when young, it matures
into a cheese with bright flowery
flavours and a softer texture.
● Chris Duckett's Caerphilly (sold
off the farm after one week, but
when bought from the likes of
Neal's Yard Dairy the cheese will
have been aged into a semi-soft,
herb- and grass-laden cheese of
immense subtlety)
● Cashel Blue (soft and creamy in
texture, the flavour is powerful,
but well rounded and structured)
● Ticklemore (hard goats' cheese
with a mild sweet flavour)
● Wigmore (firm when young, it
flows as it ages, developing soft
and subtle notes of flowers and
pasture)
● Tymsboro (creamy textured with
rich nutty flavours)
● Ragstone (light and smooth
texture with delicate clover
flavours)
● Berkswell (see above)

British Cheese Award winners
('supreme champions' they call
them)
● 1994: Innes button (soft textures, bright, mild and refreshing)
● 1995: Mrs Kirkham's
Lancashire (moist and crumbly

103

with bright flowery buttery overtones)

- 1996: Lincolnshire Poacher (close-textured with warm earthy notes and a clean tang)
- 1997: Milleens (rich and creamy, there is a salty tang to its summer pasture flavours)
- 1998: Celtic Promise (a traditional Gouda-style cheese with close texture with a herby rich, complex flavour)
- 1999: Cheddar Gorge Cheese Company's Extra Mature Cheddar (close texture with strong, earthy and meadow flavours)

supermarkets

These bastions of retail therapy have done much in recent years to improve the range and quality of the cheese they sell, with limited success. The truth is, supermarkets hate anything alive and anything which shows variation – it simply goes against everything they believe in. Their cold systems are designed to eliminate bacteria, not separate the good from the bad, and they simply don't have the expertise or time.

Increasingly, however, supermarkets are stocking a small range of specialist cheeses from small producers that compete favourably with some of the cheese offered in some delicatessens. In theory, because you are buying from a smaller producer, the quality should be better. However,

as outlined above, the ageing and keeping of the cheese are crucial. However good it is to start with, if it is not cared for and brought on, it is likely to taste dull and boring. Buy by all means, but ask yourself if what you are eating is worth the extra money. You may well conclude that the trip to a good cheesemonger is worthwhile.

Supermarket best-buys for cheese

Blue cheese is always a good bet. Few, if any, will be of the same quality as those from a speciality retailer, but this is what I buy when faced with the task:

- Roquefort (even the packet version is not bad, in part because it is a regulated cheese)
- St Agur (another blue, with some length and character)
- Stilton (a regulated cheese)
- Goats' cheese (avoid the logs and go for an individual 'button')
- Parmesan (not fantastic, but Parmesan is a regulated cheese, so it must reach a set standard)

eggs

Eggs in the UK tend to have a 'best-before' date, some also have a packed date. The packing date can be several days after laying (egg packing often being done on a different site from where the egg was laid).

BARN EGGS: account for about 5 per cent of egg production. The cages of the battery system are replaced with perches and feeders at different levels, but the diet and indoor life are much the same.

FREE-RANGE: a standard minimum, accounting for about 15 per cent of production. Regulations stipulate outside access and minimum flock sizes, but in reality many of the birds never see daylight, flock sizes are in thousands, not hundreds, and feed is generally cereal with a protein source (often soya).

FOUR-GRAIN EGGS: an attempt to specify the diet as being cereal-based and devoid of medicines, although the hens are likely to have been in a barn system.

ORGANIC FREE-RANGE: regulations are much more specific, birds have easy and continuous outside access, flock size cannot be more than 500, debeaking is banned and 80 per cent of the diet must be organic, and the remainder from permitted sources. Antibiotics, proteins and colourings are banned. Watch out, however, for eggs that might be from an organic farm but are not themselves organic.

QUAILS' EGGS: from the same intensive system as battery hens.

In the UK, egg sizing is as follows:
SMALL (under 53 g)
MEDIUM (54–63 g)
LARGE (64–73 g)
VERY LARGE (over 73 g)

butternut squash and saffron soup *with goats' cheese croûtes*

serves 4

2 onions
1 leek
4 celery stalks
2 garlic cloves
2 tablespoons olive oil
500 g (1 lb 2 oz) butternut squash
150 ml (1/4 pint) fresh orange juice
juice of 1 lemon
salt and pepper
1 litre (1 3/4 pints) light chicken stock
125 ml (4 fl oz) whipping cream
generous pinch of saffron strands,
    ground to a powder (there is no
    need to toast them as they will be
    cooked in the soup)

FOR THE GOATS' CHEESE
CROÛTES:
200 g (7 oz) fresh goats' cheese
1 garlic clove
1/2 small red chilli
1 teaspoon freshly chopped parsley
zest of 1/2 lemon
3 tablespoons olive oil
4 slices of baguette, lightly grilled

Squash is a much underrated vegetable. In Spain, on the plains of La Mancha, I have eaten a pie that was nothing more than the slow-roasted bottom half of a pumpkin. Sweet and candy-like, it made a perfect mid-morning snack. Butternut squash is one of the more consistent of the squash family and is widely available.

1 Peel and finely chop the onions, leeks, celery and garlic. Heat the olive oil in a saucepan and add the vegetables. Cover and sweat over a very gentle heat for 20 minutes, stirring occasionally.

2 Split the squash, remove the seeds and rind and cut the flesh into small dice. Add to the vegetables, together with the orange and lemon juices. Season with salt and pepper and cook gently for a further 25 minutes.

3 Add the stock, bring to the boil and simmer very gently for 5 minutes. Add the cream and saffron and simmer for a further 5 minutes, then remove from the heat and allow to cool for 10 minutes.

4 Liquidize the contents of the pan, then pass through a sieve. Reheat and adjust the seasoning.

5 Make the goats' cheese croûtes: in a bowl, lightly mash the cheese with a fork. Finely chop the garlic clove and chilli. Mash these together with the cheese, parsley, lemon juice and oil, and season. Spread on the baguette slices and serve with the soup.

chicory, Roquefort and toasted hazelnut salad *with grain-mustard dressing*

serves 4

2 heads of chicory, trimmed and the
    leaves separated
100 g (3¹/₂ oz) Roquefort, crumbled
2 tablespoons hazelnuts

FOR THE GRAIN-MUSTARD
DRESSING:
1 heaped tablespoon grain mustard
1 tablespoon Dijon mustard
3 tablespoons light olive oil
1 tablespoon hazelnut oil
1 dessertspoon red wine vinegar
1 dessertspoon clear honey
Tabasco sauce to taste

This salad is such a perfectly light way to start any meal. Dispense with a knife and fork; the leaves offer all the leverage you need and half the fun is mopping up the dressing with bread and fingers.

1 Arrange the leaves on 4 plates like the spokes of a wheel and scatter over the Roquefort.
2 Heat a dry frying pan and, when hot, toss the hazelnuts in it so they toast and take on a good golden colour. Tip on to a cold surface and, when cool, scatter them over the chicory and Roquefort. (Alternatively, you can toast them in a moderate oven until golden brown, about 5 minutes.)
3 Make the dressing: put the mustards in a bowl and whisk in the two oils, much as you would do for mayonnaise. It should have the consistency of thin cream; thin it with the vinegar and a little water if it looks too thick. Add the honey and a few drops of Tabasco sauce to taste. Spoon the dressing over the salad.

white bean salad
with black olives, grilled fennel and Gruyère

serves 4

2 fennel bulbs
salt and pepper
about 125 ml (4 fl oz) extra-virgin
    olive oil
two 400-g (14-oz) cans of white
    beans (e.g. cannellini or haricot),
    drained and well rinsed
100 g (3¹/2 oz) black olives, stoned
¹/2 tablespoon chopped shallots
1 garlic clove, finely chopped and
    mashed with a little salt
2 tablespoons finely chopped
    parsley
1 teaspoon fennel seeds
1 teaspoon Dijon mustard
juice of ¹/2 lemon
100 g (3¹/2 oz) Gruyère cheese

*If you are lucky enough to get fresh
beans in the summer, this salad is
even better than its winter version.
Canned beans are, however, one of
technology's better inventions; a darn
sight easier than all that overnight
soaking and endless boiling if all you
are trying to do is put supper for
four on the table.*

1 Trim the tops and bottoms
from the fennel heads and then cut
them vertically in 5-mm (¹/4-inch)
thick slices. Preheat a ridged
griddle pan or barbecue and grill
the fennel slices until lightly
charred, about 5 minutes. Turn
over and cook the other sides in
the same way. Transfer to a bowl,
sprinkle over with salt and pepper
and 3 tablespoons of the olive oil.
Cover with cling-film and set aside
(this will help to soften the fennel).
2 In a large bowl, combine the
beans, olives, shallot, garlic, parsley,
fennel seeds and mustard. Stir in 4
tablespoons of olive oil and the
lemon juice, and season to taste.
3 Pile the bean mixture in the
centre of 4 plates, arrange the fennel
slices around the edges and scatter
over shavings of Gruyère (made
using a swivel vegetable peeler).
Drizzle over more olive oil and
serve.

pork cooked with milk

serves 4–6

75 g (2³/4 oz) butter
1 boned loin of pork, weighing about
    1.5 kg (3¹/4 lb)
2 bay leaves
1 onion, roughly chopped
1 teaspoon fennel seeds
600 ml (1 pint) full-fat milk

*I know it sounds weird, but the
milk is transformed into a delicate,
finely balanced gravy and the meat
comes out remarkably moist and
tender. Baking meat in milk is
popular in parts of northern Italy.*

1 Heat the butter in a flameproof
casserole and gently brown the
meat all over. Add the bay leaves,
onion and fennel seeds. Pour in
the milk. Cover with the lid
(leaving a small gap), lower the
heat and allow to simmer gently
for 2 hours, turning the meat
occasionally. By this time the milk
will have become a nut brown and
reduced substantially.
2 Remove the meat and allow to
rest in a warm place. Add a wine
glass of hot water and scrape up
all the residue. Simmer for a
further 5 minutes or until reduced
by half. Strain through a sieve and
serve with the meat, thickly sliced.
Some root vegetables go well.

marinated feta, oven roast tomatoes, green beans, frisée and balsamic vinaigrette

serves 4

4 tomatoes

about 250 ml (9 fl oz) extra-virgin
    olive oil

salt and pepper

200 g (7 oz) feta cheese, thinly sliced

bunch of thyme, roughly chopped

2 garlic cloves, bashed with the flat
    of a knife

6 black peppercorns, lightly bashed

400 g (14 oz) green or French
    beans, trimmed

4 handfuls of frisée leaves (or a bag
    of frisée with other leaves)

1 dessertspoon balsamic vinegar

*Feta gets some hard knocks for being
a dull and boring cheese, but it takes
to marinating superbly well and its
salty tang is perfect in salads.
Marinated feta will keep in the fridge
for several days, its flavour only
improving in the process. Tomatoes
are best roasted at a low temperature
over a long period. They will keep
for a few days in the fridge, so it
might be worth considering doing a
larger batch.*

1 Prepare the tomatoes at least
one day ahead. Preheat the oven
to 160°C/325°F/Gas 3.

2 Halve the tomatoes and arrange
them on a baking tray. Drizzle
over 4 tablespoons of olive oil and
season generously with salt. Bake
in the oven for 45 minutes.
(Alternatively, you can cook them
in the oven preheated to
130°C/275°F/Gas 1 overnight, or
in the bottom oven of an Aga.)
Remove and allow to cool. They
will look wizened and somewhat
dried up, but nothing like as dry
as a sun-dried tomato.

3 Combine the feta, thyme, garlic
and peppercorns with enough olive
oil to cover. Set aside overnight in
a cool place.

4 Next day, blanch the beans in
boiling salted water until just
cooked, about 3 minutes. Refresh
under cold running water, drain
well, pat dry and place on 4 plates
along with the frisée. Arrange the
halved tomatoes and feta on top.

5 Combine the balsamic vinegar
with 4 tablespoons of olive oil and
season with salt and pepper.
Drizzle over the salad and serve.

Stilton, wilted cucumber and watercress sandwich
with beetroot and horseradish relish

makes 4

1 cucumber, peeled, deseeded and
    sliced
salt and pepper
1 baguette
100 g (3½ oz) Stilton, sliced
4 handfuls of watercress

FOR THE BEETROOT AND
HORSERADISH RELISH:
2 small beetroots (raw if possible)
1 tablespoon roughly chopped
    gherkins
1 dessertspoon grated horseradish
    (you can now buy this in jars)

There used to be a sandwich bar at the top of Cork Street in London that did a whole range of unusual sandwiches like this one. It's long since gone, but it was way ahead of its time, before the advent of chains that eschew anything like this individualism.

1 Place the cucumber slices in a sieve and toss with a heaped teaspoon of salt. Set aside to drain for 10 minutes.
2 Make the beetroot and horseradish relish: peel the beetroots and grate them on the coarsest setting of your grater. Combine with the gherkins and the horseradish and a seasoning of salt and pepper.
3 Rinse the cucumber well under cold running water, drain well and squeeze dry. Split the baguette lengthwise and arrange in layers the Stilton, watercress, cucumber and beetroot and horseradish relish.
4 Cut in four to serve.

spicy Cashel Blue butter

makes about 500 g (1 lb)

225 g (8 oz) unsalted butter,
    softened
225g (8 oz) Cashel Blue (or similar
    soft blue cheese)
1 garlic clove, crushed
Tabasco sauce, to taste
half a bunch of flat-leaf parsley

This dressing for grilled meats is perfect with veal, delectable with steak, a delight with lamb and stunning with pork. It is also the easiest way in the world to dress up a Tuesday night chop or two, with a salad rounding things off nicely.

1 In a mixer with the beater attachment, put all the butter, half the Cashel Blue and garlic, and a few drops of Tabasco. Blend until completely homogenized.
2 Pick the parsley and blanch the leaves for 5 seconds in boiling water. Refresh in cold water, dry off and chop coarsely.
3 Combine the chopped parsley, the butter mixture, the remaining Cashel Blue and garlic, and more Tabasco to taste. Roll into a tube in cling-film and chill. This freezes well and forms a log from which you can cut slices straight from the freezer as and when you require them.

spiced yoghurt relish

makes about 450g (1lb)

1 red onion, thinly sliced

1 cucumber, halved, deseeded and
    thinly sliced

salt and pepper

1 teaspoon toasted cumin seeds

bunch of coriander, roughly
    chopped (stems and all)

2 tomatoes, quartered, deseeded
    and thinly sliced

400 ml (14 fl oz) plain full-fat runny
    yoghurt

This is adapted from a basic raita, *used widely in Indian cooking. It goes with vegetable and meat casseroles, grilled chops and chicken, and is rather delicious just as a dip with drinks.*

1 Combine the onion and cucumber in a sieve, sprinkle liberally with salt and set over a bowl for 10 minutes. Rinse thoroughly and pat dry – this should rid the cucumber of some of its water and the onion of some of its strength.

2 Combine the onion and cucumber with the cumin seeds, coriander, tomatoes and yoghurt. Stir well and adjust the seasoning (carefully, as there is probably enough salt from the cucumber and onion).

grilled figs, spiced cream cheese, honey and toasted pine nuts

serves 4

1 tablespoon raisins

1 tablespoon grappa (or brandy or rum)

8 figs

about 60 g (2 oz) sugar

1 tablespoon pine nuts

small pinch of ground cinnamon

small pinch of ground cloves

small pinch of freshly grated nutmeg

4 tablespoons full-fat cream cheese

2 tablespoons double cream

4 tablespoons runny honey

Sadly, the figs we get here are too often dull, insipid examples of this most sublime of fruits. This recipe evolved out of an evening faced with some particularly depressing examples and led one guest to sit back and exclaim they were perhaps the best figs she had ever eaten. The sugar and honey had clearly done their work on the sweetness, but her real enthusiasm lay in the spiced cheese, so much fuller and more complex than straight cream.

1 In a small bowl, soak the raisins in the grappa and set aside. Preheat a hot grill.

2 Slice the figs in half vertically, but not quite through, so they open out like flower petals when pressed. Press the figs into a plate of sugar and set aside.

3 Lightly toast the pine nuts in a hot dry frying pan.

4 Combine the raisins, grappa, spices, cream cheese and cream and gently stir. Place a scoop of the spiced cream cheese on each plate.

5 Grill the figs until just golden and bubbling and add to the cream cheese. Spoon over the honey and scatter the pine nuts around.

vegetables,
pulses
and fruit

'*Vegetables in the Middle East do not play second fiddle as do the "two veg" to meat in England. They hold a dignified, sometimes splendid, position in the hierarchy of food. They are, in turn, mezze, pickles and salads. They can be stuffed and ranked as a main dish, an adornment to meat in a stew, or deep-fried, sautéed or steamed. In cooking, their nature is taken into account, and their flavour, texture and colour are treated with respect. They are expected to give of their best.*'

CLAUDIA RODEN, *A Book of Middle Eastern Food*

Picking fruit and vegetables from a garden is probably one of the best ways to get started in cooking them. Rows of carrots and leeks, broccoli and cauliflower; a line of strawberries, or an orchard full of apples; a greenhouse heady with the scent of tomatoes, clumps of various salad leaves just waiting for a bowl and some olive oil.

For most of us, however, the reality is the fruit and vegetable section of the supermarket, an old-fashioned greengrocer's shop, or for the lucky few a chance to buy direct. Whichever choice we are faced with, the problem remains – pick any fruit or vegetable when it is ripe and it starts to deteriorate. The quicker the time from field to plate, the better the quality is likely to be. The same can be said for pulses; although dried, the younger they are the better the texture and the flavour. A packet of year-old chickpeas is far less exciting than this year's crop.

How to limit the time before you start eating them has also become an environmental concern. Buy a bean and it may well have been flown from Africa or Central America, with all the inherent travelling costs implicit in its price, and the damage to the environment through the use of fuel. Much of this activity stems from

our seemingly insatiable demand to have total choice all of the time, which sends the supermarkets off round the world – essentially chasing the sun, which is key not only to the growth of fruits and vegetables, but also to their flavour.

And if you thought a carrot was a carrot, a tomato a tomato, think again. Many varieties exist and are being developed all the time. As the customer, we are encouraged to realize this with tomatoes, where the variety is explained along with its characteristics, but this is not the case in many instances. Parsnip we buy as a commodity, celery too. So why is British celery weak-tasting and white, when Italian celery is strong-tasting and green?

The answer lies, to some extent, in variety, but also in how it is grown, what the weather is like and what, ultimately, the customer demands. In Italy they want strong-tasting green celery with lots of leaves (which are also used in the cooking), while in the UK we seem to care little about the leaves, opting instead for pale rather tasteless specimens.

Buying fruit and vegetables is a bit of a lottery; the good thing about it is not needing any specialist knowledge. We all know a good peach when we eat one.

where to buy vegetables and fruit

Finding a supply of wonderful fruit and vegetables is an increasing challenge. For many of us, the supermarket is a primary source, and all the chains have worked enormously hard to build up the idea of choice. Sadly, in many instances the choice remains an illusion. Rows of expensive exotic fruit and vegetables aren't great, if what you really want are fantastic carrots and those offered have 'Day-glo' colouring and ultimately not much flavour.

Some supermarkets are better than others, however. Those that work closely with suppliers, often developing or rediscovering varieties in tandem with them, are the ones to watch. Much of this work gets exposure in the press and it is often the case that supermarkets known for their fruit and vegetable sections are also the better retailers overall. If their potatoes are good, then so too will be their bread.

As with all other food, speed of growth is of the essence as far as supermarkets – and hence farmers – are concerned. Plant a field with beetroot, grow them as quickly as possible and move them on to the shelves with all speed is the basic rule-of-thumb and we, the consumers, tend to lose out on taste, colour and intensity. With tomatoes or peppers, the field can be replaced by an inert substance that literally hold the roots in place, the nutrients coming from a cocktail provided through the watering system. Located under glass, there is no need to rely on seasons and when the weather is bad the heating comes on. When was the last time you bought a red pepper that gave any information on how it was grown?

The average greengrocer is seldom much better than a supermarket. He or she buys from the wholesale market, which is under the same pressures as the supermarket. The greengrocer is faced with selecting from an equally poor choice, usually mass-grown and obtained from all over the world. The concept of retailer as a source of all that is best, their buying done to bring you all that they think matches their high standards, is not often the reality.

Buying from farm shops or directly from producers in a market is perhaps the best and most satisfying way. Here the reputation of the producer is on show; if the tomatoes and salad leaves are not up to much, you are unlikely to return. However, traditional markets have been besieged by operators who never step into a field or orchard, preferring to buy from the wholesale market and then sell as if they were producers. Contrast the small stall bearing cabbages, onions and a little salading, perhaps, with a large one sporting kiwi fruit, pineapple and glossy potatoes.

Restaurant fruit and veg

Restaurants buy fruit and vegetables just like the rest of us, but they use specialist suppliers who know that their relationships with their customers and hence their business is determined by the quality of what they deliver.

No surprise, then, that over the last 10 years an increasing number of chefs have become suppliers. It used to be that a chef would oversee all the fruit and vegetables that came into the kitchen, rejecting anything that was not up to standard. The chefs-turned-suppliers were able to second-guess this stage, supplying only the best. Yet contrast this world with what the public experience. We limply wander around, accepting what we are given and rarely even commenting, let alone actually complaining.

storing fruit and vegetables

Fruit and vegetables should ideally be stored in a cool atmosphere, but most modern kitchens are only able to offer a fridge, generally too cold and dry. See opposite for advice on individual fruits and vegetables.

chemicals

Most fruit and vegetables are grown with the use of chemicals at some stage during their growth. We commonly believe that by rinsing them under clean water we are disposing of any residues. This has scientifically been shown to be far from the case. Many chemicals are designed to cling to the surface – and, in some instances, even impregnate the skin. A quick flash under a tap is unlikely to dislodge them. What water will do is help to wash off any surface dirt. If you are concerned about chemicals, buy organic or take the skin or outside layer off. With citrus fruit, where you are using the zest you really need to scrub the surface with hot soapy water before using, or opt for unwaxed specimens (most lemons are otherwise coated with a layer of wax full of fungicides), which are becoming increasingly available.

varietals

Throughout this chapter you will find much mention of varietals, or lack of them. This is an area of great change, some of it good, some bad. Undoubtedly, we now have endless examples of higher-yielding, more disease-resistant fruit and vegetable varieties that grow into perfectly shaped and coloured specimens, but flavour is sometimes not given nearly enough prominence.

Variety is good for lots of reasons – interest being one, security another. If a strawberry always tastes the same, it ultimately becomes rather dull. If we have fewer varieties, concentrated in the hands of fewer seed companies, there is a strong argument that we are exposing ourselves to more risk, through a lack of disease resistance and increasing reliance on chemicals or genetic modification.

This is a rapidly changing area, with much research and debate, and my reluctance to list too many varieties is based largely on the fact that so many of them are changing and becoming company-specific, with retailers working increasingly closely with suppliers to develop their own 'brands' of fruit and vegetable. Thus old varieties are either evolving into new ones, or disappearing altogether.

vegetables

what to look for when you buy vegetables

Look for bright, healthy-looking, firm examples, without soft spots or blemishes. Irregularity of shape or a little clinging earth is to be encouraged; uniformity may suit the supermarkets, but it suggests breeding for appearance and not for flavour. Any attached greenery helps to determine age. Colour should be strong, without slipping into the luminous. On the whole, vegetables don't smell, so you need to rely on flavour, which should be strong and vibrant, cooked or uncooked.

some points on various types of vegetable

Advice on buying most vegetables focuses on bright healthy examples. They should feel heavy, with dense colouring and no bruised or damaged parts. The following list sets out specifics for each vegetable where applicable.

ARTICHOKE, GLOBE: now grown all over the world, this is actually a member of the thistle family. For

all its size, most of the globe arti-choke is inedible; you eat the small pale part of the leaf where it attaches to the globe, discard the hairy choke and then eat the heart and, if sufficiently tender, part of the stem.

Artichokes should be firm; a stale globe artichoke is characteristically soft and pliable. Small is preferable to large if you want to eat the whole thing; large is preferable to small if you're after the heart, which is delicious.

Generally steamed or boiled, they take 30–40 minutes to cook, although prize small specimens may take less. Globe artichokes go well with mayonnaise, hollandaise and vinaigrette. If they are small and tender enough, you can eat them whole, as they won't yet have developed a choke and the whole leaves will still be tender. The Italians flatten them, dip them in batter and deep-fry them. You can

hollow them out and stuff them with scrambled eggs or salad.

Store artichokes, wrapped in damp newspaper, in the fridge,

ARTICHOKE, JERUSALEM: grown all over Europe, these knobbly tubers are usually boiled or steamed and then skinned. They are cooked in gratins, mashed or made into soup.

Look for firm, smooth examples; if they are knobbly, the wastage is greater. If you are skinning before cooking, drop them into acidulated water to prevent browning. Prime examples can be simply scrubbed, thinly sliced and served in a salad. Flatulence can be a problem with Jerusalem artichokes, somewhat lessened if they are boiled first, before being sautéed or grilled, the two cooking methods somehow drawing out the impurities.

ASPARAGUS: arguably the best is from the UK, but asparagus from Alsace, Italy and a spindly example in Spain have all had me swooning at various times of the year. Apart from the usual qualities to look out for, including vibrancy of colour and firmness, it is hard to tell the quality of asparagus from looking

at it. Its intense, vegetal flavour is unmistakable, but hard to describe. You must experiment with suppliers, and once you find a good one, stay loyal. Asparagus comes in various sizes and colours, from green to white, the latter blanched (i.e. earthed up to grow without benefit of light). Thin asparagus is known as sprue; after that the stems get larger until you reach 'jumbo'. Personal preference and availability will dictate your purchase, but the key sign to look for is the stem. Once picked, asparagus will last for two or three days if it is stored properly. After that the stem starts to dry out and look old – it is time to walk away.

AUBERGINE: long popular in Mediterranean countries and Asia, these come in a huge variety of different colourings in addition to the more usual purple. Normally grilled or fried, aubergine seems to suit Mediterranean flavours best, and is particularly popular in Greece and Turkey. Good with acidic foods like tomatoes and strong herb-driven sauces, it also works well with spices.

The appearance of an aubergine tells you little about its flavour; shiny black examples can taste remarkably limp while rather tired-looking mauve versions can taste surprisingly meaty. Generally it is better to go for specimens that are spongy rather than soft. It is said that you shouldn't store aubergines near tomatoes or apples as this will cause them to ripen too fast. Country of origin is a help, Italy and North Africa being particularly good sources, but even then the best come from suppliers who grow them in earth in view of sunshine. Hothouses and modified earth substitutes do little for flavour. Except for the Oriental varieties, which are generally long and thin or egg-shaped, the bitterness of aubergines has largely been bred out, negating the need for salting, although some still argue that salted aubergine requires less oil during cooking.

AVOCADO: these can taste bitter and remarkably soapy, or rich and perfectly balanced. Look for Hass, a variety which is generally more successful than many others. The fruit should just yield to pressure at the stem end. Don't delay, a ripe avocado becomes overripe quickly. If under-ripe, keep them at room temperature; if overripe, store them in the fridge. Sources

are now worldwide and all-year-round, so the seasonality has virtually disappeared.

BEANS: often lumped under the generic name French beans, there are many varieties, from the purple-streaked variety that turn green when boiled to the round yellow pods. To tell how fresh they are, snap one in half. No snap? Leave them on the shelf. The inside should be juicy, the skin intensely coloured. The same characteristics should be present with fresh broad beans. Store in the vegetable tray in the fridge.

BEETROOT: one vegetable that can improve as it ages. The root's flavour intensifies as it dries out, although it does tend to become rather limp. Beetroot can be stored at room temperature. In the UK, a lot of beetroot is sold already cooked, some of it pickled. Avoid the latter, as it tastes revoltingly of strong vinegar and not much else. Most cooked beetroot is excellent, requiring little more than a rinse before it is either heated – perhaps in roasting juices – or sliced or grated and mixed with other ingredients. Beware the juice of beetroot, as it stains easily.

BROCCOLI: comes in two forms: calabrese, which is available all year round, and sprouting broccoli, which appears in early spring. This latter variety used to be sold like asparagus, packaged in bundles with tissue paper. There are new varieties appearing that combine the all-year availability of calabrese with something of the flavour of sprouting broccoli. Avoid woody stalks and don't delay in the cooking; sprouting broccoli, particularly, deteriorates quickly. Store in the vegetable tray in the fridge. Remember that much of the flavour of both lies in the stalks, so don't discard these in the preparation and perhaps put them to cook a little ahead of the flowering heads.

BRUSSELS SPROUT: these should be firm, with good colouring and the stem freshly cut; if it looks dry and wizened this suggests harvesting was some time ago.

CABBAGE: comes in red, white, green, tight-leaved and mini versions (see Brussels sprout above). General rules apply for buying, but a good rule-of-thumb is that fresh cabbage should squeak when squeezed. Avoid cooking in

masses of water as this leaches out flavour and nutrients; a little water and some oil or butter is far preferable. Cabbage takes to spicing, as well as to more East European treatment with butter and caraway seeds. Savoy is a particularly good variety, having both excellent flavour and good texture. Cavolo nero, a red-black, thick-stemmed cabbage popular in Italy, is now widely available. Make sure you cook it long enough for the stems to soften, otherwise it should be treated as any cabbage. Cabbages can be stored at room temperature.

CARROT: there are different varieties, like Zino, which is sweet and juicy, or Parisienne, a squat, sweetly flavoured but more firmly textured carrot. There is not much chance of being able to decide, however, unless you buy direct from the producer – a carrot is a carrot. Carrots go well with both herbs and spices: mint, coriander and basil, as well as cumin,

cardamom and coriander seed. You will need a cool kitchen or fridge for storage.

CAULIFLOWER: white is traditional, but other colours are possible, like green and purple. Avoid anything with brown patches and consider stir-frying the florets as well as boiling and steaming them.

CELERY AND CELERIAC: celeriac, although somewhat rough in its appearance, actually tastes like sweet celery. At its best in winter, you need to cut away the tough, knobbly skin. Avoid large examples, which tend to go stringy. Celeriac can be either mashed with butter and eaten with game or meat, shredded raw and mixed with mayonnaise and mustard to make celeriac rémoulade, or steamed, boiled or roasted and served as a vegetable. It works particularly well with mustard. It can be stored at room temperature. Celery stalks should

be brittle and don't waste the leaves if you are lucky enough to get them; chopped up and added to soups and stews they provide a subtle celery flavouring. Store in the fridge and remember that celery keeps much longer when attached to its root.

CHICORY: the pear-shaped cluster of spindly leaves, which the French call endive. It is generally used in salads. Look for unblemished firm examples. In truth, however, looks can still mean the end result is rather watery in both taste and texture; the flavour should have a strong hint of aniseed and be slightly sour or bitter. When braised, this flavour mellows out, leaving a sweet, soft and buttery accompaniment to meat and fish. Store in the fridge.

CHINESE CABBAGE OR LEAF: has a mild cabbage flavour that is delicate, almost sweet. It can be used raw in salads, added to stir-fries, when it retains much of its bite, or used in stews and soups, when it becomes quite soft. It keeps well, for a week or so if stored in the vegetable drawer of the fridge.

COURGETTE: essentially a small marrow, courgettes can be coloured anything from yellow to pale green to dark green. The larger they get, the less flavour they have. Thinly sliced, they are delicious raw. Look for firm, shiny examples. The hair on their surface is a good guide as to how well they have been handled; they should prickle slightly. The flowers are a delight, deep-fried in a light batter. I avoid stuffing them, they are too good simply on their own with lemon juice and black pepper. Store in the fridge.

CUCUMBER: these shouldn't wobble, but be firm and stiff. Remove the seeds (which are not digested) and the skin if it is thick (a taste will confirm if it is bitter), but otherwise leave it on as it adds colour. Cucumber is largely water, so the texture is much improved if it is salted for 10 minutes. Perfect partners are yoghurt and mint. Store in the fridge.

FENNEL: as delicious raw as it is cooked, look for firm bulbs that often have the feathery fronds attached. These should be bright, green and healthy-looking; when faded they suggest age. Thinly slice and dress with lemon juice, olive oil and salt and pepper a short time before you sit down to eat. Generally available all year round, fennel is actually a winter vegetable in its home of Italy. Store in the fridge.

KOHLRABI: popular in Europe and Eastern Europe, it is the smooth, round and pale green swollen stem of the vegetable that we eat, usually sold without its leaves, which can be cooked much like beet greens. The taste falls between that of turnip and that of cabbage. Steam or boil, peel and serve with melted butter or a rich cream or butter sauce. Turnip recipes adapt well, otherwise peel and slice thinly and serve with a vinaigrette. Store in the fridge.

LEEK: look for bright fresh specimens with a minimum of green part, as this is largely inedible, although useful for soups and stock-making. The white part and paler green part can be steamed and served with a vinaigrette, or incorporated into other dishes where onion might be overly strong. Store in the fridge.

MANGE-TOUT PEA: small, crisp and green – don't delay on eating, as like peas they lose out on flavour quickly once picked. Store in the fridge. Snow or sugar snap peas should be treated in a similar fashion.

MARSH SAMPHIRE: avoiding woody stems, this shoreline plant should be tender enough to eat raw. Avoid any with black spots, a sure sign of age. Store in the fridge.

MUSTARD GREENS OR PAK CHOI: although a member of the cabbage family, this has a very mild flavour, best shown when steamed or stir-fried. Although used in Eastern cuisine, plainly steamed it is also delicious with Western food.

OKRA: otherwise know as ladies' fingers, these are as popular in the gumbos of Louisiana as they are in India. About 8 cm (3 inches) long, this five-sided green vegetable contains seeds and a sticky juice, so remove the stem without breaking into the pod (unless you want the stickiness, as in gumbo). Quality lies in stiffness; if it is limp, it is old and stale. Usually cooked in soups, stews and curries, okra contributes a bitter-sweet quality and a smooth finish. Alternatively, cook it with onions, tomatoes and garlic.

ONION, RED ONION, SHALLOT AND SPRING ONION: there are numerous varieties, which range from strong to mild, sweet to almost sour. Avoid anything with green shoots or any discernible softness. Evade the tears associated with peeling by creating a draught – an open window or door perhaps – the vapour released by cutting then drifts away, rather than up into your eyes. When adding onions to stock, include the outside skin as this adds colour. Adding salt to sautéing onions helps to prevent them colouring. Red onions tend to be much sweeter than brown onions.

PAK CHOI, see Mustard greens.

PARSNIP: as for other roots, look for firm, tight-skinned examples. As parsnips gets larger, they develop a woody core at their top which needs longer cooking.

PEA: freshly picked peas are one of nature's sweetest gifts, but all that sugar starts to convert to starch with speed. The same pea, even hours later, will have developed a mealy flavour. At the other extreme, large companies harvest and freeze peas with such exactitude that a few minutes outside of their allotted time and they are dispensed with. Whatever your feeling about frozen peas, there is no doubting their sweetness. It can, however, all become rather monotonous; where is the variety, the depth and roundness of the truly fresh pea? Sweetness may count for a lot in a pea, but not everything. Restaurants quite often use frozen peas for just this reason. If you get fresh peas in early summer, the pods make a superb soup. As with pulses, don't use salt when cooking a pea as it toughens the skin. Petit pois are a particularly delicate variety of pea and are rarely available fresh.

PEPPERS: green is an unripe pepper, red and yellow (or orange and a range of other variations on red and yellow) being the ripe versions. Avoid those that have a translucent colouring, there should be an intensity – a tone – to the colour. Wrinkles are acceptable, as is a rough texture in isolated places on the skin; softness, however, is to be avoided. The skin is not easily digestible and it is good practice first to roast or grill a pepper until the skin is charred, then remove this and the seeds before proceeding. Delicious with grilled meats and fish, peppers make a stunning salad with capers and olive oil, or add sweetness to a sandwich. If you are short of time, some tinned and bottled brands are good, but there are poor and overpriced examples, too, so beware.

POTATO: these must be firm and free from blemishes, blight or eyelets, although the latter can just be scraped off. There are literally dozens of varieties and usually very little help is offered to guide you. The following should help. *Floury varieties*: (baking, mashing and chips): Cara, Golden Wonder, Kerr's Pink, King Edward,

Marfona, Maris Piper, Pentland
Squire, Record, Romano, Santa,
Wilja;
Waxy varieties: (boiling): Arran
Pilot, Carlingford, Desiree,
Nicola, Purple Congo,
Roseval;
Salad varieties: Belle de Fontenay,
Charlotte, La Ratte, Jersey Royal,
Pink Fir Apple, Royal Kidney.

If mashing, use floury varieties
(the French, preferring a purée,
will use a waxier variety) and bear
in mind that baking ensures little
water is absorbed. You can cook
potato and let it cool before
mashing. When buying, don't be
put off by clinging earth,
particularly with thin-skinned

varieties like Jersey Royals, as it
seems to help retain flavour.

PUMPKIN: butternut, pumpkin,
Gem, patty pan, onion squash and
vegetable spaghetti are just a few
of the most popular thick-skinned
squashes, although there are plenty
more to choose from. Popular in
America and in some parts of
Europe for their sweet, rich,
deeply coloured flesh, which has a
flavour that is dense and earthy,
perfect for teaming with butter and
cream, lots or herbs and plenty of
spices. They last for an age in the
vegetable rack; just avoid anything
suspiciously light. Bake or roast,
first having pricked the skin to
stop them exploding. You get
more flavour leaving the skin on
and the seeds in, both of which
can easily be removed
afterwards. Pumpkins need sun for
flavour, otherwise they tend to be
watery, so look to country of
origin. In my experience, butternut
is the most consistent and small is
preferable to large.

RADISH: there are a number of
varieties, from dark red through to
largely white, but it is hard to beat
a French breakfast radish: long,
tapering, white-tipped and fiery,

vibrant and fresh-tasting. Make
sure what you buy is firm,
although you need to sample to
check for pepperiness. Buy in
bunches, still with the leaves.

SALSIFY: a popular winter-spring
vegetable on mainland Europe, this
looks something like a long thin
carrot and is usually sold in
bundles. Its close cousin,
scorzonera, is similar in taste,
although with a darker skin. The
skin of salsify is an earthy brown,
the flesh pale and, when cooked, it
tastes faintly of artichoke. Look for
firm, rigid examples and don't
worry about clinging earth – salsify
is often grown in sandy soil that
seems to stick to the skin. Scrub
and boil until tender, remove the
skin and proceed, or peel and stew
with a little water and lots of
butter or oil. Serve with
hollandaise, simply melted butter
and herbs or a cream sauce. Good
with poultry and seafood.

SEA KALE: native to the
coastlines of the UK and Western
Europe, this is not widely
available. It has thin celery-like
stalks and leaves that should be
steamed rather than boiled, and
served as you would asparagus,

with hollandaise, vinaigrette or simply melted butter.

SPINACH: the baby leaves go in salads, the more mature version being suitable for cooking. Blanching renders the leaves soft, frying in oil or butter leaves them slightly crunchy. High in oxalic acid, it is a devil to partner with wine, but softened with egg or butter the flavour is more accommodating. Frozen spinach is not that bad and is a good stand-by.

SPRING GREENS: basically a cabbage without a heart. The 'spring' reference is now largely redundant, this vegetable being available all year, although it is still best in the spring months.

SWEDE: buy firm, tight-skinned examples, although swede is a good keeper – several days, provided it is cool. The flavour is diluted with cooking in water; better to stew it in a little liquid with some olive oil or butter.

SWEETCORN: like the pea, once picked the sugars in sweetcorn start to turn to starch. Do not add salt to the cooking water, as with peas again it tends to toughen the skin. Serve with butter, or barbecue and serve with pepper and lime juice.

SWEET POTATO: the colour and texture can vary from white to orange, the latter with better flavour, creamy to grainy. Treat as for potatoes, but baking is undoubtedly the best way.

SWISS CHARD: chard is a member of the beet family, particularly popular in Italian and French cooking. The stem is the prized part, often steamed and served as you would asparagus. The leaves need to be cooked separately as they take less time and work well in soup and flans, indeed anything rich and eggy. Its taste is similar to, although more robust than, spinach. Both stems and leaves are good served with cream, butter and cheese, and in flans.

TOMATO: of all vegetables it is the tomato – actually a fruit (as are aubergines and peppers) – that has seen concentrated efforts on the part of retailers and growers to widen the range of varieties and increase the quality. However, this has not always been to good effect. So-called 'vine-ripened' tomatoes may smell nice, but the aroma comes not from the tomato but from the vine. Therefore not all vine-ripened tomatoes are necessarily tasty. The number of varieties may seem large, but many of the characteristics are fairly similar; sweetness balanced with acidity, a good flesh-to-seed ratio, thin crispy skin. As with many vegetables, ripeness when picking is of paramount importance if you want your tomato to taste of something. Don't store tomatoes in the fridge as they will only go furry. If they go off after a few days stored at room temperature, you should have either eaten them sooner or not bought what you did. If in any doubt, buy cherry tomatoes, as they tend overall to be sweeter, and have better acidity and bite.

TURNIP: part of the cabbage family, in the UK they use the root and in the rest of Europe it is the leaves, wilted into a sauce to accompany meat or dress pasta. Keep your purchases small; once a turnip gets much bigger than a golf ball it loses most, if not all, of its sweetness.

saladings

For all saladings, avoid anything that is wilted or blemished. A mixture provides interest and variety. If buying prewashed in a bag, check the sell-by date; leaves rarely last longer than it says they will. If you are buying whole heads, don't worry too much about the outside leaves, as they are bound to be slightly wilted. Peel back a few and check inside.

The best way to store most salad is loosely wrapped in a plastic bag in the fridge. The exception to this is bunched watercress; wrap the stems in damp newspaper and then the whole lot in a plastic bag. Remember that salad is susceptible to changes in temperature; if it sits in the boot of the car while you have a coffee in the sun, it is unlikely to recover.

One of the more useful gadgets to come on to the market is a salad spinner. Essentially, the salad sits in a basket which in turn sits inside a drum. Spin the basket and the salad stays where it is while the water flies out of the sides by dint of centrifugal force. A clean tea-towel and a bowling motion with

an extended arm is the simplest alternative. Be gentle when you wash all salad, as it has a tendency to bruise

What goes with what? In composing a salad you want variety and contrast, so choose leaves that are sweet (Little Gem), bitter (radicchio) and peppery (rocket or watercress). Colour, too, is important: bright green, dark green, red. You also need variety in texture, so if you have some crunch, look also for something delicate and smooth.

The following are my favourites:

ROCKET: peppery and delicate, fashionable and expensive. It is remarkably easy to grow.

RED CHARD: bright green leaves, dark red stem, slightly bitter and crunchy texture. Not often sold

singly, but usually part of a bagged salad selection.

MIZUNA: popular in Japan, it has a spiky leaf and a chilli – rather than peppery – heat.

BABY SPINACH: as the name suggests, an undeveloped spinach leaf. It has a mild bitterness and a buttery texture, and is very prone to bruising.

LAMB'S LETTUCE (ALSO CALLED MÂCHE): one of the sexiest salad leaves, it has a very delicate texture and flavour.

CHICORY: good all-year crunch with a delicate bitterness (it is a delight with blue cheese).

LITTLE GEM: now almost as ubiquitous as round lettuce used to be, it has a creaminess and richness as well as a faint sweetness and lots of crunch. It also keeps well.

COS/ROMAINE: traditional in Caesar salad, but also good where your dressing is thick (it should cling to the large leaves well). The stems can be quite robust, so don't worry too much if you ditch the outside leaves.

WATERCRESS: one of the leaves most susceptible to damage, the inherent pepperiness of watercress is a delight. If you find watercress growing, harvest it carefully; if it's from contaminated water, it can give you an upset stomach.

ROUND LETTUCE: often limp in texture and fairly tasteless. If you grow it in the garden, however, it can be superb.

ICEBERG LETTUCE: lots of crunch and a good shelf-life, but utterly tasteless.

FRISÉE: a key ingredient in a good warm salad, frisée has a delicious bitterness and its net-like form means it picks up whatever it is dressed with, much like pasta. It also has a delicious bite to it.

mushrooms and truffles

Fungi generally offer rich, sublime eating, strong enough to be served on their own but also beguilingly willing to work with other ingredients: think of chicken and morels, or truffles and potatoes – truffles and anything, come to think of it. Both mushrooms and truffles need careful inspection when buying, particularly wild mushrooms, which can harbour nasty wrigglies. Water is to be avoided when cleaning as they absorb it only too readily; a damp cloth is preferable.

cultivated mushrooms

Button, open cup, flat, field, whatever name is used they are invariably a cultivated mushroom, *Agaricus bisporus*. Uncooked, these mushrooms have virtually no flavour, but when cooked take on an enormously meaty flavour and texture, deep and earthy. Combined with garlic, parsley, butter and cream, they make a wonderful accompaniment to potatoes, pasta, poultry and game.

Chestnut mushrooms are similar to the more ordinary cultivated mushrooms, but brown in colour and with a slightly stronger, woodland flavour. Portobello mushrooms are their grown-up cousins and are suitable for stuffing.

Oyster mushrooms have a very subtle, delicate flavour – some might say no flavour at all. They do, however, have a very meaty texture that holds up in cooking. Try them fried with noodles and Oriental flavourings, in a pilaf, in a ragout with other vegetables, or with pasta, although you will need lots of garlic, parsley and butter to allow them to give of their best.

wild mushrooms

These are generally available in the autumn, but spring mushrooms (like morels) are a true delight. Wild mushrooms are harvested and transported all over the world; they are also frozen, so their season has become eroded. They are widely available by mail order as, being light, they incur small transport costs. Look for blemishes and any softness which might suggest rotting. Dried mushrooms are of a uniformly high quality in terms of flavour. You will pay

more for appearance; the perfect mushroom shape commands a premium, worth paying if you are going to see them on the plate perhaps, but when adding to stews save money by buying broken pieces.

CHANTERELLE: also known as *girolle*, these have a wonderful buttery richness and a delicate, almost smoky flavour, their aroma faintly of apricot. Cooked with garlic and cream, they are superb with veal or chicken, as a filling for an omelette or made into a tart.

CEP: along with the chanterelle and morel, considered among the finest mushrooms for cooking. Often dried in Italy, there they are referred to as *porcini*. The drying process concentrates their flavour, which is very aromatic and accompanied by an extreme meatiness, while at the same time having great delicacy. Recipes abound, risotto perhaps being the most famous. Large fresh specimens are often sliced lengthwise and fried in butter, with a little garlic and parsley, and dressed with lemon juice. Fresh, they should be firm, vibrant and without blemishes; as they age, they become slightly sticky and

have a decaying aroma. If buying dried, avoid lots of little pieces; the best still retain a mushroom shape.

MOREL: this arrives in spring and for a short time morels are available along with asparagus, the two kings of the vegetable world sitting together. Unmistakable because of their brown sponge-like caps, they have a strong but elegant aroma and surprisingly subtle flavour. Usually split to help cleaning, they can be fried but are best cooked *à la crème*. Morels dry well.

PUFFBALL MUSHROOM: these come in a number of guises, the best being the brilliant white giant puffball. Slice them, dip the slices in egg and breadcrumbs and fry in butter. The flavour is delicate, the texture almost crunchy.

oriental mushrooms

SHIITAKE MUSHROOM: these tend to be quite mild when fresh, similar to the oyster mushroom.

Bought dried, however, the flavour is hugely concentrated. They need to be reconstituted in warm water (see page 208) and the stems discarded (they tend to be tough). Much used in both Chinese and Japanese cookery, they go particularly well with steamed fish and red meat.

DRIED CLOUD OR WOOD EAR: is similar to JEW'S EAR mushrooms, rather gelatinous and with a delicate flavour. Usually sold dried, they should be reconstituted in tepid rather then hot water to keep their flavour. They are good with chicken and pork.

truffles
These fungi which grow entirely underground have an enormous, meaty sweet aroma, their flavour curiously piquant but ethereal. They come in various guises, but the best are undoubtedly the black truffles of Périgord and the white truffles of Piedmont. Just to confuse matters, however, there are also summer truffles, which

although good have nothing like the power and pungency of their autumn cousins.

You can buy truffles canned or in jars, but there is little point. Truffle oil is also popular, particularly with chefs, but use it sparingly as it is very powerful. There are many brands, but look to see if it is white truffle oil (very strong) or black truffle oil (less strong). The latter can be useful if you want a slick of oil on the plate; the former if you are happy with a few droplets.

If you are lucky enough and can afford fresh truffles (they are one of the world's priciest ingredients), use restraint; the best thing is to finely grate them over pasta or scrambled eggs, or slip them under the skin of a roasting chicken. If placed in a bowl with eggs or rice and covered, truffles will scent the eggs or rice deliciously.

pulses

The dried ripe edible seeds of any leguminous plant, pulses offer stunning eating, robust flavours and much nutrition. Although

dried, watch out for old examples, which will need more soaking; best to buy from the last season's harvest. And don't think one chickpea is the same as another; there are different varieties, some offering superior eating. These are likely to be sourced in delicatessens and ethnic stores. Look for a shop with a high turnover. The tinned product, particularly that from Spain or Italy, is usually excellent. In these countries, you can often buy pulses precooked by the shopkeeper; the tinned version is only that using modern technology, in this case to excellent effect. It is best to drain all tinned pulses and rinse them thoroughly.

With the exception of some types of lentil and split peas, all dried pulses first require overnight soaking in plenty of cold water. As well as starting the rehydration process, this helps to soften the impurities that make pulses difficult to digest. As you start to boil them, a white scum floats to the surface and you need to remove this with a slotted spoon; if you allow it to be boiled back into the water it only makes the pulses difficult to digest again. It is hard to discuss pulses without reference

to flatulence. In my experience this problem is much alleviated by buying young pulses and cooking them correctly. Salting should be done after the pulse has been cooked; it otherwise tends to toughen the skin .

ADUKI BEAN: small, red-brown, with a little white thread down one side, these have a nutty flavour and are good in salads. Chicken is a good partner, particularly with some spices like cumin, coriander and ginger.

BLACK BEAN: not kidney beans, black beans are really black and have a strong earthy flavour. Particularly good with bacon and pork, they are popular in Asian cooking, where they are salted, which completely alters their texture and concentrates the flavour.

BLACK-EYED BEAN OR PEA: kidney-shaped with a black dot, these beans have a slightly smoky flavour and go well with mushrooms and, curiously, potatoes. They, too, benefit from the use of spices and are easily cooked in 30 minutes without the need for soaking, provided you get young beans.

BUTTER BEAN: these need to be cooked for about 1 hour. They make a good creamy soup, but are quite bland. Superb with a mustard-flavoured vinaigrette and chopped shallots and parsley, you can buy them halved and skinned, which is by far the best way.

CHICKPEA: another favourite of mine, the Spanish brands are easily the best (they are called *garbanzos* in Spain). They need 1–2 hours' cooking. With a delightful nutty taste and texture, they go well with spinach, bacon, chorizo and chicken. Mint goes surprisingly well with them (just think of hummus), as do parsley and coriander.

HARICOT (CANNELLINI, BORLOTTI AND FLAGEOLET): need to be cooked for about $1^1/_2$ hours. Delicious in salads, stews and in Tuscan-style bean and pasta soups. They are also superb with lamb, particularly when partnered with tomatoes and lots of rosemary and garlic.

LENTIL: for me, the king (or queen) of pulses, particularly Puy lentils (native of France but now often from Canada). These are almost like peas – sweet and juicy. Green and brown lentils are also delicious, but are, for my money, not quite as succulent. Lastly, yellow lentils, which are usually sold split. The outer skin is removed and the lentil naturally splits in two. These have a tendency to collapse when cooking and are excellent in soups and dals. Lentils do not need soaking. If you wish to preserve the shiny look of Puy lentils, coat them in hot oil before adding water and don't overcook them. Cooking times: for Puy about 30–35 minutes; for green and brown, about 30–40 minutes; for yellow, about 15–20 minutes. Flavours that work well with lentils: aubergines, mushrooms, fennel, cream, anchovies, bacon, sausage.

MUNG BEAN: the source of beansprouts, the split versions are perhaps the most popular beans used in dal in India. They have a good nutty flavour and works well with onions, garlic and spices. They are superb in soups.

RED KIDNEY BEAN: again about $1^1/_2$ hours to cook, these are essential in *chile con carne*, good in salads with shallots and make a great winter soup. They work well with beef and chilli as well as bacon. Red kidney beans can be particularly difficult to digest and it is received wisdom that they need to be boiled initially for 10 minutes over high heat in order to 'eliminate potential toxins', but I (and many other people) find this quite unnecessary.

SOY BEAN: extremely nutritious, these have a rather mealy texture and take an age to cook, easily 2 hours. Better to use haricot and get your soy fix with the sauce.

SPLIT PEA: both the red and green variety are good in soups and stews, require little or no soaking and cook quickly. They have a mealy taste, which performs well with butter and spices.

fruit

Fruit is one area in which supermarkets have excelled, developing new varieties and working closely with growers to ensure what looks good actually tastes good too. Seasons have become confusing, however, with

source markets being developed all over the globe in the search for all-year availability. Your only clue is the country of origin on the label and your own sense of the seasons. Strawberries in December may seem obvious, but what about apples in April? By this date, what you are being offered here tends to come from the southern hemisphere.

what to look for when you buy fruit

Look for brightly coloured, vibrant examples with unblemished skins. They should feel heavy in the hand and in most instances should smell of themselves. This is partly dependent on temperature, a chilled peach smelling less strong than a warm one, but there should still be a pleasant, fresh aroma.

Greenery and leaves are useful indicators of age, the leaves generally wilting rather more quickly than the fruit. Ultimately you need to eat the fruit to tell if it is good. The flavour should be piquant, well balanced, sweet and with a full long taste. The fear is often that the fruit will be under-ripe, but it can also have a fermented, 'boiled sweet' flavour, suggesting that it is past its best.

APPLE: there are many varieties, with new ones being developed all the time. Characteristics differ greatly, from the crisp russetted skin and creamy texture of a Cox's Orange Pippin to the sweet crunchy flesh of a Gala, the rustic but very delicious Egremont Russet or the refreshing and crunchy Braeburn. Buy carefully – blemishes in the skin will expand. A good and ripe apple will have a faint aroma around the stem; press lightly with your finger if it is elusive. If you still get nothing, it is probably better to reject it.

APRICOT: the stronger the colour, the sweeter the flavour. Buy indi-vidually if you can, selecting firm glowing fruit. If you are lucky, it is a delicious fruit eaten straight from the tree, but we more usually think of cooking it into tarts, pastes, fill-ings for almond meringues, jams or as the sweetness in a bitter chocolate cake. Apricots make good ice-creams, sorbets and soufflés.

BANANA: often sold under-ripe, a banana will ripen at room temperature in a day or two. If you keep them in the fridge they will blacken. Store them separately from other fruit as they give off a gas that encourages other fruit to ripen over-quickly.

BLACKBERRY: eat one, you should have a full voluptuous taste of late summer, the juice richly unctuous and with a firm but balanced acidity. It is more usual, however, to have to cook them, the only way of eating ripe ones being to wander along hedgerows looking for choice specimens.

BLACK-, WHITE AND RED-CURRANT: generally tart and in need of both sugar and cooking, look out for a good fruit-to-stem ratio and berries that are tight and brightly coloured.

BLUEBERRY: available all year, but less expensive (and better) in the summer. Taste before buying, as they can be remarkably dull.

CHERRY: a firm favourite of mine, but finding a full-flavoured cherry can, at times, be an uphill task, not least because appearance gives little away. Even darkly coloured, bright examples have been disappointing. Insist on
tasting and don't rely on your supplier, for the cherry is an elusive fruit.

CRANBERRY: consistent and farmed, the cranberry needs sugar, and quite a lot of it, even to get off the starting block. Often frozen, there seems nothing to distinguish the fresh version other than its hand-harvesting. Bulk cranberries, which go for juicing and freezing, are harvested using water, great red lakes of the berries scooped up for processing.

DATE: sitting in their round-ended box on almost every Christmas table, dates had a hard time of it, until, that is, we started to get fresh dates from Israel, which are much more attractive and decidedly more delicate to eat. Their meaty texture and full, round flavour makes them equally good in sweet and savoury dishes. Try them with chicken in a Moroccan-inspired tagine, in cakes

and brownies, or stuffed with cream cheese (full-fat), perhaps flavoured with an orange liquor.

FIG: as sweet as nectar, as soft as raspberries – for the short season from September through to the New Year there is nothing to beat a fresh ripe fig. Eat one first if you can, as even soft figs can be disappointing. Serve them slightly warm, as this enhances their flavour. Figs partner nuts and candied peel, fortified wines and cream. Lightly grilled, with a dusting of sugar, they are a delight. Serve with dry-cured ham or duck for savoury dishes; with cream or caramel or as a tart for desserts.

GOOSEBERRY: while often cooked with sugar, a dessert gooseberry is a startling surprise, its sweetness perfectly matched by its curiously fleshy texture and flavour. The best test is to eat one, but a good sweet gooseberry smells sweet. They are fat to bursting and come in green, gold and purple.

GRAPE: often sticky and sweet-smelling on the outside, in the case of muscat grapes, or those left purposely on the vine so they wilt

slightly, sometimes alarmingly so. The skin is crucial and can often be bitter and thick, so taste. Verjus (literally the juice before it is turned into wine), available from some good delicatessens, makes an excellent sauce for poultry and game.

GRAPEFRUIT: from tart and unpleasant through to sharp and delicious, the pink varieties are often more reliable. They are excellent in salads, particularly with avocado.

GUAVA: peeled and eaten raw, these have a gentle nutty texture and a honeyed flavour, which is not surprising given their subtle pink colour. They are often used in dishes with cream cheese and cream.

KIWI: the epitome of *nouvelle cuisine*, kiwi has been ridiculed but somehow remains with us. To look at, it is a deliciously delicate, translucent green, with dainty black seeds – a pretty fruit that has the added advantage of keeping extremely well. Its season (most come from New Zealand) is quite short, but it ripens gently in the correct conditions. It works well in

Chinese dishes (it did originate there), meringues, crème brûlée and fruit salads.

LEMON AND LIME: both lemons and limes can be decidedly more subtle than we are used to. Look for large examples of both, the skin being thicker and less regular than normal examples. Look, too, for unwaxed organic examples, which can be packed with flavour.

As with much fruit, buy those that are heavy for their size.

MANGO: possibly my favourite fruit, a ripe mango, particularly from India (look out for Alfonso and Bangapalli), is truly one of life's simple pleasures. Roll up your sleeves, take a sharp knife and get to work. Look for slightly giving fruit, which should smell sweetly of itself. Mangoes have large stones, which you need to work around carefully. There is no easy way, but leave no flesh behind, it is too precious. Make it into fools and ice-creams if you tire of the fruit

by itself; try it with crab, prawn and duck, the latter particularly with ginger, sesame seeds and spring onion in a chilled salad.

MANGOSTEEN: with flesh white as snow and a sweet, heavenly aroma, the mangosteen (the lychee and rambutan are related but not nearly as good) is one of the most sublime fruits. Run a knife around the middle, peel away the top and eat like a hard-boiled egg. The fruit is best eaten like this, but can also be chopped into salads; it partners avocado well and lemon juice brings out the flavour.

MELON: there is an enormous number of varieties on offer, from Honeydew to Galia to Charentais, the latter being a favourite of mine. All tend to be sweet and refreshing, but Charentais have a more overt melon flavour. Gently press them around the stem; you should get a distinct aroma.

NECTARINE, see Peach.

ORANGE, TANGERINE AND KUMQUAT: we have oranges all year from all over the globe, but the best come in the first few months of the year from Spain,

Morocco and Cyprus. As the spring and summer months approach, there always seems to be better fruit about. Tangerines and the various hybrids like clementines (the best) are a traditional Christmas fruit but, as with so much, the season seems to get increasingly extended both at the start and at the finish. It is, unfortunately, hard to tell the quality of an orange from the outside. Take a Seville, for example, which looks as dull as ditchwater – one good reason why on traditional market stalls a few are usually halved for display. Even then, however, the task is not easy. The Seville season is remarkably short, only about six weeks.

PASSION FRUIT: one of the most fragrant of fruits, go for large dark, dimpled fruit. Remove the top and scoop the pulp out with a spoon (a jug of cream helps to add richness). To use in cooking, scoop out the pulp, heat it gently in a pan and work vigorously through a sieve. The best dishes are soufflés and ice-creams, but for ease and decadence, simply mix in a glass with rum and sugar syrup for a refreshing, if alcoholic, summer drink.

131

PAWPAW: this makes one of the best breakfasts, when the weather is hot, if dressed with lime juice. The flesh itself is delicately flavoured, somewhere between melon and avocado; indeed, most melon recipes can be adapted. Peel and remove the seeds, although they do you no harm. Pawpaw goes well with yoghurt, ginger, coriander, ham and chicken, and even smoked fish.

PEACHES AND NECTARINES: look for heavy, pale-coloured fruit that have a strong aroma (white peaches tend to have more flavour than yellow). They should be firm to the touch (soft fruit implies woolliness) but not too firm. The supply of ripe peaches and nectarines is one of the great leaps to have been made by the supermarkets recently. Dropped into a glass of wine or champagne, slices of peach or nectarine make an instant and rather delicious dessert. If either fruit is a little hard and under-ripe, slice and place in a bowl, pour over some light, boiling syrup and allow to cool, the peaches will cook as the liquid cools. If you are really unlucky and the fruit is even firmer than that, slip it into boiling syrup, return this to the boil, cover, remove from the heat and allow the fruit to cool in the syrup.

PEARS: these should be firm to the touch, heavy in the hand and with a light delicate aroma. Varieties to look out for include Williams, Comice and Rocha. Any sign of squashiness is to be avoided. A ripe pear gives slightly around the stem. Pears make fantastic tarts, but also have a real affinity with cheese – pear and Stilton being a personal favourite. Pear often benefits from lemon zest and juice, as in a pear sorbet.

PERSIMMON: looking for all the world like an unripe tomato, the persimmon or Sharon fruit is something of an enigma, straddling the fruit and vegetable categorization much like the tomato. A ripe example is slightly giving and sweet-smelling around the stem. The Sharon fruit version comes from Israel and is sweeter when firm than the more traditional Mediterranean version, which should be soft before you eat it. Indeed, it is so soft it is often sold in partitioned plastic trays to protect it. Slice and serve with a vinaigrette, or in combination with avocado and watercress or rocket. Spoon the flesh out of whole fruit, adding cream as you go.

PHYSALIS: one of the most attractive fruits to look at, with its orange berry and gauzy calyx, no wonder it is popular in so many restaurants on a tray of petits fours. The flavour is quite tart, which is why it is so suitable for coating in sugar. Physalis work well in cakes with nuts, and can be made into a tart but rather delicious jam.

PINEAPPLE: these are at their best during the late winter months, which is an advantage given the scarcity of other fruit. Pineapple should smell sweetly and the area around the stem should yield slightly to pressure. To peel, top and tail and then, holding the fruit vertically, run a sharp knife down the outside; then cut into slices and remove the core. You cannot set raw pineapple with gelatine and it is not easy to freeze. Simmer it gently first, allow to cool and then proceed. They do not ripen after harvesting, so make sure what you buy is already sweet-smelling.

become impregnated with the tiny spines that lie underneath the large spikes. Sliced and sprinkled with lime zest and juice, the prickly pear makes a good dessert.

QUINCE: a good quince is intensely fragrant, almost overpoweringly so, and should have a downy dusting over its skin. You cannot eat quince raw but, when cooked by themselves or with other fruit like apples and pears, they contribute a decadent aroma and flavour. If it doesn't smell, don't buy it. They are very useful in jams because of their high pectin content. In Spain they are made into a paste called *membrillo*, to eat with cheese, but versions of this exist in many countries.

RASPBERRY AND LOGANBERRY: two of the most glorious of fruits, with their seductive colour and rich yet refreshing flavour. Particularly good varieties include Glen Prosen and Glen Moy. With cream or without? There may be all sorts of ways of using raspberries – to make vinegar, for jam, in cakes – but, in truth, what better way of enjoying them than to eat them

PLUMS: avoid bruised or damaged skins and look for weighty fruit with a healthy shine to the skin. Tough skins sometimes cover delicious fruit and can always be peeled away; if this is difficult, pour over boiling water, leave for 2 minutes and then skin. If cooking with plums, crack a few of the stones and include these in the cooking, as their presence markedly improves the flavour. Good varieties include Mirabelle, Reine Claude and the much-overlooked damson.

POMEGRANATE: this is hardly a fruit at all, but a cluster of tiny seeds, yet find a ripe pomegranate (it is hard to tell as there is not much aroma, so you need a knife to slice one open) and you are in for an experience: sweet and sour, part grape, part lemon and lime. I have eaten them juiced mid-morning in hot Mediterranean markets, just the thing to refresh,

as well as in more elaborate desserts closer to home. In the Middle East, they use it to make a syrup not unlike balsamic vinegar, as well as in soups. It goes well with duck and pheasant. If you need to remove the seeds, quarter and then bend the skin backwards over a bowl and the seeds will pop out; just ensure you remove any of the yellow membrane, which is the bitter part.

PRICKLY PEAR: the skin is to be avoided, but inside that the orange flesh of the prickly pear is well worth the effort of getting through, although it is hardly the grandest of fruits. The taste is rich and unctuous; lime juice improves things. To peel, slice off each end and then cut the length of the skin, without going into the flesh too much. Lever each side down so the fruit lies in the flattened skin of the fruit. Take care not to touch the skin, or your own skin will

133

fresh. The quality of a raspberry will only truly reveal itself on the tongue.

RHUBARB: this comes in an early forced version and later as a more strongly coloured main crop. It requires quite a lot of sugar. If in doubt, dip a stick into some sugar and eat; it should taste good.

STRAWBERRY: in general we mean cultivated strawberries, but all are derived from the frais de bois, or wild strawberry, which is still to be found in woodland and cottage garden alike. The breeding process, however, was quite difficult and the modern varieties have only recently come on stream. These can often look alarmingly bright and jolly, with little flavour or texture to back them up. Trial and error is an inevitable part of strawberry buying, but look out for varieties like Cambridge Favourite, Elvira and Pegasus.

TAMARILLO: plum-shaped, with a skin that is dark red, almost black, the flesh is soft, with blood-red juice and a strong, tart flavour. They are best eaten by themselves with a spoon, but can also enliven

a vinaigrette, when squeezed, or add sharpness to a fruit salad.

WATERMELON: enormously refreshing but, while not exactly tasteless, certainly lacking in much character. Crush to make a refreshing juice, or eat and spit – the pips are rather an integral part.

Peeling and coring fruit

Swivel fruit peelers are inexpensive pieces of equipment and ensure an even, smooth cut. Buy several – they are inexpensive, so many hands can be put to work. Even children are happy to peel fruit and it is much safer than a knife. Corers, which allow the core to be removed cleanly and simply so the fruit remains whole, are also useful and give a much cleaner finish than a knife.

Stoning fruit

To remove the stone from peaches, nectarines and plums, cut around their 'equators' with a sharp knife and then gently twist the fruit. The stone will remain in one half, quarter that and the

stone should come out easily; if it does not, it's likely that the fruit is not ripe.

Removing fruit skins

To remove the skin of peaches, nectarines and plums, plunge them into boiling water for 2 minutes, remove and allow to cool. The skin should then come away easily.

To obtain the kernel of an apricot, crack with a rolling pin, mallet or hammer and remove the tough outer coating.

Pineapple skin makes a good serving plate for the fruit cut into chunks or for other fruit and ice-cream. Cut vertically down through the leaves and body and scoop out the flesh. The halves can be frozen and used again.

Seville oranges may be for marmalade, but they are also the perfect oranges to use in savoury dishes. Duck à la orange, for example, should never be made with anything but Sevilles, although a kumquat comes close.

directory

Fruit and vegetable seasons in the UK

With the use of glass and plastic tunnels, heating and work on varieties, the 'season' for various fruits and vegetables has been greatly extended. Major retailers are now global shoppers so, if you are not overly concerned about where what you want has been grown and the consequent cost, it is possible to buy anything pretty much throughout the year. The quality and certainly the price, however, may well vary substantially from one month to the next. The list below is aimed at those wanting to make informed decisions about what they buy. Asparagus in March is possible, but likely to be expensive and not on a par, in terms of quality, with that available in April, May and June.

Available all year

(in many instances this is because the ingredient has been stored, rather than harvested, all year round): avocado, cabbage, carrot, chicory, greens, mushrooms (although not wild), onion, potato (although not salad or new), spinach and watercress; apple.

JANUARY: beetroot, Brussels sprout, celeriac, chard, Jerusalem artichoke, leek, parsnip, shallot, turnip; apple, cranberry, orange, Seville orange, forced rhubarb.

FEBRUARY: beetroot, Brussels sprout, celeriac, chard, Jerusalem artichoke, leek, parsnip, shallot, turnip; banana, forced rhubarb, pineapple.

MARCH: beetroot, celeriac, Jerusalem artichoke, leek, parsnip, sprouting broccoli, turnip; forced rhubarb.

APRIL: cauliflower, courgette, leek, sprouting broccoli, turnip; outdoor rhubarb.

MAY: asparagus, broad bean, cauliflower, courgette, cucumber, lettuce, marsh samphire, new potato, pea, radish, sprouting broccoli; gooseberry, rhubarb.

JUNE: asparagus, aubergine, avocado, broad bean, cauliflower, courgette, cucumber, French bean, lettuce, marsh samphire, new potato, pea, radish, runner bean, tomato; cherry, gooseberry, rhubarb, strawberry.

JULY: artichoke, aubergine, beetroot, broad bean, cauliflower, celery, chard, courgette, cucumber, French bean, lettuce, marsh samphire, new potato, pea, radish, runner bean, sweetcorn, tomato;

apricot, blackberry, black and redcurrant, gooseberry, greengage, raspberry, strawberry.

AUGUST: aubergine, beetroot, broad bean, cauliflower, celery, chard, courgette, cucumber, French bean, globe artichoke, , lettuce, pea, radish, runner bean, sweetcorn, tomato; apricot, blackberry, blackberry, blueberry, gooseberry, loganberry, plum, raspberry, tayberrry.

SEPTEMBER: aubergine, beetroot, cauliflower, celery, chard, courgette, cucumber, fennel, French bean, leek, lettuce, parsnip, pumpkin, radish, runner bean, sweetcorn, tomato, turnip; apple, blackberry, blueberry, pear, plum.

OCTOBER: aubergine, beetroot, Brussels sprout, cauliflower, celeriac, celery, courgette, cucumber, fennel, French bean, leek, lettuce, parsnip, pumpkin, radish, runner bean, shallot, sweetcorn, tomato, turnip; apple, blackberry, pear.

NOVEMBER: beetroot, Brussels sprout, cauliflower, celeriac, celery, chard, fennel, kale, leek, lettuce, parsnip, pumpkin, shallot, tomato, turnip; apple, damson, pear, quince.

DECEMBER: beetroot, Brussels sprout, celeriac, chard, fennel, Jerusalem artichoke, kale, leek, parsnip, pumpkin, shallot, turnip; apple, pear, quince.

In the UK, as well as other parts of the world, there has been growing interest in organic fruit and vegetables, as well as pulses. My general comments on the area of organics are covered in the Introduction. Here it is worth pointing out the availability of box schemes and the growing importance and availability of so-called 'farmers' markets', an idea taken from the US. Details of where to find either of these can be obtained from the Soil Association on 0117 929 0661.

Box schemes vary enormously, both in how they operate and in where the produce comes from.

There are now literally hundreds to choose from, some coming and going at an alarming rate. For more information there is a book, *The Organic Directory 2000–2001*, published by Green Books, £7.95, which is a regional guide to what is out there. A visit to the website www.theorganicdirectory.co.uk may also answer some of your questions.

My advice is to look for certified suppliers, but the certifying bodies and their requirements do vary. I buy my pulses from Brindisa, which has a stall at Borough Market in London on Fridays and Saturdays; ring 020 7403 0282 for details. I also buy quite a lot of vegetables there. There are organic suppliers and a few wholesale suppliers who open to the public because of the market. Seek out the likes of sea kale, English asparagus and salsify.

The best supermarkets for fruit and vegetables are Marks & Spencer and Waitrose, the former particularly for soft fruit. For tinned items, look for producers from Italy, Spain and France. Ditto with bottled vegetables like grilled artichokes, roasted red peppers and mushrooms. They may seem expensive, but you are likely to be paying for the quality of what is inside. Health-food shops have a high turnover of produce, so pulses, grains and similar store-cupboard items are often better sourced there than in supermarkets.

vegetables, pulses and fruit
recipes

penne with chilli, rosemary and potatoes

serves 4

1 onion, finely chopped
4 tablespoons olive oil
2 garlic cloves, finely chopped
500 g (1 lb 2 oz) waxy potatoes,
    peeled
large bunch of parsley, chopped
1 scant dessertspoon chopped
    rosemary
1 red chilli, finely chopped
1.5 litres (2³/4 pints) chicken stock
300 g (10¹/2 oz) penne
salt and pepper
2 tablespoons freshly grated
    Parmesan, plus more to serve
extra-virgin olive oil for drizzling

I know this combination sounds unlikely – two starches together, what on earth am I thinking about? I was doubtful, too, until persuaded by Alastair Little, a chef whose approach to food has been something of a guiding light for me. Somehow the starch of the pasta shows up the creaminess of the potato. The origins of this dish lie firmly in Italy's peasant tradition, the herbs and spicing providing interest and flavour.

1 Gently sauté the onion in the olive oil for 15–20 minutes without allowing it to colour. Add the garlic, potatoes, parsley, rosemary and chilli, and stir together so they are well coated in the oil.

2 Add the chicken stock and bring to the boil. Simmer uncovered until the potatoes are almost, but not quite tender.

3 Add the penne and season with salt and pepper. Bring back to the boil and simmer for 5 minutes. Cover with a lid and set aside for 10 minutes, by which time the pasta should be cooked; if not, return to a gentle heat and simmer until it is tender. By this time most of the liquid will have been absorbed.

4 Stir in the 2 tablespoons of grated Parmesan, adjust the seasoning and serve with more Parmesan for sprinkling over, as well as extra-virgin olive oil for drizzling.

grilled radicchio with goats' curd cheese, *toasted sourdough and caper berries*

serves 4

2 small heads of radicchio
about 125 ml (4 fl oz) extra-virgin
  olive oil
salt and pepper
4 slices of sourdough or good-
  quality country-style bread
100 g (3½ oz) goats' curd (soft
  fresh) cheese
2 tablespoons caper berries, well
  rinsed
100 g (3½ oz) black olives
1 lemon, quartered, to serve

1 Preheat a hot grill. Cut each radicchio head lengthwise into eighths, so its segments are still held together by its stem. Lightly oil a shallow roasting tray with olive oil and arrange the radicchio segments so they are not overlapping. Drizzle over some more olive oil, season with salt and pepper, and grill until lightly browned. Turn the radicchio over and brown on the other side.

2 Grill the slices of bread until lightly browned on both sides. Spread with the cheese.

3 Pile some radicchio in the middle of each of 4 plates and lay the goats' curd cheese toast on top. Scatter over the caper berries and olives, season with more salt and pepper and drizzle over a couple of tablespoons of olive oil per serving.

4 Serve with a lemon quarter on each plate.

aubergine, basil, spinach and chilli salad *with yoghurt dressing*

serves 4

2 aubergines
large handful of basil leaves
3 tablespoons olive oil
4 tomatoes, sliced
225 g (8 oz) baby spinach
1 garlic clove
salt and pepper
200 ml (7 fl oz) yoghurt
1 red chilli, deseeded and finely
    chopped
1 heaped tablespoon pine nuts
1 lemon
good bread, to serve

1　Preheat a hot grill. Cut the aubergines across into slices about 1 cm (¹/2 inch) thick. Grill until slightly charred on both sides, transfer to a bowl and cover with cling-film. If working in batches, make sure to cover the bowl again each time. If you can barbecue the aubergines, so much the better.

2　Roughly chop the basil leaves and add these to the bowl, together with the olive oil, tomatoes and spinach leaves.

3　Mash the garlic with ¹/2 teaspoon of salt, whisk this into the yoghurt and add the mixture to the aubergine together with the chilli.

4　Heat a dry frying pan and, when hot, toast the pine nuts until they just begin to colour. Add these to the bowl.

5　Toss everything well together, squeeze over the juice of the lemon and serve with lots of good bread.

aubergine, mozzarella and crispy sage 'sandwiches'

serves 4 as a starter

2 small aubergines
4–5 tablespoons extra-virgin olive oil
1 buffalo mozzarella
2 tomatoes
1 garlic clove, finely chopped
salt and pepper
1 tablespoon chopped parsley
12 basil leaves, finely shredded
juice of 1 lemon
12 large sage leaves
about 100 m (3^1/$_2$ fl oz) milk
seasoned flour, for coating
vegetable oil, for frying
125 g (4^1/$_2$ oz) caper berries

1   Slice the aubergine across into 1-cm (^{1}/2-inch) discs, brush these with olive oil and either grill or fry in a little oil on both sides until golden brown. Set aside.

2   Slice the mozzarella as thinly as possible and then trim the slices so they are about the same size as the aubergine slices.

3   Skin and deseed the tomatoes (the skinning is made easier if you drop them into boiling water for 30 seconds and then refresh them in cold water). Chop the flesh into small dice. Using the flat side of the knife, mash the garlic with a little salt.

4   To assemble the 'sandwiches', layer the aubergine and mozzarella as you would a club sandwich (see page 79): 3 slices of aubergine, interleaved with 2 of mozzarella.

5   Combine the diced tomato, garlic, parsley and basil with enough olive oil and lemon juice to bind and to taste. Drizzle this mixture over the aubergine stack and around the plate.

6   Dip the sage leaves in milk, then in seasoned flour, then again in the milk and finally in the flour again. Heat 1 cm (^{1}/2 inch) of vegetable oil in a pan and, when hot, deep-fry the leaves until golden – this takes only a few seconds.

7   Scatter the leaves on top of the aubergine stack, together with the caper berries, and serve.

home-salted cod *with chickpeas and spinach*

serves 4–6

1 kg (2¹/4 lb) cod fillets (skin on)
about 225 g (8 oz) coarse salt
1 onion, finely chopped
2 carrots, peeled and finely diced
4 tablespoons olive oil
two 400-g (14-oz) tins of chickpeas
2 ancho chillies, soaked in warm
    water, deseeded and finely
    chopped
2 garlic cloves, finely chopped
250 ml (9 fl oz) chicken stock
1 kg (2¹/4 lb) spinach, stalks removed
2 tablespoons finely chopped
    parsley
zest and juice of 1 lemon
pepper
Aïoli (see page 43)

1 Two days before you want to serve: place the cod, skin side down, in a plastic container, sprinkle salt liberally over the exposed flesh and place in the fridge for 24 hours.

2 Next day, most of the salt will have become brine, liquid having been extracted from the fish. Rinse thoroughly and place in a large basin of water for 24 hours, replacing the water four times.

3 About an hour before you want to serve, gently sauté the onion and carrots in the oil for 20 minutes without allowing them to colour. Add the chickpeas, chillies and garlic, and turn to coat them in the oil. Add the stock, bring to the boil and simmer, uncovered, for 20 minutes, or until most of the stock has evaporated.

4 Add the spinach, parsley, lemon zest and juice, toss well and simmer for 5 minutes more.

5 Cut the cod into portion-sized pieces, lightly oil them and season with pepper only. Fry them in a little more oil on both sides for 2 minutes, or until cooked (it flakes readily when forked).

6 Serve the cod on top of the chickpea mixture, together with a generous dollop of aïoli.

grilled leg of lamb steaks
and 'creamed' haricots with garlic and rosemary

serves 4

4 lamb leg steaks

FOR THE MARINADE:
2 anchovy fillets, gently mashed
2 garlic cloves, lightly bashed
zest and juice of 1 lemon
1 teaspoon finely chopped chilli
100 ml (3¹/2 fl oz) olive oil

FOR THE 'CREAMED' HARICOTS:
two 400-g (14-oz) tins of haricot beans
250 ml (9 fl oz) whipping cream
2 garlic cloves, finely chopped
1 teaspoon finely chopped rosemary
salt and pepper

Buying tins of beans is convenient, particularly for small numbers. It is worth seeking out the better brands, however, and shops specializing in Italian or Spanish cuisine are good hunting-grounds.

1 The day before: combine all the marinade ingredients and mix well. Coat the steaks thoroughly with it, cover and refrigerate overnight.

2 Next day: take them out of the fridge well ahead to allow them to get back to room temperature.

3 Prepare the 'creamed' haricots: combine the drained and rinsed beans with the cream, garlic and rosemary in a saucepan. Bring to the boil, reduce the heat and simmer, stirring occasionally, until the cream thickens, about 15 minutes. Season with salt and pepper. Keep warm.

4 Preheat a cast-iron griddle or barbecue until hot, brush the marinade off the steaks and grill them for 4 minutes each side.

5 Serve the steaks with the beans.

baked almond-stuffed peaches

serves 4

4 peaches

100 g (3¹/₂ oz) amaretti biscuits, crumbled

1 egg

2 tablespoons roughly chopped blanched whole almonds

2 tablespoons light brown sugar

butter, for the baking dish

1 Preheat the oven to 180°C/350°F/Gas 4. Halve the peaches and remove the stones. Combine the amaretti, egg, almonds and sugar. Stuff the peaches with this mixture.

2 Generously butter an ovenproof dish and arrange the peaches in it, cut sides up. Pour in 150 ml (¹/₄ pint) of water and bake, uncovered, in the preheated oven for 30 minutes, or until the peaches are tender but short of collapsing.

3 Serve at room temperature.

mango and passion fruit trifle

serves 4

8 amaretti biscuits, roughly broken
200 g (7 oz) panettone
8 tablespoons very sweet thick
    sherry, preferably Pedro Ximenez
2 mangoes
4 passion fruit
150 ml (¼ pint) whipping cream
45 g (1½ oz) caster sugar

1 Put half the crushed amaretti into the bottom of 4 glasses. Break the panettone up into bite-sized pieces and divide equally among the 4 glasses. Drizzle a tablespoon of sherry into each one.

2 Remove the skin from the mangoes and roughly chop the flesh. Add this to the glasses, together with the pulp scooped out of the passion fruit.

3 Whip the cream with the sugar until standing in soft peaks, fold in the remaining sherry and spoon over the top of the other ingredients.

4 Top with the remaining amaretti biscuits and serve.

pasta,
grains
and
bread

'For Italians, pasta is part of the ritual of daily life that unfolds around the dinner table. It is at the table that one's need for sustenance transforms itself into shared pleasure. Often at the centre of that table is an abundance of golden, glowing pasta.'

VIANA LA PLACE and EVAN KLEIMAN,
Pasta Fresca

Agnolotti are the stuffed pasta of Piedmont, traditionally made on a Monday using the meat left over from Sunday lunch. Sitting in the cool of restaurant Guido in Costigliole d'Asti in June, I considered this fact momentarily before eating some of the most sublime pasta ever. The restaurant is rather proud of its agnolotti... and rightly so. It takes them a day to make the stuffing, a complex and refined dish of veal, pork and beef with gentle spicing, herbs and seasoning. Greed can be good, I thought, and asked for more, moving on to a secondo of beef braised in red wine that you could cut with a spoon. Piedmont is the most glorious culinary region of Italy.

It is hard to imagine our lives without pasta, even if the experience above was a little more special than usual. It is the convenience food made for modern life, with its instant sauces, store-cupboard friendliness and amazing versatility. There is some idea that the Chinese taught the Western world about pasta through their rice noodles, but evidence is strong that the Etruscans and Greeks were munching their 'lagna' quite happily before Marco Polo even thought about his world tour. Indeed, it is a common

misapprehension that the Italians were the only European pasta lovers – Spain, the Arab countries and Russia all show evidence of utilizing the dough made from flour and water in a form we would readily recognize today as pasta.

types of pasta

There is not much to pasta, so how do you decide which one to buy? First it is worth considering the fresh versus dried debate. We tend to perceive fresh as being better, which is understandable given the implied criticism that

dried is somehow less fresh, or possibly not fresh at all. However, most Italians rarely eat fresh pasta – which is something of an indication – preferring the texture, versatility and practicality of dried.

Dried pasta is made from hard durum wheat (that is, semolina, one of the hardest wheats) and water, or at least it once was. Now dried pasta also incorporates softer wheat flour and can include eggs – dried pasta's advance into what was once fresh pasta's domain. In the north of Italy, fresh home-made pasta was usually a combination of hard and softer flours and eggs, to be dressed with rich buttery or meat sauces. In the poorer south, fresh pasta is still tradition-ally durum wheat and water, eggs being expensive and therefore not included. Try making fresh pasta with durum wheat and water; it's very hard work. This rough pasta, rolled by women dressed in black sitting in their front doorways, would be dressed with vegetable sauces rich in olive oil.

Given the simplicity of ingredients, there is enormous variation in product and you only have to look at supermarket shelves to be confused. Supermarket own-brand, or one of the more recognizable high-street brands? Should it be some of the deliciously wrapped artisan spaghetti, at twice or even three times the price, or a modified pack of egg-rich 'fresh' tagliatelle?

Dried supermarket pasta used to be pretty terrible, manufactured in this country to a recipe designed for our so-called 'uneducated palates'. These days, however, most supermarket pasta is manufactured by one or other of the large Italian companies. Still, the recipe gets tweaked to fit perceived expectations, in terms of both taste and texture, as well as price constraints. Soft flour is less expensive than durum, for exam-ple, which can make the finished product look better value.

The other vital ingredient is time and that, too, costs money. Industrially made pasta is combined in vast quantities, yet the kneading so inherent in its manufacture can be fast or slow and can take place at high or low temperatures, all of which affect the final result. It is then pushed through a die cast in the required shape. These can be made from metal or from super-smooth Teflon, the latter a faster but less satisfactory method. Finally, and perhaps most important, is the drying. Done at speed, the end-result can lack body and substance, while pasta that is dried slowly tends to more closely resemble the dry natural conditions of a southern Italian farmhouse baking in midday sun.

Neither the supermarkets nor the big brands are particularly keen to part with this information, so the packaging will tell you little... only vague claims to authenticity, usually couched in meaningless flowery language. Most want to sell on the perceived position they have in the market. In reality, all the brands are to a greater or lesser extent looking at colour, stickiness, starchiness – and, if you are lucky, what the Italians call *anima* or 'soul'. Ask almost any Italian about pasta and their eyes drift heavenwards as they warm to the subject. They insist that pasta must have *anima*, a combination of taste, texture and body; the pasta must have presence, be of itself. It is not easy to define *anima*, being the sum of several different aspects, but it is what defines good – as opposed to indifferent – pasta.

what to look for when you buy

Colour should be a consistent pale golden-yellow, with tiny flecks; the latter are an indication of how much whole wheat is in the dough. Too much and the whole-wheat sensation takes over; too little and the pasta lacks body and substance.

On the stickiness front, a plate of drained, correctly cooked good-quality spaghetti, for example, should wriggle around like a bowl of snakes and, when pinched between thumb and forefinger, spring back rather than collapse.

The pasta needs to be correctly cooked to perform; overcooked pasta yields results that are just as disappointing as inferior pasta cooked correctly. To test the starch content you need to stir the hot cooked pasta with your finger for 20 seconds or so and then remove it. Your finger should not be sticky or slimy.

As for 'soul', this is really an evaluation of all of the above. If the cooked pasta has good colouring, wriggles like a live snake and lacks any kind of sliminess or stickiness, then it has soul. With the better brands, this soul means the pasta will hold well when it is cooked; with the less successful ones, the pasta tends to collapse into a sticky mess quite quickly.

Egg-rich dried pastas are growing in popularity, providing the richness of fresh, with the convenience of the dried. In many cases, the egg element is dried pasteurized egg; when whole fresh eggs are used this will be stated on the packet. This does not mean the pasta is better, but it is more likely to be.

I once ate dinner with a group of Italian chefs on the tiny island of Pantelleria in the middle of the Mediterranean. Our second course was pasta dressed with a sauce of fresh sardines and they all waxed lyrical about the dish, not just the

sauce but the pasta. The chef was summoned and the source of the pasta demanded, most anticipating some local artisanal producer. The chef smiled and said it was De Cecco, one of the most popular brands in Italy.

Since then I have experimented with other brands, but find myself coming back repeatedly to De Cecco. Not only are the flavour and texture good, but they hold up well in cooking, which is important as the time from when you finish cooking to actually serving can be quite long and the pasta needs to be quite robust. It also has *anima*.

In my experience, it is only the Italians who understand this, which is why my advice is to buy from an Italian manufacturer. Even then there are good and not-so-good brands. The former are, however, easy to recognize and the ones you are likely to find in good Italian delicatessens.

So how come some are so expensive? In many instances you are paying for the packaging. However, the recent emergence of *pasta artisanale* is not to be frowned upon. Although often twice as expensive, these pastas tend to be produced from excellent flour and mineral water, and are

dried at a lower temperature over a longer period, producing something that has more texture and body. Experiment and taste. You'll soon make up your own mind.

coloured pasta
Dried pasta comes in a range of different colours, although few are authentic. Spinach will produce green pasta, tomato red; but you will also find turmeric-coloured pasta and even a pink, beetroot-coloured version. Black is possibly the most authentic, originating from Venice, where cuttlefish ink is used to colour the pasta a jet black, the accompanying sauce being made of fish, or perhaps squid. It makes for dramatic eating, sending lips and teeth momentarily black. Personally I'd rather have my pasta uncoloured, leaving the sauce to work on a pale background. One of the most striking Italian meals I ever had was pasta with a dense inky-black sauce of cuttlefish in Verona, the only relief being green specks of parsley.

cooking pasta
How much to cook? About 100 g ($3^1/_2$ oz) is sufficient as a first course, 150 g (5 oz) if it is to be a

main course. It is worth bearing in mind that pasta is relatively cheap, so if you have to throw a little away before you make the final dish, it won't cost that much. Far better to do this than have a mound of under-dressed pasta which you will be too full to eat anyway.

The larger the saucepan and the more water you cook the pasta in the better. The reasoning behind this is that once you add the pasta to the boiling water you want the water to return to the boil as soon as possible. If the ratio of water to pasta is too small, the pasta doesn't return to the boil quickly enough, resulting in something mushy and quite unappetizing. As for the adding of oil to the water, there is no real

foundation for this whatsoever; it simply makes no sense. Far better simply to use more water, and that's free. Pasta needs salt and lots of it, a generous 2 to 3 tablespoons for every 4 litres (7 pints) of water.

Is this the only way to cook pasta? Well, no. You can follow the above method, returning the water with the pasta to the boil and cooking for 2 minutes. Turn the heat off, cover with a tea-towel followed by a tight-fitting lid and leave for the same length of time as you would normally cook the pasta. The water will be much clearer and the pasta will retain more of its starch and goodness.

When is it ready? The only sure way is to taste. What you are looking for is, of course, the classic

al dente state, i.e. tender but still firm to the bite. Pasta continues to cook unless it is cooled, so take it out a little earlier than you might otherwise do if you are going to add it to a sauce. You can always cook it for a little longer in the sauce.

Dressing pasta is a subject of much debate. The water in which the pasta has cooked has both body and flavour. While there is often a tendency outside Italy to think the pasta should be drained of every last drop of water, this is not the case in Italy. The water can often help to emulsify the sauce and ensures that the mixture is not too dry. Combining some of the drained water also helps to retain the heat; cold pasta is not much fun.

For this reason, drain the pasta into a bowl or another saucepan. Then you have the choice of adding some of the drained water to let down (dilute) the sauce (the pasta will go on absorbing moisture from the sauce as it continues to cook while still hot). The dressing should be done immediately, while the pasta is still hot, and always remember that the flavour of the pasta is as important as the flavour of the sauce.

Parmesan? Not if you are dressing the pasta with seafood. Some of the vegetable sauces take it, others not. Consider Parmesan as a seasoning rather than an ingredient – that way you are likely to use the correct amount.

size and shape

Up to a point, the shape and size of pasta for a particular sauce do not matter that much; it is the general rules that are important. There are now literally hundreds of shapes and sizes, far too many to remember. The general rules are as follows.

The small-sized pasta are for broths and light soups. Larger, but still short, lengths are for more robust and chunky soups and stews, like *pasta e fagioli*. Long thin pasta, like spaghetti (easily the most popular shape in Italy), should be dressed with light oil-based sauces, as these allow the pasta to remain separate. Long thicker and flat pasta, like tagliatelle, is more usually served with sauces incorporating cream, cheese, eggs or meat. Medium-sized tubes go well with vegetable sauces, while larger tubes, like penne, go well with rich sauces and in baked dishes.

fresh pasta

Fresh pasta, so simple, is surely one of life's great culinary experiences. Strands of feathery-light and rich tagliatelle, dressed with some of autumn's first wild mushrooms, or rich gleaming parcels enveloping anything from the freshest ricotta to thick dark game sauce. Every time I make it, I wonder why I do not do so more often. The answer is fairly simple. It takes a lot of time and turns your kitchen into a flour pot, particularly if (like me) you endeavour to get children involved. It may seem mad at the start, but it is a great way of involving children in Sunday lunch – just make sure you are prepared and everything else is ready.

You can, of course, buy fresh pasta, either from pasta shops or supermarkets. Some of it is quite good, and makes a change from dried pasta. My advice, however, would be to stick to straight – rather than stuffed – pasta. I know of only a handful of places where the stuffing is up to standard; most of the time it is dry and tasteless. This is certainly true of any of the mass-produced stuffed pastas, which are simply not worth considering. The same can be said for any of the 'dried' stuffed pasta, which all taste powdery and anaemic.

While there is little to beat fresh tagliatelle made with golden-yellow free-range eggs, one of the main reasons for making your own pasta is so you can stuff it with delectable items like pumpkin or spiced cheese, and serve it with nothing more than melted butter in which you have lightly sautéed a handful of chopped fresh sage leaves.

If you are going to the trouble of making your own pasta, you need the very best ingredients possible. Buy the best eggs you can afford and track down Italian 00 (*doppio zero*) flour to mix with the harder durum flour, called fine Italian *semola dura* (semolina, or anything else for that matter, will not do).

storing pasta

Dried pasta can be stored pretty much indefinitely, although conditions should be dry. Dried pasta with egg tends to have a shorter shelf-life. Fresh pasta should be just that, cooked and eaten on the day it is made, otherwise the whole point of it rather disappears.

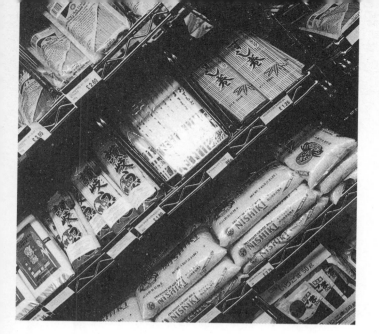

noodles and dumpling wrappers

Popular throughout the Far East, noodles come in soups, salads, as one-bowl meals and sometimes to accompany a whole range of dishes. They can be made from rice and wheat flour, buckwheat and bean paste, with and without egg and are sold dried, fresh and precooked. To buy the best, head for ethnic stores, although super-markets are increasingly stocking the larger brands. The standard overall is very high, texture being a prime consideration to most

cuisines of the Far East. If you brave an ethnic store, ask for help; there is usually somebody who speaks English, if your Chinese, Thai or Japanese is not up to much.

Noodles come in a vast range of shapes and sizes, fresh and dried. Allow around 100 g ($3\frac{1}{2}$ oz) per person. If you are buying fresh, they can be frozen and cooked directly from frozen when you come to use them. Often noodles are boiled, drained and rinsed in cold water and then stir-fried, cooked in a soup or steamed. Cooking times are generally less than for pasta. This is because the flour tends to be softer if it is wheat, while rice and bean flour both cook more quickly anyway or need only soaking in hot water.

CELLOPHANE NOODLES: these are made from ground mung-bean flour, although sometimes also from rice and potato flour. They are so called because, when dry, they look like cellophane. Brand instructions may vary (often poor translations can be misleading), but in general they are soaked in hot water for about 15 minutes. They absorb a lot of water, so the starch content is not overt and they are often served alongside rice dishes.

EGG NOODLES: these are usually made from wheat flour and eggs, and are common in soups, dressed with sauces and stir-fried, when they can be served either quite brittle or soft. Shape and size vary greatly, from thin and round, to broad and flat. Some of the larger brands are rather mean on the egg content. Egg noodles should taste distinctly eggy and rich.

RICE NOODLES, STICKS OR VERMICELLI: typical in rice-growing areas, these are generally thin, white and slippery. If bought dried, they should be soaked for a few hours and then do not require much cooking, if any. Most rice

noodles are so delicate they only need soaking in hot water before dressing with a sauce or stir-frying with other ingredients.

RICE PAPERS, SPRING ROLL WRAPPERS AND WON TON WRAPPERS: rice papers are similar to rice noodles in that they are made with rice flour and water. Brittle, until lightly brushed with water or soaked, they are then stuffed. Won ton wrappers are made from wheat flour and water and then rolled paper-thin. They are pliable so need no soaking before being stuffed; they are then steamed, deep-fried or boiled in a soup.

SOBA NOODLES: made with a combination of buckwheat flour and wheat flour, these are very popular in Japan, where they are either eaten cooked and cold and dipped into a variety of soy-based sauces, or served in a bowl of hot broth.

UDON NOODLES: also Japanese in origin, these are long and narrow, not unlike thin tagliatelle in shape; they are made from wheat flour and handled in much the same way as spaghetti.

rice

Rice is a cereal grass grown on marshy flooded land throughout the world, but particularly in Southeast Asia, China, Japan, India and parts of the USA, as well as in parts of Italy and Spain. It is a versatile plant and adapts well to different habitats, but does require water and rather a lot of it.

There are literally thousands of varieties of rice, numerous ways to cook this humble grain, and myriad dishes – from the basic plain accompaniment to something as rich and opulent as truffle risotto, or Spanish paella imbued with that most expensive of spices, saffron.

To buy rice you need first to consider the correct rice for the dish. Rice is essentially graded into short-, medium- and long-grain varieties. Within these categories, however, there are subsections; basmati, for example, is a particularly fragrant long-grain rice.

LONG-GRAIN RICE: most suitable as a plain rice to accompany curries and other dishes, or in a pilaf or biryani, and in Chinese-style fried-rice dishes.

MEDIUM-GRAIN RICE is suited to those dishes, like paella and risotto, where the rice is meant to absorb some of the cooking liquid. It can also be used for puddings, where it contributes more flavour and texture than short-grain rice.

SHORT-GRAIN RICE is suited to puddings where the intention is that the rice should partially collapse and release starch to impart a creaminess to the dish.

Rice is sold as a commodity, usually by large multinationals whose brands are known worldwide. The quality swings from the dull and boring, to good – some might even say impressive – but it depends on which type of rice and what you are cooking.

When buying rice, not only do you want it to contribute flavour but also texture.... will it be dry, fluffy, absorbent, sticky or creamy? For a pilaf you want it to be fluffy, for a risotto or paella, absorbent; and you want whichever characteristic to be constant. A fluffy rice that becomes sticky by the time it reaches the table is not a good rice. Some will argue about the textural differences between Arborio risotto rice and Vialone Nano, but to my mind the main difference is the latter holds its shape and character longer, which is why restaurants prefer it.

Spending money on rice needs to be seen in context. More rice is eaten around the world than any

other food, and few types are very expensive. Against that, if you eat rice infrequently you are unlikely to enjoy the marginal benefits of spending ever-increasing amounts of money on it. Far better to perfect your cooking technique.

what to look for when you buy

With all rices, the grains should be unbroken, of similar size, texture and colour, and not dusty. The aroma should be sweet and pungent, not dull and tired. Which brand to buy depends on availability, price and the marginal enjoyment. If you eat risotto a great deal, you may well be able to appreciate the difference between Arborio and Carnaroli, but the latter can be twice the price – and do you obtain twice the enjoyment?

PILAFS, PLAIN RICE FOR CURRIES AND STEWS: undoubtedly the top rice in this area is basmati, with its unmistakably clean and pure aroma. It holds its shape, is long and elegant, tastes as good as it smells, and marries well with other ingredients. The quality is usually evident in the aroma, which should be rich, full and rounded, but with

a crystal-clear quality. The same can be said for Thai fragrant rice, although this tends to be slightly sticky (not the same as soggy), the grains remaining separate. American long-grain rices are also generally good, although to my mind not as full-flavoured.

RISOTTO RICES: the three main varieties are: Arborio, Vialone Nano and Carnaroli, although in Italy you will come across rather more, including the likes of Roma and Baldo. The regionality of Italy shows itself in risotto-making, as elsewhere; if you live in an area growing Baldo, that's what's in your risotto. Start with Arborio, the most widely available, and then compare and contrast with the other varieties.

PAELLA RICES: the home of this great dish is the east coast of Spain and here you find the greatest Spanish rice of them all, Bomba, which comes from the beautiful Calasparra region. The rices from this area tend to be shorter than risotto rices but behave similarly, absorbing liquid.

BROWN RICE: a generic term for any rice that has not had the outer bran layer removed. They

153

generally have a more nutty flavour but take an age to cook. They are good for you, but you tend to feel that when you are eating them, which takes some of the pleasure away.

PUDDING RICE: use a short-grain rice by all means, but you are likely to get more flavour and texture using a medium-grain rice, either an Italian risotto rice or paella rice from Spain (see previous page).

PAR-BOILED RICE: the process may sound modern but is actually 2,000 years old. The paddy, which is rice that has been threshed from the stalk but is still in the husk, is soaked for several hours and then steamed for about 10 minutes. Then it is dried and milled. The process forces some of the nutrients in the outer husk back into the rice grain and a hard shell is formed on the grain, which reduces its tendency to stick during cooking.

EASY-COOK RICE OR PRECOOKED RICE: this is rice partially cooked, then chilled, dried and packaged. It means a shorter cooking time for the consumer, but also gives less character and

texture. Almost no rice-eating nations would consider it, which says enough for me.

WILD RICE: this is not actually rice, or even a grain, but a grass, and although it used to grow wild, it is now cultivated. It absorbs more liquid than white rice (up to four times its volume), which means a little goes a long way (about 125 g/4^1/$_2$ oz serves four). Its nutty, earthy flavour suits game and red meat, and wild rice is also good for stuffing vegetables.

STICKY RICE: used in Japanese and Chinese cooking, the high starch content of this variety of rice makes the grains stick together – so that it is handy for gathering up in chopsticks.

If you buy rice in a supermarket, you are likely to get a range of brands, from the good down to the indifferent; paying a little more is likely to give you infinitely better quality. Ethnic stores are far better hunting-grounds, with a better range, quality and turnover. The same is true of risotto and paella rices, which are better bought from Italian or Spanish delis.

storing rice

Storage instructions are very much the same as for any other dry goods: in a dry cupboard, away from natural light. Avoid trying to stockpile too much; although rice is fairly indestructible, it will nevertheless deteriorate over time.

cooking rice

Rice is cooked in a number of ways, from the creamy risotti of Italy, to the biryanis of India, from the fluffy paellas of Spain to the congees, or rice gruels, of China. Some rinse the grains thoroughly before cooking to rid the rice of excess starch, others abhor the practice. I would always rinse basmati rice, for example, but would never even consider doing the same to a risotto or paella rice.

There are two principal basic methods of cooking the grain, either in quite a lot of water which is drained off at the end, or by the 'absorption method'. In the former, the rice is added to boiling salted water, simmered until tender and then drained. Remember to allow for the expansion in volume of the rice and to use sufficient liquid (rice

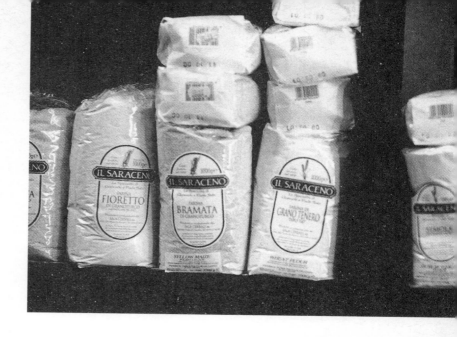

grains can extend to as much as three times their original length and will also expand in proportion). Quite a lot of the starch in the rice will also be released into the water, leaving the grains separate and fluffy. In some Indian kitchens the rice water is then turned into a spicy broth, lest anything should be wasted. It tastes pretty good, too, for something so frugal.

In the absorption method, a quantity of rice is added to a set amount of water (or stock, etc.), the pot is sealed and the rice cooked for a set period, until all the moisture has been absorbed. The main advantage of this method is that it requires very little attention once everything has been assembled. As a rough guide, you require two parts water by volume to one part rice. Often rice prepared this way is first partly cooked in butter or oil; some flavourings. like onions, chillies or spices, can also be added at this stage.

If you think a rice cooker will solve your problems, just think about how much rice you eat; it needs to be quite a lot to justify the accommodation of such a large piece of kit.

grains

In general, health-food shops are the best source for most grains, as quality tends to be good and turnover high. If in doubt about the age of what is in your cupboard, my advice is to bin it; it is likely to have been there at least twice as long as you think it has and is hardly expensive. The more familiar grains are dealt with in detail below; for others, like the more unusual buckwheat, millet, oats, quinoa, rye and spelt, the general rules apply: buy frequently, use a shop with a high turnover and remember that grains are not inert – like pulses, they deteriorate over time.

BARLEY: we see it most often as pearl barley to thicken soups and stews, yet this ancient grain also

appears malted in both brewing and distilling. You can buy whole-grain barley, but its cooking time is long, a few hours. Pearl barley can be fashioned into a type of risotto, cooked in the same way but for longer.

BULGUR WHEAT: made by parboiling grains of wheat and then passing them through rollers, this is an excellent store-cupboard item. Because it is partially cooked, it is very quick to prepare, has great texture and a nutty, mealy flavour that goes as well in salads (tabbouleh) as with stews and casseroles. For the best, head for an artisanal or organic producer. A great deal depends on the quality of the grain and how it is rolled, industrial rollers being less forgiving than stone. Health-food shops tend to have a good

155

turnover, which lessens the risk of stale bulgur wheat, an experience to be missed – it is akin to stale fermenting bread. Look for one that contributes a strong nutty flavour and has real bite.

COUSCOUS: this is not in itself a grain at all, but grains of semolina that have been rolled and coated in wheat flour to keep them separate. Semolina, in turn, is flour ground from hard or durum wheat, the kind of wheat used in eggless pasta. Because of its high protein and gluten content, durum wheat is incredibly tough to work – see the section on making fresh pasta on page 162.

Eating real couscous, as opposed to precooked or instant varieties, is a revelation. It has bite and texture, with a delicate wheat flavour that almost bursts in the mouth when you bite into it. It makes quite a change from the rather pappy instant couscous we put up with, but then there is the convenience – couscous is time-consuming and hardly exciting to cook. The best is to be found in Middle Eastern stores, but even there the attractions of the instant variety have had their effect.

OATS: popular in northern Europe, Scotland and Ireland, their widespread use there is the direct result of their liking for cold damp weather. Oats are also nutritious and cook into a jelly-like consistency, with a somewhat grim and grey colouring. Oatmeal is the kernel and comes in various sizes, producing a rough or smooth texture. The flour can be used to make biscuits, but not bread unless mixed with wheat flour (for all its good qualities, oats contain very little gluten). Oats and their by-products (oatmeal and oatflakes) are packed with flavour and much overlooked in flavour of wheat.

POLENTA: pale yellow, sometimes almost white, with a curiously deep mealy flavour and texture, polenta can be cooked into a comforting rich creamy mash, or allowed to cool until solid and then sliced and grilled, fried or made into a gratin. Its affinity with other ingredients – mushrooms, cream and butter to mention just three – makes it an ideal accompaniment. Fashioned into a cheese-rich porridge, it transforms a winter stew, or as char-grilled slices it takes on a completely different character with grilled fish or

vegetables. Polenta has both its devotees and detractors; in the past, societies existed throughout northern Italy devoted to its consumption and yet others cannot see the point.

Also known as cornmeal in America, it comes in instant-cook varieties which lack the bite and texture – not to mention flavour – of the real thing. Convenience however, dictates its prevalence, certainly outside Italy. You should look for an Italian brand and preferably one sold in an Italian shop.

Things to whisk into soft polenta: cream and nutmeg; Parmesan and Taleggio; butter and milk. Uses for grilled polenta: with a salad of goats' cheese, olives and cherry tomatoes; with grilled vegetables and pesto; with grilled fish and salsa verde.

WHEAT: together with rice, this cereal grass makes up the main source of man's food grains. Wheat (*Triticum*) comes in literally thousands of varieties, but is generally divided into three distinct groups. First is *T. monococcum* or *einkorn*, now grown only in parts of Africa and some northern parts

of Europe. It is of limited use in modern cooking and is generally grown only on poor soil, where other wheats will not flourish.

The other two categories are much more important. *T. durum* is pasta wheat, believed to have developed from its more basic cousin, emmer wheat – the ancient simple ancestor of today's wheat. It is a hard wheat with a high gluten content (see below) and excellent keeping qualities. Apart from making pasta, it is also used for high-protein bread.

Finally, and most importantly, there is *T. aestivum*, bread wheat. It has thousands of varieties, often the result of man's breeding, and is grown throughout the world, where the plant has adapted and also been adapted to varying conditions. The stronger flours used for bread-making come from this group, as do the softer flours for making biscuits, cakes and pastry.

Gluten is a key element of wheat. It is a protein consisting of a mixture of glutenin and gliadin, and it is what gives bread texture by producing an elastic dough, allowing it to rise in the baking. Wheats high in gluten are commonly referred to as 'hard

wheats'. Durum wheat is also hard, and although it too has a high gluten content, it is hard in the physical sense; when it is rolled, the grains splinter into slender chips that are glassy in appearance.

Wheat is usually sold as flour: plain, wholemeal, self-raising and strong flours; and every brand, it seems, is different. Flours also vary wildly between countries, from the hard wheat of Canada to the softer wheat of mainland Europe. Depending on the country you are buying in, flour will variously be labelled 'strong bread', 'soft' or 'cake'. In Italy, for example, a much more specific system is used: *tipo* 0 or 00 (zero and doppio zero, see page 150).

Wholewheat flour is normally a strong flour in which the whole grain is milled, nothing being either added or removed. The nutritional qualities of this flour are undoubtedly very high, but it has a rough-and-ready texture. Stone-ground is, as the name suggests, ground with old-fashioned stones, rather than being milled with modern steel mills, the latter producing a much finer texture, but, some argue, less flavour.

bread

Basic bread is easy to make and involves only three ingredients: flour, yeast (or another raising agent) and water... Or is it four, time being also rather crucial? In the last 50 years, substantial and lasting damage has been done to this basic foodstuff. Industrial processes have ripped it apart, bringing us a tasteless cheap, pappy concoction. Not all is bad news, however, as out of this morass of mediocrity there is an emerging band of artisanal producers determined to put

character back into bread.

Throughout mainland Europe, a great deal of the bread we consume is dry, tasteless and dull. Even in France, the once famous baguette is now often baked from frozen dough; in Spain and Italy, the average daily bread is regularly dull and relatively boring, while little pockets of interest – parts of Portugal, for example – consume bread that is infused with texture and flavour that rightly make it a food by itself. A slice of good bread should leave you feeling nourished and satisfied, even when eaten by itself.

If buying ingredients to make your own bread, the following applies. Wheat, the most common flour used for bread, is often produced on an industrial scale and plied with chemicals to control its growth. Don't think that by buying wholemeal flour you are avoiding this thorny issue; wholemeal flour often has a greater percentage of chemical residues in it, a consequence of the flour being made from the outer layers of the grain. An organic flour is, therefore, worth seeking out.

As to which flour you should use, a hard wheat – common in North America – is easier to bake with; while a softer wheat – more common in Europe – is harder to bake with, but tends to have better flavour. A hard wheat has more protein, which develops the gluten and helps the bread to rise. Flours are very different, depending on the type of wheat used and the milling: stone-grinding leaves flour more gritty, and many would say with more flavour. Higher-yielding strains of flour exhibiting less character have found increasing favour, but there is now a backlash – with more difficult, but also more interesting, flours being produced. Good hunting-grounds are, again, health- and whole-food shops and good delicatessens.

Yeast is the most popular raising agent used and there are many who say fresh yeast provides more character than dried. A baker friend, however, swears by dried yeast, saying consistency is more important, given yeast's relatively small influence on the final flavour. He, however, makes all his bread with a sourdough starter, or leaven, a mixture of flour and water – and usually some dough from previous bread – as well as something for the natural yeasts present in the flour and atmosphere to work on, like crushed apples, for example.

Leaven gives bread a natural sourness and more depth, body and interest; the analogy, perhaps, is with cream and crème fraîche (see page 91). Popular in Eastern Europe in rye breads, you also find leaven in the darker French breads, like *pain de campagne*, as well as in some better baguettes; on the west coast of America, where the term San Francisco sourdough has become popular; and in Britain, where a small band of bakers are using sourdough.

Water is also important, its chemical make-up and – in some instances – additions affecting both the flavour and the behaviour of the bread. Most good bakeries will purify water, so it is worth considering bottled water if you are making your own.

Although there is nothing complicated about baking bread, it is a huge and fascinating area. Practice is required, as are a great deal of patience, particularly as you start to make more complicated breads, and time – you cannot rush a good loaf.

what to look for when you buy

If you are buying your own bread, look for a loaf that has an interesting crust, with good colour and texture. This should be as true for a crusty *pain de campagne* as for soda bread, even though the crust of the latter is not actually 'crusty'.

Pick the loaf up; in general, if it is surprisingly light, beware. With the exception of loaves like brioche, good bread tends to have some weight. There should be a significant ratio of crust to inside, as a great deal of the flavour comes from the crust. The interior should be white, but not brilliant-white, the sign of bleached flour; something grey or beige is preferable. The dough should be springy and, if you press it, it should bounce back.

When you taste, the flavour should be bright and exciting, the texture equally alive; if the bread sticks to your teeth, becoming pappy, dull and unexciting, you are on to a bad thing. Good bread also keeps well, at least for a few days, if loosely wrapped in plastic, although the crust is likely to soften. (French baguettes are the exception here, but then they are designed to be bought and consumed within hours.) Both the flavour and the aroma of good bread concentrate on nutty, wheaty, satisfying roundedness.

directory

pasta

The best place to buy pasta is a good Italian deli; for a marginal increase in price over supermarket offerings, you'll find better texture and flavour. Brands to watch out for are De Cecco, Spinosi, Martelli and Lucio Garosalo from Napoli... the list could be endless. Ask Italians living here for their favourite brand. I find it hard to recommend any fresh pasta other than that at Lina Stores in Soho, 18 Brewer Street, W1R 3FS (020 7437 6482) and Valvona and Crolla, 19 Elm Row, Edinburgh EH7 4AA (0131 556 6066).

rice and Oriental noodles

Head for ethnic supermarkets and try to ask for some help. This can, of course, be difficult because of the language – or, rather, lack of it.

other grains

Italian delicatessens are good sources, as well as health-food shops, the latter tending to have a high turnover. They are also good sources of flour for bread-making. Remember that bread is seldom more than flour, yeast and water, and the most influential of these in terms of taste is flour. Pick some mass-produced brand and you are likely to make mass-tasting bread, which hardly seems worth the effort.

Look out for Principato di Lucedio Black Venus Rice and Bartolini farro (emmer wheat). Spain is one of the best producers

of rice: contact Brindisa on 020 7403 0282 for stockists of the likes of Cooperativa del Campo Calasparra rice, a delight and the only rice for paella.

bread

Good sources include: & Clarke's, 122 Kensington Church Street, London W8 4BH (020 7229 2190); Alexander Taylor of Waterside Bakery, 10–11 Waterside Street, Strathaven, Lanarkshire ML10 6AW (01357 521260); Baker and Spice, 46 Walton Street, London SW3 1RB (020 7589 4734); De Gustibus, 53 Blandford Street, London W1H 5RF (020 7486 6608); Derwen Bakehouse, Museum of Welsh Life, St Fagans, Cardiff (01222 573500); Flourpower City, 238 Hoxton Street, London N1 5LX (020 7729 7414); Veales of Conway, 124 Vale Street, Denbigh, Denbighshire (01745 812068); The Village Bakery, Melmerby, Penrith, Cumbria (01768 881515).

pasta, grains and bread recipes

basic fresh pasta dough

You will need a pasta machine to make this dough.

makes about 1.5 kg (3¼ lb)

800 g (1³/4 lb) 00 (doppio zero) flour

400 g (14 oz) semola dura (hard fine Italian semolina, other types will not be hard enough)

12 medium eggs (preferably free-range and organic if possible)

1 Combine all the ingredients in a food mixer fitted with a dough hook and process until they form a ball. If the dough is too wet, add a little more 00 flour; if it is a little dry, add a few drops of water. You can use a food processor, but the results are not nearly as good. Better to do it by hand if you lack a food mixer.

2 Turn the dough out on a board and knead it for 10 minutes – any less will not do. Form it into a ball, wrap in cling-film and chill in the fridge for at least 1 hour or up to 4 (if you leave it any longer there is a chance the eggs will oxidize).

3 Break off a golf-ball-sized piece of dough. Liberally dust the pasta machine with 00 flour and then, starting on the thickest setting, roll the piece of dough through the machine several times, reducing the setting each time until you pass it through on the thinnest. This is much more easily achieved with two people as you need to keep the pasta moving through continuously. If it gets too unmanageable, simply cut it in half and carry on. Once rolled, you need to dust whatever surface you are putting it on with semola, otherwise it will stick. The semola comes off the pasta when you put it in boiling water.

4 Cut the sheet of pasta into appropriate shapes: rectangles for lasagne; long strips for noodles, etc., dusting both pasta and surfaces with semola as you go. Remember, the more rough-and-ready your shapes are the more appealingly home-made they look.

5 Repeat the rolling and cutting processes with the remaining dough.

6 Fresh pasta needs cooking, but not much. If you are making lasagne, it still needs a couple of minutes in boiling water to cook the flour through before layering. It is, however, very easy to overcook fresh pasta, so take care.

pappardelle with mushrooms, cream and garlic

serves 4

4 garlic cloves
200 ml (7 fl oz) double cream
150 g (5 oz) button mushrooms
2 tablespoons olive oil
75 g (2³/4 oz) butter
2 tablespoons chopped parsley
salt and pepper
freshly grated nutmeg
500 g (1 lb 2 oz) egg-rich
    pappardelle
grated parmesan cheese, to serve

1 Smash the garlic cloves with the flat a large knife and place in a small saucepan with the cream. Bring to the boil and simmer gently for 2 minutes. Remove from the heat and set aside.

2 Slice the mushrooms thinly and gently sauté them in the olive oil until they wilt and start to give up their juices, about 5 minutes.

3 Strain the cream over the mushrooms and stir in the butter and parsley. Season with salt, pepper and nutmeg, and cook over a moderate heat until the mushrooms are tender.

4 Cook the pappardelle in plenty of boiling salted water until just al dente, i.e. tender but still firm. Drain and toss with the mushroom sauce. Adjust the seasoning and serve with Parmesan.

linguine and fresh sardine sauce

serves 4

500 g (1 lb 2 oz) linguine
salt and pepper
1 kg (2 lb) fresh, very fresh, sardines
about 125 ml (4 fl oz) extra-virgin
    olive oil
2 garlic cloves, thinly sliced
2 chillies, deseeded and finely
    chopped
2 tablespoons finely chopped
    parsley
1 tablespoon pine nuts, lightly
    toasted in a dry frying pan
juice of 1 lemon

Grilled sardines are one of the pleasures of summer, either on holiday or at home, their rich full flavour cut with nothing more than lemon juice and something icy-cold – beer or wine. This is a dish I once ate on a trip to Sicily: the light was fading on a night at the end of the summer, and I could hear the lapping of the sea all the way through the following winter.

1 Put the pasta to cook in plenty of boiling salted water.

2 Scrape the scales away from each sardine and slide a knife down behind the head and along the backbone towards the tail, pressing lightly with your free hand to guide the knife. Repeat on the other side to end up with 2 fillets.

3 Heat 4 tablespoons of olive oil in a large shallow frying pan. When hot, but not too hot, add the garlic, chilli and parsley. Lay the sardines, skin side up, on top and lower the heat. Simmer gently for 5 minutes, or until the sardines are cooked through.

4 When al dente, i.e. tender but still firm, drain the pasta and toss with the sardines. Drizzle over more olive oil, scatter with the pine nuts, season with salt, pepper and lemon juice, and serve.

hare sauce for pappardelle

serves 6 – 8

1 dressed hare, cut into pieces
salt and pepper
6 tablespoons olive oil
2 onions, finely chopped
2 carrots, finely chopped
2 celery stalks, finely chopped
squeeze of tomato purée
2 garlic cloves, finely chopped
1 bouquet garni
one 400-g (14-oz) tin of chopped
    tomatoes
1 bottle of red wine
1 litre (1³/4 pints) chicken stock

Hare is not an easy meat to cook, the saddle and legs needing different cooking times and methods. With this classic Italian sauce, however, you get the best of all worlds, a stew that is thick, unctuous and robust. Combined with the pasta, the dish softens the hare's intrinsic gaminess and richness, giving a dish that is well balanced and surprisingly light.

1 Season the pieces of hare with salt and pepper and lightly brown them in 4 tablespoons of the olive oil in a large heavy-based pan. You will probably need to do this in two or three batches, depending on the size of your pan. Set the pieces of hare aside.

2 Add the remaining olive oil to the pan, heat and gently sauté the onion for 10 minutes without colouring it.

3 Add the carrots and celery and continue cooking gently for a further 10 minutes. Add the tomato purée and cook until the sauce deepens slightly in colour.

4 Add the garlic, toss once and then add the bouquet garni, tomatoes with their liquid, red wine and chicken stock. Return the pieces of hare to the pan. Slowly bring to the boil, lower the heat and simmer for 2 hours, uncovered.

5 Remove the hare from the pan and allow to cool until you can comfortably handle it, then shred the meat from the bones and return it to the sauce. Continue to cook, uncovered, until it reaches a thick syrupy consistency, 15–20 minutes more. Take care if reheating, as you may need to dilute with a little water to prevent it catching. Adjust the seasoning before serving.

rice with squid and mussels

serves 6–8

1 kg (2 lb) mussels, cleaned and
   scrubbed (discarding any open
   ones that don't close on being
   tapped)
4 tablespoons olive oil
800 g (1³/₄ lb) squid, cleaned and
   cut into tablespoon-sized pieces
salt and pepper
2 garlic cloves, finely chopped
400 g (14 oz) Valencia rice (or a
   risotto rice)
one 400-g (14-oz) tin of chopped
   tomatoes
1 litre (1³/₄ pint) hot chicken stock
pinch of saffron threads, dissolved in
   a little hot water
1 tablespoon chopped parsley
3–4 lemons, halved

1 Put the mussels in a saucepan,
cover with a lid and place over a
moderate heat, shaking well. The
mussels take 4 to 5 minutes to
open. Remove the lid and set the
mussels aside to cool.

2 Heat the olive oil in a
flameproof casserole. Season the
squid with salt and sauté for 5
minutes. Stir in the garlic and rice
and sauté for 2 minutes.

3 Add the tomatoes with their
liquid and the stock. Bring back to
the boil, stir once and simmer for
20 minutes.

4 Meanwhile, remove the mussels
from their shells, leaving a dozen
or so intact for decoration. (Any
mussels that have not opened
should be discarded.) Strain the
liquor from the saucepan, taking
care to leave any grit behind.

5 A couple of minutes before the
end of rice cooking time, stir in
the strained liquor and the mussels
along with the saffron and its
soaking liquid. Adjust the
seasoning, stir in the parsley and
serve with a lemon half.

spiced bulgur wheat pilaf

serves 6–8 as an accompaniment

4 tablespoons olive oil
1 onion, chopped
500 g (1 lb 2 oz) bulgur wheat
1 teaspoon each ground cumin,
    coriander, turmeric and ginger
one 400-g (14-oz) tin of chopped
    tomatoes
salt and pepper

1 In a large heavy-based saucepan, heat the olive oil and gently sauté the onion in it for 10 minutes, or until softened.

2 Add the bulgur wheat and continue to cook for a further 2 minutes, stirring frequently. Add the spices and cook for 2 minutes more, or until the spices lose their raw aroma. Add the tomatoes with their liquid and 350 ml (12 fl oz) of water. Bring to the boil. Season, turn down the heat and simmer for 15 minutes, uncovered. (You may need a little more water towards the end of the cooking.)

3 Remove from heat and set aside for 10 minutes, covered with a clean tea-towel, before serving.

risotto with beef and red wine

If you can't find beef stock, you can use a 225-ml (8-fl oz) tin of consommé diluted with water.

serves 4–6

1.2 litres (2 pints) beef stock
45 g (1½ oz) butter
3 tablespoons finely chopped
   pancetta
2 garlic cloves, finely chopped
1 teaspoon finely chopped rosemary
2 teaspoons finely chopped sage
115 g (4 oz) minced steak
salt and pepper
325 ml (11 fl oz) red wine
450 g (1 lb) risotto rice
freshly grated Parmesan cheese

1 In a saucepan, bring the stock up to simmering point.

2 Put one-third of the butter in another large heavy-based saucepan along with the pancetta and garlic and cook gently, without colouring, for 5 minutes. Add the rosemary and sage, cook for 1 minute more and then add the meat, mashing it up with a fork and turning it to colour, still on low heat. Season with salt and pepper.

3 Add about 250 ml (9 fl oz) of the red wine and simmer until the wine has almost all been absorbed or evaporated.

4 Turn the heat up and add the rice. Stir to coat it well. Then add the stock in stages, about a ladleful at a time, and cook, stirring as you add the liquid, until the rice is almost tender, 20–35 minutes depending on the type of rice. Add the remaining wine and finish cooking.

5 Off the heat, stir in the rest of the butter and Parmesan to taste, cover and leave to stand for 5 minutes. Serve with more cheese.

soda bread

makes 1 loaf

450 g (1 lb) plain flour, plus more for
   dusting
1 teaspoon salt
1 teaspoon bicarbonate of soda
about 350 ml (12 oz) buttermilk

The buttermilk that gives Irish soda bread its characteristic flavour, while widely available in Ireland, can be quite difficult to come by elsewhere. One solution is to make your own: combine 30 g (1 oz) of fresh yeast with 30 g (1 oz) of caster sugar, stir in 1 litre (1³/4 pints) of full-cream milk at room temperature, cover with a tea-towel and set aside for 2 days at room temperature. The resulting taste is much the same as that of buttermilk.

1 Preheat the oven to 230°C/450°F /Gas 8.

2 Combine the dry ingredients in a large bowl, make a well in the centre and pour in the buttermilk. Stir together, aiming for a sloppy but workable dough. You may need a little more (or less) milk depending on your flour.

3 Turn out on a floured surface, shape into a mound and cut a cross in the top. Bake for 15 minutes and then turn the oven down to 200°C/400°F/Gas 6 and bake for 20–30 minutes more, or until cooked (the bottom sounds hollow when tapped).

6

vinegars,
oils, herbs
and spices

'Olive oil is the very soul of a salad,
and far beyond this, for it is one of the finest
natural foods and medicines ever bestowed
upon man.'

EDWARD and LORNA BUNYARD, *The Epicure's Companion*

'The cook who does not habitually use some
sort of bouquet garni is probably not worthy
of being called a cook, and it will not do
to substitute commercial "mixed herbs" or
powdered bouquet garni from a packet.'

TOM STOBART, *Herbs, Spices and Flavourings*

I always have two or three vinegars to hand, at least three oils, a garden full of herbs and a cupboard restocked regularly with a selection of spices. It is to these ingredients I turn every day to provide variety and interest. No dish is ever the same, the Chianti vinegar imparting a different flavour from that of the one from the Veneto, a little more cumin than coriander, rosemary used in greater profusion than sage or thyme, whereas last time it was the other way round.

All these flavourings should provide an identity, which must be in balance with the other tastes in your dish. You are trying to achieve a depth and complexity of flavour, without any single element being too forceful. Experiment and taste, and don't forget the role of water – a dash of vinegar in a hot pan will evaporate with speed, better to follow with a splash of water and see if the resulting sauce needs more vinegar.

With such flavouring ingredients, small producers should be favoured over large, cottage rather than factory. Except for spices, perhaps, and that is only because the production process is essentially one of drying, involving little more than taking a large quantity of spice, drying it and bagging it. In the case of oils and vinegars, and for more interesting herbs, small really is better.

vinegar

Vinegar is made when alcohol combines with bacteria to create acetic acid. The bacteria grow to form a thin skin called the 'mother' and the process after that is continuous, the mother re-used as a starter for other batches of vinegar. The alcohol can come from a number of different sources – beer, cider, wine or rice – and can be combined with other flavouring ingredients, such as herbs, nuts and fruit. Vinegars can be a subtle and delicate means of introducing variety of flavour.

A good vinegar, irrespective of its base, should taste full and rounded, the acidity being balanced by other flavours: fruit in the case of fruit vinegars and wine characteristics in the case of wine vinegars. The acidity should provide focus, but should not be overly astringent. Above all else, it should smell and taste invigorating, not flat and dull.

balsamic vinegar

There are two versions of balsamic vinegar, one traditional and the other commercial. The former, true balsamic vinegar, is made from the juice of the Trebbiano grape which is slowly evaporated and fermented in progressively smaller barrels. It can only be made in an area centred on Modena in Italy and takes years, often 15 to 20, to reach maturity. Consequently it is extremely expensive – expect to pay enormous amounts for really old balsamic, labelled as '*aceto balsamico tradizionale*'.

On the other hand, commercially produced balsamic is hardly aged at all and will have caramel added to introduce the required sweetness. The price is a good guide, but after that you have to taste. Most commercial balsamic is fairly easy to identify, with its lack of balance, off-flavours and generally cloying texture (the caramel). Spend more on the better vinegar and use it less frequently.

cider vinegar

This comes in a commercial (clear) or more home-produced version which can be cloudy. Its

relatively low acidity makes it particularly good in salads, the apple flavour coming through very gently. It is also good for pickling and for flavouring with herbs. It can also be used as a refreshing summer drink: sweeten it with sugar, add some mineral water and lots of ice.

flavoured vinegars

While straight vinegars can provide great complexity in a dish, you can go one step further by flavouring the vinegar with fruit, spices, herbs, even nuts, as in walnut vinegar. This latter is a salad favourite, much more subtle than too-powerful walnut oil. Flavouring is easily done, in no more than a few minutes, although the vinegar generally has to sit for a few weeks to develop.

Fruit vinegars

Raspberry is probably the most popular of the fruit vinegars, but there are others, like strawberry, blackcurrant, pear and mixed berries. The fruit should not be too predominant, a hint or suggestion being preferable, otherwise it can taste cloying. The base vinegar is usually wine vinegar, the fruit being gently crushed and left to infuse with the vinegar for several days. It is then strained, boiled and bottled – a process that is remarkably easy to do at home.

Useful in providing variety in vinaigrettes, fruit vinegars can also be used to deglaze roasting pans and as part of a basting mixture for fatty meats, the sharpness of the vinegar helping to cut the richness of the meat. More

commercial vinegars are likely to use fruit concentrates, which tend to lack much subtlety.

Herb vinegars

Wine vinegar is, again, the most common base for these flavoured vinegars. Select unblemished herbs, place in the vinegar and seal. Leave for at least a week or two before use. If the herbs wilt you can always replace them with fresh. There is no limit to which herbs may be used: tarragon is the most popular, but thyme and rosemary are also good. Chillies, too, make for interesting vinegar, particularly aromatic chillies.

malt vinegar

This comes in two forms, traditional and industrial. The latter, called non-brewed condiment, is likely to be the one used in your local fish and chip shop, and its origins lie in a petrochemical plant somewhere; it is a by-product and to be avoided at all costs. True malt vinegar used to be as varied and interesting as wine vinegar, but its manufacture requires time and a corresponding cost, which has led to malt vinegar tasting rather sharp, astringent and boring. Its affinity with fish and chips, however, is undisputed. Some smaller breweries are trying their hand at malt vinegars, but as yet they are few and far between.

rice vinegars

These come in two main forms, a Japanese version that borders on being sweet, mellow and soft, and Chinese rice vinegar, which tends to a sourness with quite a high acidity. It is as well not to mix the two; use one or the other as specified in a recipe, as their flavours are very different.

wine vinegars

These should have flavours reminiscent of their origins: light and sharp in the case of champagne; rich and full in the case of Rioja; or strongly fruity in the case of sherry. The result should be a vinegar of depth and roundness, with a balanced taste that is sharp, but with the background flavours following up quickly. The traditional centre of wine vinegar manufacture is Orléans in France, where a lengthy fermentation process is still followed. If the bottle says 'Orléans method' you're likely to pay much more, but also have a more complex and balanced vinegar.

oils

In culinary terms, oils are fatty substances in liquid form derived from a number of plant sources. Olive oil is a clear favourite in my kitchen and the one I use most, but there are plenty of other sources, from peanuts (groundnut oil) to sunflowers to coconuts.

Oils can be an extremely concentrated form of energy, as well as a source of fatty acids, although in a highly refined oil many of the fatty acids are stripped out. Much is made of the beneficial qualities of some oils over others, but they all remain a concentrated form of fat. The nutritional chemistry of oils and fats is complex beyond the scope of this book, but to over-simplify, fatty acids fall into three categories: saturated (bad), monounsaturated (somewhere in between, but also with their own added health benefits) and polyunsaturated (good). Unfortunately, oils high in polyunsaturated fats tend to be fairly bland in taste, but this can be beneficial, as when making mayonnaise for example, when highly flavoured oils tend to exhibit their inherent bitterness.

OILS HIGH IN SATURATES: *avocado, coconut, palm*
OILS HIGH IN MONO-
   UNSATURATES: *olive oil*
OILS HIGH IN POLY-
   UNSATURATES: *corn, grapeseed, groundnut, safflower, soya, sunflower*

When oils are heated, their characteristics change, depending on their burning points. Sesame seed oil, for example, has a very low burning point and even a gentle heat will begin to destroy the subtleties inherent in the oil; the same is true of walnut and hazelnut oils. Other oils, like groundnut and sunflower oil, have high burning points and tend, therefore, to be used widely in Chinese cooking, where stir-frying is done at a fairly high temperature.

A great deal of the oil available is intensely refined and processed to ensure it has almost no flavour at all. This is particularly true of the brand names you will find on supermarket shelves. The oil is produced from any number of world-traded commodities, from seeds to cereals, nuts to fruits. For character and diversity, you need to find an oil that is the result of a

first cold pressing. Once heat is applied, most of the subtleties in an oil disappear. Look out for small producers and taste, taste and taste again. It is only by comparing oils that you will be able to make a judgement. A first cold pressing of hazelnut oil will be just that; the quality of the nuts will, however, vary from one producer to the next.

The enemies of oil are light, heat and damp, an excess of any of these leading to deterioration, which will inevitably result in the oil becoming rancid. Don't be tempted to buy too much oil at a time and keep whatever you do buy away from excess light and heat in a cool, dry environment. This used to mean a larder, an area absent from most modern kitchens. A fridge is not really suitable as the oil will solidify, which is not ideal, although it will become liquid again when it warms up.

some common vegetable oils

Almond oil
Very delicate, for which read pretty much tasteless, this oil is, however, clean-tasting, with any almond flavour generally non-existent. These characteristics mean it is often used in baking and confectionery, and is useful for greasing the inside of cake tins when you are baking delicate sponges.

Flavoured oils
Often using as its base olive oil, or a mixture of olive and a neutral oil like sunflower oil, the flavourings range from chillies and spices to herbs. It is easy to make your own flavoured oil: simmer the oil with your chosen flavourings over the gentlest of heats for 10–20 minutes and allow to cool. Strain and bottle.

Grapeseed oil
As its name suggests, this – the cleanest-tasting of the flavourless oils – comes from grape pips. Its neutrality and delicate flavour – for which read none at all – make it a popular oil for mayonnaise, but it is also superb as an all-rounder, for frying and for dressing, where you want the other ingredients to shine.

Groundnut, peanut or arachide oil
One of the most elegant of oils, this has an attractive ungreasy texture and neutral flavour which make it a very good all-rounder. Its high smoke-point makes it suitable for stir- and deep-frying, and it is also used in baking and the making of mayonnaise. Its neutrality also makes it a good partner for use with other stronger-flavoured oils, like walnut, hazelnut or sesame seed.

Hazelnut oil
Delicious and extremely expensive, this oil is a delight when used in relatively small quantities on salads (a good opportunity to bulk out an expensive oil with a cheaper neutral-tasting oil). The addition of toasted hazelnuts to the salad adds interest in both flavour and texture.

Pine kernel oil
Made from pine nuts, the flavour of this oil is delicate and its price is enormous, as pine nuts are still largely harvested by hand.

173

If you do decide to fork out, however, it makes the most sensational vinaigrette, or can be drizzled – sparingly – over grilled fish.

Pumpkin seed oil

Dark in colour and not dissimilar in flavour to sesame seed oil, pumpkin seed oil is popular in parts of Eastern Europe. Strong in flavour, it is best used to dress other foods after cooking, more as a condiment than as a cooking oil. For example, splash it over roasted pumpkin wedges or stir it into a butternut squash risotto just before serving.

Safflower oil

Deep in colour, the flavour of this oil is actually surprisingly strong, almost too strong even for mayonnaise, and it has a distinctly cloying texture. Its main claim to fame is that it is higher in polyunsaturates than any other oil.

Sesame seed oil

When cold-pressed and unblended, sesame seed oil has a glorious nutty texture and well-rounded flavour. I use it with soy sauce and ginger to make an Eastern-style vinaigrette. In the East they use the version based on toasted seeds, which is much stronger both in colour and in flavour; indeed sometimes it is too strong. Use it sparingly, or combine it with a flavourless oil. Toasted sesame seed oil burns at a low temperature, so add it when you have finished the stir-fry or just before serving grilled fish.

Sunflower oil

One of the most popular oils, sunflower is light in colour, has a neutral flavour and is ideal when you do not want the oil to add any flavour to the food you are cooking. For the same reason, it is also useful if you are wanting to dilute other oils, like sesame seed oil for example.

Walnut oil

Popular in south-west France, this oil has a short shelf-life and will turn rancid in a matter of months. I am not a fan, as I find the flavour too strong and would much prefer a walnut vinegar, which has a far more subtle taste. You may well disagree, however, in which case other uses include baking and bread-making, where broken walnuts are used, as well as drizzling over steamed vegetables.

olive oil

Thick and unctuous, its colour anything from deep cloudy-green to clear midsummer gold, where on earth would we be without olive oil? Next to salt and pepper, it is the ingredient I use most frequently, even for breakfast. In the middle of summer, what better way to deal with toast than douse it in olive oil, rub in the flesh of a deep red tomato – a fruit after all – and sprinkle over some Maldon sea salt. Sunshine on toast, I'm ready for anything after this little feast.

The question is, however, which oil? Where once we went to the chemist for a specimen-sized bottle intended to soften the wax in sore ears and, hence, refined to absolute flavourlessness, these days supermarket shelves are groaning with olive oils, not just from Italy, but also from Greece, Spain and France. Buy from a good delicatessen and you'll probably also be faced with five-litre tins. Are they good value? (They generally give you five litres for the price of four.) Is it to be a blended oil, or something from a single estate? Is it to be extra-virgin (see opposite) or pure, and what about the variety of olive?

The most important aspect of choosing an olive oil is finding the one you like. Tuscan single-estate oils are the current vogue, but I know plenty of people who dislike the fiery, grassy, peppery flavour that many of these oils have. Some people prefer to have the rougher edges filed down, and for them a blended oil is probably more suitable. Other people favour the elegance of French olive oil. As a general rule, the further south you go the more peppery, grassy and herbaceous the olive oil becomes. This holds true of the region around the Mediterranean, but olive oils are now being produced in South Africa, New Zealand and Australia, as well wine-producing countries like Argentina.

Acidity is what makes olive oil taste bitter and unpleasant. The higher the acidity, the more fatty the oil will taste in the mouth. Low acidity gives it a smooth silkiness. Olive oil is graded on this basis – along with other factors, like whether it actually tastes very nice, as well as how the oil is extracted from the olive. Spain, it is worth noting, has a system for grading extra-virgin olive oil similar to that used to grade wine in many European countries.

Remember, if an oil is blended, say in Italy, it becomes Italian olive oil, even if part of that blend originated elsewhere. Unbelievable as it may seem now, when severe frosts in the mid-1980s killed off a great many Tuscan olive trees, olive oil production remained curiously stable.

Grades of olive oil

Olives are pressed using a variety of different methods, from those that have remained the same for centuries to ultra-modern computer-controlled systems. Once the olives are ground, the traditional extraction method is to spread the ground pulp on stacked mats and then press down using a hydraulic press. The more industrial approach is to use a centrifugal system, where the

paste is spun in a drum, throwing the liquid off as it turns.

The best oil is cold-pressed, but heat-treating olives extends quite substantially the amount of oil they yield, although the quality will fall. Unless the label says the oil has been cold-pressed, it is possible that either system has been utilized. Look also to see if the label says something along the lines of 'product of more than one country'.

Olive oils can be, and often are, mixed: refined with unrefined, extra-virgin with virgin or not-so-virgin. As consumers, we tend not to see the huge variety of grades, generally being faced with extra-virgin or olive oil, but much use is made of the others in catering.

EXTRA-VIRGIN: oil obtained from the first cold pressing of the olives. The oleic acid content cannot be more than 1 per cent and in many olive oils it is substantially less, around 0.5 per cent. The oil must have a perfectly balanced aroma and flavour.

FINE VIRGIN: the oleic acid content must be below 1.5 per cent and the oil must have a similar perfect aroma and taste to

175

extra-virgin. In order for this oil to qualify as extra-virgin the only requirement is that the acidity level is below 1 per cent. This can be achieved by chemical manipulation and currently there is no legislation to prevent this. With a substantial price difference between the two grades, the attractions for some producers are obvious. Just because it says 'extra-virgin olive oil' does not mean it is good.

SEMI-FINE OR ORDINARY VIRGIN: with a maximum oleic acid content of 3 per cent, this oil is also sold as simply 'virgin olive oil'. Its aroma and taste must be good, rather than perfect.

PURE, NOW SIMPLY CALLED 'OLIVE OIL': a combination of both refined and virgin olive oils.

SINGLE-ESTATE OILS: vary from year to year and will tend to have strong dominant characteristics that will soften over the coming year. Colour, too, will vary, depending on the year, country and the colour of the olives when they are picked. This grade of olive oil is the most similar to wine, in that it varies from one year to the next.

BLENDED OILS: whether extra-virgin or simply pure olive oil, these are designed to be consistent from one year to the next. Many of the international brands, like Berio and Cypressa, as well as the supermarket own-label oils, are excellent and, for many, quite strong enough in terms of character.

Which type of olive oil to use when

Olive oil can vary from deep green to light gold in colour and from pungent and peppery to fruity and quite light in flavour. When to use which oil is a matter of taste, although it seems a shame to use a strong pungent oil for frying. Most of the characteristics will be lost as the oil is heated, although some chefs maintain a good strong olive oil gives a richer, caramelized finish to whatever you are frying. For many of us, a great deal comes down to money. A single-estate oil can cost four or five times as much as a blended oil.

A day in the death of an olive

Throughout the summer months the olive ripens, turning from pale green through a rosy hue to violet and finally black. The olive is picked any time from September through to March, depending on location, either by hand into baskets, knocked into nets spread on the ground or by machine. In the case of the latter, a machine literally grabs the tree and shakes the fruit from it. As a result, the tree is grown more like a bush to assist in the process; a gnarled tree trunk the size of an elephant's leg is not exactly easy to shake. The olives are then taken for crushing, the time delay being kept to a minimum to limit oxidation.

When the olive is picked depends very much on the producer. A green olive contains very little oil and has a sharp flavour, whereas a black olive has lots of oil but tends to taste flat, unexciting and have an increasingly high acidity level. Optimum picking time is somewhere between the two extremes and varies depending on location and the style of oil a producer wishes to achieve.

The taste, colour and aroma of olive oil are dependent on location, type of olive, when it is harvested and how. I once visited the first day's harvest of my favourite Spanish olive oil, Nunez de Prado.

There the olives are picked by hand from the organic groves, the trees being revisited by the pickers to obtain olives at exactly the correct stage of ripeness. They are then taken to the *almazara,* where they are still crushed by old-fashioned conical granite grinding stones. While we sat at a long table in the storage area for lunch, surrounded by expectant wooden vats, the first load of olives arrived. We ate in the most glorious environment, the aroma of freshly crushed olives hovering in the air, while the grinding stones hummed in the background.

Once ground, the olive pulp is spread out on hemp mats, which are then stacked up to a few metres high and pressed with a mechanical press and the juice extracted. This juice is made up of oil, water and vegetable matter. In some instances, the oil is sold unfiltered so it is just left to settle, separated and bottled; in others, there is some form of filtration. If the oil you buy is cloudy, it is usually unfiltered.

As you might imagine, old-fashioned pressing like this is now the exception rather than the rule, most olive oil being extracted by more mechanical means. The principle is much the same, but the process is continuous. Instead of grinding the olives, they are crushed to a paste in a stainless-steel vat, churned up into a mass and then spun at great speed so the oil comes out by means of centrifugal force. There is nothing wrong with the process, but it is fairly industrial. This is still extra-virgin olive oil and it is a purely natural oil.

What remains after the oil has been extracted is a mass of olive, pip and pulp. By adding water and heating this mixture, further extraction takes place, but this is no longer cold-pressed. This heated extraction can be done a few times, the end-result being deterioration in quality and an increase in acidity each time. What you end up with is called 'residue oil', chemicals being used to wring the final oil from the paste. What happens to this? Most is further treated and used for commercial packaging of foods, or for manufacturing soap and other toiletries.

Storing olive oil

Does olive oil improve in the bottle like some wines? No, sadly it is rather unstable and over time its characteristics level out, becoming less pronounced. This is not to say that an olive oil that is 12 months old is necessarily poorer in quality than one that is two months old, but the inherent characteristics will not be as pronounced. Is there a limit? Yes, at about 18 months. Good producers put a 'best before' date, or a date of harvesting or bottling.

The number-one enemy of the oil is light and the second heat, but light is the crucial one to watch. Store the oil in dark bottles and a cupboard is better than exposed shelves. Above your cooker is not a good idea.

A brief round-up of the styles of olive oil from the main European producing countries:

SPAIN
Top of the list in terms of production, Spain produces generally well-balanced oils. Those from the north of the country tend to be slightly bitter, with a well-rounded nuttiness. Oils from the south are full of tropical fruit flavours and flower aromas. The southerners tend to use Arbequina and Picual olives.

177

ITALY

Next in line in terms of volume, Italy's principal producing area is Tuscany, from which we receive a great many single-estate oils, often from the Chianti vineyards of the region. Typically full of freshly mown hay aromas and with a strong peppery aftertaste, varieties like *leccino* (characterized by its butteriness), *frantoio* (pepperiness) and *moraiolo* (depth and grassiness) can be too assertive for many. Tuscan oils tend to be better known than the softer oils of Umbria and Liguria (home of pesto), which are full of fruit and lack the astringency. Puglia, too, produces rounded and fruity oils, largely from the Coratina olive; these are well worth looking out for.

GREECE

Third in the league table, Greece is also, per capita, the largest olive oil consumer. Crete was one of the areas used in early research into the healthy properties of olive oil, as they have one of the lowest rates of heart disease in the world. The oils, usually from the Koroneiki olive, tend to be big and rounded, with lots of herbaceous flavours. They are also remarkably inexpensive for what they are.

FRANCE

France is not a big producer of olive oil; indeed much of the country north of Provence never considered using it for cooking until relatively recently. Why bother when their butter is so exceptional? Still some of the oils from Provence, in particular, are elegant, fruity and have a delicate smooth finish, coming from varieties like the Picholine and Tranche olives.

Tasting olive oil

The correct way to taste olive oil is very similar to the tasting of wine. A little oil is poured into a white saucer, to observe colour, and then into a small glass so you can access the aroma and taste a little to access flavour. You can use your hand for the latter two stages and dip a piece of plain white bread into the oil for tasting, if you prefer. It is said that the correct way to taste oil is in the little dimple formed at the base of your thumb if you stretch the fingers of your hand outward and lift your thumb as high as it will go. The heat of your skin enhances the aromas and flavours – but it can all get quite messy.

I recently did a tasting of four oils in Tuscany with a group on a week's cooking course. There were one blended supermarket oil, two basic estate oils (one from Umbria, one from Puglia) and a boutique oil from Tuscany. Twelve of us tasted and opinions varied widely, although almost all found the Tuscan oil too assertive. Later that day we ate the Tuscan *ribollita* (see page 196), a country stew of sausages and vegetables over which we drizzled the various oils. Our opinions all changed, particularly for the supermarket oil, which lost a great deal of its flavour; the two successes were the rounded fruity oils from Puglia and Umbria.

What to do with boring oil

Add some peeled garlic cloves, lemon zest, sprigs of herbs, chillies, or toasted spices, say cumin or coriander. Allow to stand for a week and then strain. Use this flavoured oil in salad dressings.

herbs

Fresh herbs are now very easy to buy, although the quality is often debatable and certainly the price high in some supermarkets, where a few strands of tarragon or basil seem to cost more than what you intend flavouring with them. Herbs need sun, which is why many of them grow wild in hot countries. What we are presented with, in pots or in plastic containers, is usually grown and harvested in a vast greenhouse, the herb encouraged with artificial light and heat, and earth replaced by a more neutral medium, jute for example. The produce of this system, unsurprisingly, smells and tastes insipid and lacks punch and power. Compare these types of herbs with something grown in the Italian soil and you will see what I mean.

The other alternative is to grow them yourself through the summer months, either in a garden or on a window ledge. This is perfectly satisfactory for the main herbs like parsley, thyme, rosemary, bay, tarragon, lovage, sage and mint.

Fresh and dried

Generally, herbs are better fresh than dried; indeed some herbs simply lose their aroma and taste when dried, mint for example. Some, like oregano, thyme and bay, dry well. The rough rule is to dry oily or hardy herbs; the more delicate ones are better frozen (freeze the fresh herb and then smash them up so they take up less room).

What to look for when buying fresh herbs

Look for strong, green, fresh, vibrant examples, which should smell strongly if brushed or bruised.

Storing fresh herbs

Most herbs are remarkably resilient and will keep well, wrapped loosely in a plastic bag and stored in the vegetable part of the fridge, except basil, which is inclined to wilt. My Italian delicatessen wraps the stems in wet tissue paper and then foil, and covers the leaves with a plastic bag secured around the stem with a rubber band. Many herbs can be kept like cut flowers, standing in jugs of water.

Storing dried herbs

The enemies of dried herbs are light, heat and moisture. You need to keep them in opaque jars, or store glass jars in a cupboard. Avoid excessive heat or moisture, so away from the cooker or window is also a good idea.

Drying herbs at home

You can make your own dried herbs, but choose a sunny day, before the herbs have flowered. Wait for the dew to dry off and then cut at the stem and blanch for 30 seconds in boiling water. Allow to dry over several days in an airing cupboard or hot press. Remove the leaves from the stems and store in airtight dry jars.

Bouquet garni

This traditional flavouring consists of a bunch of mixed herbs, containing parsley, thyme and a bay leaf. The bouquet can be fresh or dried, the latter generally contained in a muslin or paper bag. In practice, it can be made up of whatever herbs you choose, the important point being to ensure that the herbs you use complement the dish you are cooking.

Some common herbs

BASIL: this pungent peppery herb is surely one of the glories of the summer. Look for oily, waxy leaves that have a strong aroma, particularly if you run your hand over the leaves. Basil does wonders for a tomato salad and is a main ingredient in pesto and pistou – the former Italian, the latter French in origin. Shredded into salads, it adds a sweet pepperiness, and tossed with pasta, garlic and olive oil it makes a near-instant sauce. Basil comes in a number of varieties, including a bush basil with small leaves and a purple-coloured version that makes up in colour for what it sometimes lacks in flavour. The flavour of basil disappears with heat, so add it at the end if using it in hot dishes. Thai or holy basil is less aromatic and more spicy, but it too should be added towards the end.

BAY: this waxy leaf from a tree of the laurel family has a pungent and powerful flavour. It is a common mistake to attribute star status to the dried version, but in practice both fresh and dried versions are equally good and almost as strong. Bay requires fairly long cooking to get the best of its flavour and should not be eaten as it is actually toxic.

CHERVIL: delicate in both taste and texture, this has a slight aniseed flavour. It must be used fresh, very fresh, and works well with fish and egg dishes, and added late to hot dishes.

CHIVES: with their mild onion flavour, chives provide a strong but delicate flavour to salads. When added to hot dishes, they wilt quickly, losing pungency. Fantastic with potatoes, they also work well with cream, cheese, eggs and fish. The tiny supermarket growing pots are particularly hopeless, with limp stalks that have no texture and little flavour.

CORIANDER: the leaves do not take well to cooking. Far better to use the stems and roots, which are more robust and tend to keep their flavour, adding the chopped leaves at the end of cooking. The taste is distinct, citrusy and remarkably strong, so use it with caution. The seeds are dried and also used (see Spices, page 189).

DILL: its affinity with fish is well shown in *gravad lax*, the subtle aniseed flavour providing just the right note to cut the oily fish, but dill also goes well with potatoes, cream and eggs. Add at the end of cooking, or it tends to lose its pungency. The seeds are dried and also used (see Spices, page 190).

FENNEL: similar to dill, although stronger and not as subtle or delicate a flavour, this is particularly good with fish. The seeds are dried and also used (see Spices, page 190).

LEMON GRASS: lemony certainly, but more reminiscent of peel than juice, and with a delicate fragrance, it is often used in clear soups, providing cleanness and some spiciness. It is also pounded and added to Thai and Indonesian stews, working particularly well with shellfish and pork. Buy firm but moist stalks, as it does dry out.

LIME LEAVES: popular in Thai cookery, this is the leaf of the Kaffir lime tree. Available fresh,

dried and frozen, they are normally cut finely for cooking. The cutting is best done with scissors rather than a knife.

MARJORAM: this grows wild around the Mediterranean and comes in two forms, the much sweeter and more powerful sweet or knotted marjoram and the less powerful pot marjoram. It is superb in marinades and works well with grilled fish and meats, particularly lamb. Tomato is a natural partner. It has a sweet floral aroma and taste that do not survive long cooking or high heats, so add towards the end for best effect.

MINT: this is possibly the most difficult herb to buy as the varieties are numerous and not all taste that good. In the Lebanon I have had mint sprigs with hummus that were so peppery they almost brought tears to my eyes. This is what is needed in savoury dishes and too often mint is of the sweet applemint, spearmint variety, which in my view is not so good. Aroma will give you the biggest clue; after that don't hold back. If you are going to use mint, do it with confidence. A note on the English approach to mint, as in mint sauce, mint with new potatoes and mint with peas; I cannot see the point. Far better to make it into a salsa so you can taste the herb and unleash its full potential.

OREGANO: mild when grown in northern Europe, surprisingly pungent when grown in southern areas, the pepperiness becoming quite predominant, oregano is often sold dried in bundles, in which case it works well in slow-cooked dishes. Add it with caution, however, as it can be overpowering. Used fresh it depends on your source; taste before you add, and do so towards the end of cooking. It is particularly good with tomatoes and cheese.

PARSLEY: there are two varieties, curly- and flat-leaved, the latter (also known as Italian or Mediterranean parsley) having better texture and flavour. Don't be too timid about using parsley; a whole bunch in a soup can be a delight. Stems, too, have lots of flavour, particularly if you are cooking with it. Finely chopped with lemon zest and garlic it becomes *gremolata*, to be sprinkled liberally over grilled meat, vegetables or fish and traditionally over *osso buco*.

ROSEMARY: powerful and much underrated, rosemary's affinity with lamb is well documented, but it works equally successfully with chicken, beef, vegetables and fish. With sautéed or roast potatoes it is a dream, particularly if they are fried in or brushed with goose fat.

SAGE: too often served with calves' liver and not much else, this is a superb herb, no better

181

than when the whole leaves are dipped in milk and flour and deep-fried to make pre-dinner crisps of fine texture and flavour. Lightly sautéed in butter, sage makes a near-instant sauce that is as good with a grilled pork chop as it is with poached skate.

SUMMER SAVOURY: this has quite a bitter flavour, with vague suggestions of thyme. Popular in sausages, it certainly has an affinity with pork and is also used in stuffings and together with other herbs. It is also popular with pulses and peas.

TARRAGON: along with basil, this is my favourite herb in summer – the only time to use it, unless it is poached in vinegar as the basis of béarnaise sauce. It must be French (not Russian) tarragon, but is easily identified by its fine, elegant aroma and flavour. Its aniseed character is curiously elusive, almost teasing. Chicken adores it, but pick leaves into a green salad for a really refreshing end to a meal.

THYME: what doesn't go with thyme, the powerful, resinous herb that adorns so many of the dishes in Mediterranean cooking? From a winter stew or *daube* to a summer barbecue, this herb seems good at all times of the year. Keep an eye on the variety. There is a distinctly lemony thyme, of which I am not greatly fond; other varieties can lack punch.

CHOPPING HERBS
A chef's knife or *mezzaluna* is required, the curve in the blade being necessary to get sufficient roll. Pile the herb or herbs on a chopping board and roughly chop them. Then pivot the point of the knife on the board and use your left hand to guide the blade, while chopping backwards and forwards. With a little practice and care, you can really get up to quite a surprising speed.

HERBS AS SEASONING
Concerned about your salt intake? Herbs provide seasoning as well as flavour to other foods; used bravely, that is quite liberally, you will find that less salt is required to draw out inherent flavours.

spices

What we commonly call spices are the intensely aromatic parts of certain plants, normally the bark, berries, buds, pods, roots, seeds or stems. They can either be fresh, as in chillies or ginger, or dried, as in chilli flakes or dried ginger – many spices coming in both forms. Spices should, in whatever cuisine, be used as a seasoning, no one spice predominating. We tend, I think, to be too quick to divide the world's cuisines into spicy and not spicy. Spices, when used correctly, bring enormous complexity and character to many dishes.

New Year resolutions never work for me; I fall at the first post, usually on the day I make them, certainly the day afterwards. Instead, I kick off the year with a ceremonial spice-throwing session; into the bin with every spice I own. I watch cascading cumin seeds, their speckled colouring flickering like water, the faint smell making me think of dusty, parched India. I listen to the clatter of coriander seeds, the plop of star anise, the rattle of cloves and already the idea of *rogan josh* is floating inside my head.

This could all be a rather

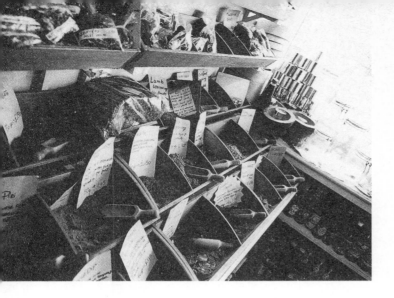

depressing start to the year, but the exercise is followed by one of my favourite shopping trips. Almost before the sack with spent spices has hit the bin, I am on my way to my local ethnic shops. Here I move along the shelves, robot-like, greedy to a fault, loading up one spice after another – black peppercorns, a bag the size of a dinner plate; then cardamom, pale and whole, the surface bright and healthy; plump fennel seeds, I am already imagining the momentary fix as they are dry-fried and ground on my return home, the heady perfume running straight up my nostrils.

Spices, of whatever type, have an unmistakably bright, full-bodied aroma that excites and makes the taste-buds yearn for more. Their ancient role as a currency (think of peppercorn rent) is almost extinct, although not for spices like saffron which are still used as a cash crop by farmers in the plain of La

Mancha in central Spain. There I was once shown a bag of freshly dried saffron – a black bin bag full – which had me reeling from the pungency. 'This,' the farmer told me with pride, 'is for my daughters' weddings.' He had three daughters.

What to look for when you buy

All spices are traded in a mysterious world, closed to most of us, but their potency brings alive every dish in which we use them. Particular combinations conjure up distinct images: five-spice powder blended with soy, ginger and garlic, unmistakably Chinese; cumin and coriander as uniquely Indian as roasting chillies and accompanying flour tortillas are Mexican. Or they don't, depending on where, when and how you buy them. That jar of paprika – a spice particularly prone to dull staleness because it is

sold ground – may have been harvested and ground months ago, if not years... not quite what once it was.

How to tell? Colour and aroma are crucial – both should zing with life and vibrancy. So, too, should the taste. Test all three of these properties and if any read dull it's time to ditch the goods or look elsewhere.

Spices have a definite shelf-life, at least a length of time when they are at their best. After that, it's downhill all the way. What makes a spice spicy? Apart from the dry vegetable matter, spices contain quantities of essential oils which, over time, oxidize and deteriorate, producing a dull, stale aroma and flavour. We pick up pungency using our noses. The nose is a particularly finely tuned receptacle, but when working in tandem with our language, which is vague and almost entirely related to other tastes and aromas, it can seem somewhat clumsy. Cumin, for example, has a strong anise flavour that is intense and quite raw, but how to tell good cumin from not-so-good cumin? The simplest answer is to couch the response in terms of intensity. Smell good-quality cumin and it is stimulating, exciting, almost alive; if the spice is stale, the experience tends to be a dull one.

Some spices grow wild, others are cultivated, but common to all is the need to harvest and store correctly. Given the enormous variety of sources that any one importer faces, a great deal of the system is built on trust and past record. In part, this is the reason why 90 per cent of the wholesale spice trade is conducted with whole spices, which are far easier to monitor and less easy to adulterate than ground spices.

Schwartz is one of the largest worldwide suppliers of spices. Standing in one of the company's booking-in areas is the closest I have come to a spice nirvana. Walking through this vast warehouse, my taste-buds were gently massaged by a vast range of spices. Pepper here, cumin there, then both all at once – with the addition of coriander, cardamom, cloves... the list was endless. This company sources spices from all over the world and imports all but a small percentage whole into the UK, where the grinding is done on a site in Oxfordshire, after much sifting and sorting, testing and analysing.

The company's senior buyer, Mike Clarke, gives whole spices a shelf-life of four years, ground spices get two years. He reckons the average age of a jar of Schwartz spice on a supermarket rack to be about 18 months – which doesn't leave a lot of life on your shelf, particularly if you buy spices ground.

Where to buy

Finding out about spices is no easy task. Questions like when and where they were bought, from whom, where they were ground, how they were stored and for how long, how careful was their cleaning (in the sense of retaining taste rather than eliminating harmful insects and bacteria), are not ones to which most shopkeepers will be able to provide the answers. So it is vital to buy from a source you can trust.

The best advice I have been given by chefs, spice importers and Indian friends – Indians after all, understand spices better than anyone else in the world – is to buy from ethnic stores. This advice holds throughout Europe. Turnover is high, ensuring freshness, customers are a discriminating bunch and most

of the spices sold are whole.

The neat rows of glass jars in supermarkets may look pretty, but as we have already seen some of them have been there for quite some time. I have done a comparative tasting of cumin, cardamom and coriander, one of each from ethnic stores, the others from a supermarket, and in every case the supermarket version was decidedly lacking in aroma and slightly less focused in flavour.

One difficulty in buying from ethnic stores is the quantity; it may not seem particularly expensive, but if you are not a high spice user, most of what you buy is likely still to be in the packet 12 months later. If you are buying in bulk, check the packet to make sure there is no debris like dust or bits of leaf.

There is still a remarkable amount of mystique attached to spices and it remains devilishly difficult to unravel the often long journey most spices make. For example, the best coriander comes from India, but the journey it makes once harvested can take weeks, if not months. The fully ripe seeds are harvested in the early morning, before the heat of the sun makes them split. It is only

after being dried, threshed and sieved that the sweet, woody, almost caramel spiciness begins to come through and the seeds are then bagged up and head off en route to ships with destinations all over the world. Weeks, or months, later they arrive in warehouses, to be ground or packed whole before they eventually end up in the shops.

Some spices are grown wild, others are cultivated. Cardamom grows wild in southern India, for example, while in Guatemala I have seen fields and fields of it being cultivated. The best is said to be grown in southern India, the distinctly mellow aroma giving way to a strongly bitter flavour which softens out. If the quality is less good, the aroma and flavour are distinctly harsh. In India, cardamom is known as 'the queen of spices', after pepper, which is 'the king'. Elegance of flavour is an inherent quality to look for.

What to buy

You should always buy spices whole. The aroma and flavour are contained in the essential oils and sugars within the seed, pods, berries, roots, stems, bark or buds. As soon as the structure is broken, both begin a relatively rapid deterioration, hence a loss of flavour and aroma. You might recognize ground coriander as coriander, but the intense lemon-and-lime – some say orange-rind – flavour will largely be gone, as will the freshness. Coriander should make you sit up and notice its fresh aroma.

Spices that cannot normally be bought whole are cayenne pepper, paprika, turmeric and five-spice powder (there is version of this called *panch phoron* in India, but it uses a rather different mixture of spices). This is because the grinding to a suitable fineness is problematical or difficult to do on domestic grinders; and, in the case of chilli, the dust is really quite potent.

Namita Panjabi, owner of several Indian restaurants, bases her spice-buying on her upbringing in India: 'There women travel about – still do in rural areas – with large pestles and mortars to grind the whole spices the family have bought. This ensured quality and freshness. In India, spices are very much seen as a perishable food, there is a time for chillies, around January and February, when they are harvested and dried, and that is when you get rid of the old and buy in the new to store for the following year.'

She imports her own, and they are prepared in the kitchen along with all the other food, using a gigantic granite pestle and mortar. Stand beside them while the grinding is in progress and you are transported to another world, heady with the piquant liquorice aromas of anise, the warm woody smell of pepper, the orange and ginger aroma of turmeric. Her advice to the consumer? 'Head for ethnic shops, buy one of the bigger brands but, more than anything else, experiment and use your nose. Spices should smell fresh and invigorating, bright and alive, not stale or dusty, tired or lacklustre.'

If you insist on buying spices

185

ground, look for a supplier that imports spices whole and does the grinding within the country to which they sell; at least that way the time-lag is as short as it can be… and the risk of adulteration lessened – trading standards tend to be higher and more closely monitored in developed rather than developing countries. Remember that, in most cases, adulteration simply means adding a harmless substance, usually part of the spice normally extracted, to bulk it out. You simply end up using a lot more.

What to buy if you happen to be travelling in a spice-producing country? The best example of what not to buy is saffron. Every year thousands of people are conned into buying large – more than they will ever use – bags of 'saffron' in countries like Turkey, for which they will have paid seemingly nothing. The bag will largely be coloured by turmeric, the remaining contents certainly not saffron, but more probably safflower. Harmless, but also tasteless. If you are buying abroad, buy from a reputable retailer, not in a market frequented largely by tourists. Watch carefully for where locals shop.

Storing spices

Spices are harvested annually. If you restock the main ones once a year, discarding everything as you do, your spices will be as fresh as they can be, short of importing your own.

Glass jars let in light, which speeds deterioration – although this is clearly not a problem if the jars are stored in a cupboard. Something that keeps light away from the spice is more suitable. It should be airtight, as contact with the air allows a loss of flavour due to evaporation of the more volatile substances. Spices should also be kept in a dry environment, as dampness only encourages mould.

The next time you consider eating in your local curry house or ordering a takeaway, consider the following: many high-street so-called 'Indian' restaurants do not buy whole spices, or even ready-ground spices, but tubs of spice mix. Uniformity of product? You bet, buy one spice mix, add a few bits and pieces and you have a 'curry'.

Grinding spices

Small quantities can usually be handled using a pestle and mortar (one of the best kitchen 'gadgets' I ever invested in). In a remarkably short space of time and with relatively little energy, you can have a fine powder.

Alternatively, and for larger quantities, a coffee grinder is one of the best ways I know. Consider buying a separate grinder if you use spices a lot, otherwise you are forever cleaning it as you move from coffee to spices and back again. A tip for final cleaning is to add a few bits of bread and do a quick pulse; the bread picks up the vestiges of spice or coffee.

Spices like cumin, coriander, star anise, cloves, peppercorns, caraway, fennel and fenugreek benefit from a light frying in a dry frying pan before grinding; this helps to release the essential oil so crucial to the aroma and flavour. There are also many who suggest that the risk of food poisoning is reduced by using this procedure for all dried spices, as they can make a good home for bacteria.

Heat a frying pan over a moderate heat and, when good and hot, add the spice, stirring or tossing so the heat is evenly distributed. Cook for 2 to 3 minutes, or until the spice loses its raw aroma and takes on a rounded fruitiness.

Spice mixes

Whether it is curry powder, garam masala, Cajun seasoning, five-spice powder or *ras al hanout*, the mistake buyers often make is to buy a proprietary brand, as they tend towards a rather bland aroma and flavour. In an Indian household, the garam masala will be made in a particular way, the mix arrived at over years, if not generations, some households preferring, for example, a higher proportion of cumin or coriander.

With a coffee grinder and whole spices, you are into a whole different league.

The same can be said of harissa and the red and green curry pastes for Thai cooking. Buy them ready-made and your dish will end up tasting rather bland and uniform, certainly more so than if you make them up yourself.

Fresh spices

When buying fresh chillies, ginger and galangal, to name just a few, look for bright, unblemished, weighty and vibrant examples.

some common spices

ALLSPICE: the name gives the game away – although a single berry, its flavour is a pot pourri of cloves, cinnamon and nutmeg, with more than a hint of pepper. Used in soups and stews, it gives a warm, gentle flavour.

ANISE: you can't get far away from its liquorice characteristics, which is probably why it tends to turn up more usually in sweets. However, it has a surprising affinity with fish, particularly when used alongside cream or butter.

CARAWAY: this has a soft, round flavour which is warming and slightly citrusy. The aroma is surprisingly pungent. Use it in soups and with winter dishes of beans and cabbage, in breads and with apples and pears. It is traditional to eat Munster cheese with toasted caraway seeds, but why stop at Munster?

CARDAMOM: initially the mellow aroma catches you out – cardamom has a lemony, citrus jewel-like flavour, almost like rose-water and as delicate, but searingly penetrating. It is widely used in both sweet and savoury dishes. Green cardamoms are considered the best; white cardamoms are blanched and less powerful; brown cardamoms are not really cardamoms at all, their flavour correspondingly rather coarse. Whichever you are buying will come in a pod, the seeds can be prised from within or the pod discarded when you are eating.

CASSIA: similar to, although coarser than, cinnamon, it the outer bark of the same tree. The flavour is sweet and aromatic, and useful in both sweet and savoury dishes.

CHILLIES: I feel I need to confess my addiction to chilli. It all began with just a little to pep things up and the habit grew. Somehow with each incremental increase I felt better, and before I knew what I was doing, things had got out of hand.

To some, the word 'chilli' evokes feelings of fear and loathing, to others it is an essential ingredient, as crucial as pepper and salt and sugar. Chillies are about heat, but this is to simplify their role and should not be their primary function in a dish, because they are also about flavour. They are just one ingredient and their role is not to grab the limelight, but to work alongside all the other elements. Fold chilli into crab and it brings out the richness; marinate chicken pieces in olive oil, garlic and lemon juice with chillies and it makes the flesh more full-bodied, somehow more succulent and rich; toss mussels in chopped chilli, parsley and garlic before dressing pasta and their meaty, sweet texture is transformed.

For mind-numbing, searing, blow-your-socks-off heat, scoff a habanero or Scotch bonnet chilli if you dare. I did once and never will again. It scores 300,000 Scoville units (the chilli heat version of the Richter scale for earthquakes) and I visited hell for hours afterwards. What idiot in me suggested I do such a foolhardy thing I still cannot fathom. A red sweet pepper, on the other hand, scores a Scoville zero and you can't get more seductive than that, its rich, fruity flavour so wonderfully beguiling. Between both extremes, though, there is a world of sweet, fruity, smoky, lemony, even green-tea flavours, perfect for all those summer dishes that want zip and zing.

For most of us, however, shopping for chillies is usually done staring into a hopper of bright fresh red, green or somewhere-in-between fruits, with no idea of what we are looking at. In my experience, most chillies sold in supermarkets tend to be particularly mild; in ethnic stores, however, exercise caution as their chillies are generally more potent.

There is only one sure way to test a chilli and that is to eat some. However, there are a few rules and exceptions, so always be on your guard. Dark green are hotter than light green, but both are hotter than red, the colour a chilli goes as it ripens. Chillies become sweeter and their flavour more rounded and full-bodied the riper they are. Sweet is a relative term, however. Thin pointed chillies tend to be hotter than blunt ones.

If you are a cautious user, my advice is to go for a branded sauce. Tabasco is probably the most famous, but there are others. The advantage with these is their predictability – control is essential when dealing with an obsession.

The best remedy for chilli burn is to drink or eat dairy products, not beer or water, which can make things even worse. Yoghurt is particularly soothing.

To reduce the chilli heat of a chilli, cut out the seeds and the membrane holding them to the chilli. The tip is said to be milder than the stem end. To be honest, though, I think it is much better to find a chilli that suits your taste. Be sure to wash your hands after handling chillies, if you rub your eyes it can be painful.

In chilli-loving countries, children do not start munching their way through habaneros as soon as they stop drinking milk, the process is a gradual one. If you are not used to cooking and eating chillies, start slowly, adding more or not as you wish.

WINES TO GO
WITH CHILLIES.
The heat in chilli comes for a substance called capsaicin, which is said to produce endorphins in the body that block out pain and give a sense of well-being. Unfortunately, they tend to knock wine out too. Removing the seeds and the membrane helps to reduce the power of chillies, wine lovers take note.

Beer and curries are well-known partners but actually not very well suited, the sparkle

tending to accentuate the chilli heat (this is also true of champagne and sparkling mineral water). Far better, I think, to look to those wine-producing areas where chilli is used in the cooking. South America is an obvious contender, but also southern Italy, Spain and parts of the Middle East. Wines from these regions tend to be richer, more full-bodied and often with a significant amount of wood. They also tend to be traditional red-wine-producing regions and, in my experience, red wine tends to be better with spicy foods.

CINNAMON: unusually, cinnamon is the bark of the tree. Buy the quills, which are the best bit of the bark, and are hand-rolled as they dry. You can package them up like cigars at Christmas time as an alternative to pot pour-ri. Cinnamon has a spicy butteri-ness, with a hint of wood smoke and should smell sweetly. It is one of those spices equally at home in sweet and savoury dishes. Great with lamb, perfect with rice, a star in fruit salad, it shines with chocolate and is good on toast

with sugar and hot, melting butter – one of the best tea-time treats (although you will need to buy ground cinnamon for that particular indulgence).

CLOVES: nibble a clove and you are in for a shock – it is sharp, fiery and bitter, with a fair chilli-whack of heat. Cook it, however, and these characteristics become much more subdued, although it retains a dark, rich, assertive flavour. Cloves are used in both sweet and savoury dishes, with apples in particular.

CORIANDER SEED: the taste is mildly sweet, with a burning, orange-peel flavour that is subtle but full-bodied. Not many Indian dishes skip on the coriander and it is popular, too, in Europe and America for pickling. In the Middle East it is particularly popular with lamb.

CUMIN SEED: with its strong, long-lasting, slightly bitter flavour, cumin has a warm, approachable character, enhanced when it is dry-roasted. It is widely used in both Indian and Middle Eastern cook-ing, and has a particular affinity with lamb. Ground, it is often incorporated into meat dishes, especially in conjunction with coriander.

DILL SEED: with an aroma similar to caraway and a flavour that is less pronounced and rather warming, dill is often used in digestive mixes and for pickling. The seeds are delicious incorporated into bread, lightly toasted and sprinkled over potato salads or seafood, a welcome addition to soups and stews, and also good in cakes and pastries.

FENNEL SEED: with a warm anise flavour, these often partner pork, but are good, too, with vegetables. They are also a key ingredient in Indian *paans*, spice mixtures chewed after eating to aid digestion. Green to yellowish-brown, the seeds have lighter-coloured ridges.

FENUGREEK: the seeds need to be dry-roasted to rid them of their bitterness, but after that they exhibit a light, bright aniseed aroma and flavour.

GALANGAL: this rhizome has a lemon-and-pepper flavour which is quite citrusy. There are actually two types, lesser and greater: the former have a bigger aroma but a less dominant flavour. There is a pleasant sourness to galangal, a spice widely used in Thai cooking. If unavailable, the usual and correct advice is to substitute ginger, even though it lacks the sharp tanginess of galangal.

GINGER: the root of the plant is a series of fat creeping rhizomes, not unlike a swollen hand, and this is the spice. Widely available in its fresh form, it is also commonly sold dried and powdered. It has a warm, welcoming aroma with a hint of woodiness. The taste is hot and pungent. Often used with garlic in savoury dishes, it adds richness and depth. It is also much used in sweet applications, like gingerbread and biscuits, when it is often used in dried form. Ginger also comes crystallized as a sweetmeat, and can also be covered in chocolate.

JUNIPER BERRIES: bitter-sweet, when describing these it is tempting to refer to gin, but then juniper is used in gin's preparation so that is not surprising. There is a pine-needle flavour to juniper, with a slight chilli-heat. Particularly suitable with game, beef, pork and veal, it works well when combined with rosemary and garlic, and red or green cabbage.

MACE: See Nutmeg and Mace.

MUSTARD: the seeds of the mustard plant are usually described as black, even though they are more of a brownish colour or white, and remarkably different in character (both are used to make mustard). Bite into a brown seed and the taste is slightly sour, then strongly pungent. The white seed, on the other hand, is initially sweet, with mild full-bodied pungency. Steep both in lemon or lime juice and add to salad dressings, or fry in hot oil to release their peppery nuttiness. Most commercial mustard is fairly bland, tasteless stuff, with little peppery kick. One glaring exception is Colman's English Mustard, which is both fiery and with a good rounded flavour.

How to tell good from bad? The only way is to taste. Prepared mustard should have depth and body, be relatively complex and have length and a strong peppery pungency. After that it is down to personal taste.

NUTMEG AND MACE: the mace is the lacy aril which surrounds the seed; nutmeg the kernel. Mace is the more refined of the two, but both have a rich, warm aroma, the taste bordering on medicinal. Widely used in sweet and savoury dishes, both spices go well with veal, potatoes and pasta, as well as with sweets, biscuits and cream cheese.

PEPPER: the black version is faintly smoky and definitely nutty. The aroma is pungent with a pointed searing heat and the flavour is agreeably complex. Its pungency is its power and, although generally used in savoury dishes, it works wonders on a bowl of strawberries. While black pepper is the unripe green berry of the *Piper nigrum* bush left to ferment and then dried, the white version comes from the ripe red berries soaked so the red skin can be removed. White pepper tends to be more refined in both flavour and aroma.

Green peppercorns are the berries harvested while still unripe, but there is no drying. Their aroma and flavour are mild and fruity with a hint of spice. Pink peppercorns are not really a peppercorn at all, being the soft berry of the *Schinus terebinthifolius*, and the flavour is somewhat resinous.

SAFFRON: a deceptively powerful spice, too much can render a dish medicinal, as the inherent bitterness can become curiously unpleasant. Highly aromatic, it tastes earthy yet very much of the sun, which is curious given that it is harvested in the depths of winter. Always buy the whole stigmas of the crocus (*Crocus sativus*), as the flavour is better and it is easier to tell the quality – a deep even colour is required. Before using either strands or ground saffron, lightly toast them in a spoon over a flame or soak in hot liquid or lemon juice. Saffron cakes are famous, but its main use is with fish and poultry.

Why does it cost so much? It is painstaking to harvest, which has to be done by hand, and the conditions are inhospitable to say the least... icy cold and muddy. Cultivation also strips the land of nutrients, requiring it to be left fallow for several years afterwards.

STAR ANISE: providing a warm, sharp liquorice flavour, this is a key ingredient in Chinese five-spice powder; it also used in Vietnamese cuisine and is particularly good with fish and poultry.

TURMERIC: the slightly musky aroma of turmeric often hides its pungency, orange rind and ginger sneaking out from behind its invigorating pepperiness. Although popular in Asian cooking, we are more used to seeing it in Indian food, where its affinity with vegetables, particularly beans and lentils, is much employed. Combined with seasoned flour, turmeric makes an excellent coating for fish, with a brilliant colour and quite a gingery taste. Watch out for the vibrant colour of the spice, which stains easily and permanently.

VANILLA: the pod of a climbing orchid which originated in Mexico; the Aztecs are credited with developing the necessary sweating and drying process that develops the vanillin, responsible for the distinctive tobacco-like taste. Rich and mellow with a sweet, gently perfumed flavour, it is used in sweets, ice-creams, chocolates and custards. Look for supple swollen pods, which will dry out over time.

directory

What should you be paying for olive oil?

Blended oils, supermarket own-brands, as well as more famous international brands like Berio, Carbonell and Cypressa, will cost about £5 per litre. Many are excellent, particularly the supermarkets', which have boldly moved away from Italy and started to source from Spain and Greece. For a single-estate oil, the price is more likely to be between £10 and £30. There is no inherent reason why the £30 bottle is 'better' than the £10 bottle, however. That is a value judgement only you can make. For my money, the interesting development in recent years is the increasing emergence of single-estate oils from Spain and Greece, which are often substantially cheaper than the Italian oils.

Sources for oils and vinegars

& Clarke's, 122 Kensington Church Street, London W8 4BH (020 7229 2190); Carluccio's, 28a Neal Street, London WC2H 9PS (020 7240 1487); The Conran Shop, 81 Fulham Road, London SW3 6RD (020 7589 7401) and 55 Marylebone High Street, London W1M 3AE (020 7723 2223); Harrods, Knightsbridge London SW1X 7XL (020 7730 1234); Harvey Nichols, Knightsbridge, London SW1X 7RJ (020 7235 5000); La Fromagerie, 30 Highbury Park, London N5 2AA (020 7359 7440); Lina Stores, 18 Brewer Street, London W1R 3FS (020 7437 6482); Mortimer & Bennett, 33 Turnham Green, London W4 1RG (020 8995 4145); Neal's Yard Dairy, 17 Shorts Gardens, London WC2H 9AT (020 7240 5700) and 6 Park Street, London SE1 9AB (020 7407 1800); The Oil Merchant, 47 Ashchurch Grove, London W12 9BU (020 8740 1335); Saponara, 23 Prebend Street, London N1 8PF (020 7226 2771); Selfridges, 400 Oxford Street, London W1A 1AB (020 7629 1234); Tom's, 226 Westbourne Grove, London W11 2RH (020 7221 8818); Valvona and Crolla, 19 Elm Row, Edinburgh EH7 4AA (0131 556 6066); Villandry, 170 Great Portland Street, London W1N 5TB (020 7631 3131).

Buying herbs

Supermarket herbs tend to lack power and punch and they are also relatively expensive. Italian delicatessens invariably have a supply of flat-leaf parsley and basil. Vegetable shops are also good for herbs, but inspect before you buy; as quality can be variable. The likes of coriander and lemon grass are far better sourced in ethnic markets. There are both small and large outlets, like Wing Yip (see right).

Buying spices

Indian-owned and -run supermarkets are by far the best, with good quality and a high turnover of products. Otherwise, try The Cool Chili Company (mail order, 020 7229 9360); Peppers By Post (01308 897892); Wing Yip, 395 Edgware Road, London NW2 6LN (020 8450 0422) and branches nationwide; The Spice Shop, 1 Blenheim Crescent, London W11 2EE (020 7221 4448).

WHICH BRAND OF SPICES: One of the best known, albeit expensive, is Rajah. Others to look for are Netco, TRS. Why these in particular? They are the ones most widely used by the top half-dozen Indian restaurant chefs in Britain.

vinegars, oils, herbs and spices
recipes

red chicken curry, *Thai style*

serves 4

3 tablespoons vegetable oil

4 garlic cloves, finely chopped

200 ml (7 fl oz) chicken stock

400 g (14 oz) boned chicken thighs, thinly sliced

3 tablespoons nam pla (Thai fish sauce)

200 ml (7 fl oz) coconut cream

FOR THE RED CURRY PASTE:

6 red chillies (or to taste), deseeded and chopped

1 teaspoon freshly ground coriander seeds

1 teaspoon freshly ground cumin seeds

4 garlic cloves, finely chopped

3 lemon grass stalks, the dry outer husks discarded and the core finely chopped

4 coriander roots, chopped

3 Kaffir lime leaves, chopped

3-cm (1¹/₄-inch) piece of galangal, peeled and finely chopped

1 dessertspoon nam pla (Thai fish sauce)

The spice paste in this dish is what makes it so wonderfully bright and sharp. I always feel healthier after Thai food, which is one of the hallmarks of true Thai cooking; it should be invigorating. If you can't find coriander with its roots still attached, use the stems in favour of the leaves, as the latter will dissolve in the cooking. Thai fish sauce is widely available in better food shops and many supermarkets.

1   Make the curry paste: combine all the ingredients in blender or food processor and blitz to a paste.

2   Heat the vegetable oil in a wok or large frying pan and, when hot, add the garlic. Sauté until golden and then add half the red curry paste (the rest will keep for about a month in the fridge). Fry for about 30 seconds, then add the chicken stock, chicken and fish sauce.

3   Bring to the boil, lower the heat and simmer until the chicken is cooked through, about 5 minutes.

4   Stir in the coconut cream and heat through before serving with rice.

charmoula

makes about 300 ml (¹/₄ pint)

2 garlic cloves, roughly chopped
2 tablespoons ground cumin
2 tablespoons sweet paprika
1 dried chilli, deseeded and finely
    chopped
4 tablespoons coarsely chopped
    parsley
4 tablespoons coarsely chopped
    coriander leaves

4 tablespoons white wine vinegar
juice of 1 lemon
salt
extra-virgin olive oil

In Morocco, fish is usually prepared using a marinade called charmoula or chermoula. It is also delicious when used as a salsa to serve with grilled fish and meat.

1 Combine all the ingredients except the oil with salt to taste in a blender, and blitz to a rough purée, adding just enough olive oil to blend.

2 Gently heat the purée in a pan, but do not allow it to boil.

3 Allow to cool and use either as a marinade, particularly with fish and poultry, or as a sauce.

cherry tomato, ricotta, basil
and olive oil sauce for pasta

serves 4

250 g (9 oz) ricotta
300 g (10¹/₂ oz) cherry tomatoes
bunch of basil, roughly chopped
150 ml (¹/₄ pint) extra-virgin olive oil
salt and pepper
Parmesan cheese, to serve

This is a favourite raw summer sauce for pasta, best eaten in the heat of the day when the lightness of the ricotta really does shine through.

1 In a large bowl, mash the ricotta lightly with a fork. Quarter the tomatoes and stir them in, together with the basil and olive oil. Season with salt and pepper.

2 Toss the mixture with cooked pasta and serve with freshly grated Parmesan.

chilli oil

makes about 500 ml (18 fl oz)

12 dried red chillies
500 ml (18 fl oz) extra-virgin olive oil
2 sprigs of fresh rosemary
3 garlic cloves, thinly sliced
1 teaspoon cumin seeds

1 Soak the chillies in hot water until soft. Drain and combine with all the other ingredients in a small pan. Place over a very gentle heat for 20 minutes. Remove from the heat and allow to cool.

2 Strain before use. Once strained, the chilli oil can be kept in the fridge for a few weeks.

ribollita

150 ml (1/4 pint) olive oil
one 400-g (14-oz) tin of cannellini
    beans, drained and well rinsed
1 onion, thinly sliced
1 carrot, thinly sliced
1 celery stalk, thinly sliced
4 garlic cloves, finely chopped
sprig of fresh rosemary
sprig of fresh thyme
2 dried red chillies, broken up
12 pure pork sausages
salt and pepper
1/2 Savoy or white cabbage, cored
    and thinly sliced

TO SERVE:
6 slices of good country bread
1 garlic clove, halved
extra-virgin olive oil

This is a classic dish from Tuscany that makes the most of the region's fantastic vegetables. Pouring olive oil over hot food, particularly where there is lots of liquid, is one of life's great simple pleasures. The essence of the oil remains, and all the subtleties are brought to the front. If ever there was a time to splash out on an oil that is rich, full-flavoured and peppery, it is with this essentially peasant stew. It is best made a day in advance, refrigerated and then gently reheated.

1 Heat the olive oil in a large flameproof casserole, add the beans, onion, carrot and celery, and sauté gently for 10 minutes without browning.

2 Add the garlic, cook for a further 2 minutes and then add the rosemary, thyme, chillies, sausages, salt and pepper, together with 1 litre (1 3/4 pints) of water. Bring to the boil, lower the heat and simmer for 1 1/2 hours.

3 Add the cabbage, bring back to the boil and simmer for a further 45 minutes.

4 Traditionally, the bread is grilled, drizzled with olive oil and put in the bottom of soup plates, the soup then being ladled on top. I prefer to grill the bread, rub it with garlic and olive oil and serve it on top. Each person can then dip it into the liquid as they choose.

5 Serve with lots of extra-virgin olive oil and douse liberally.

ciabatta

makes 2 loaves

500 ml (18 fl oz) warm water
1 sachet (15 g / ½ oz) of dried yeast
1 teaspoon caster sugar
900 g (2 lb) bread flour
2 teaspoons salt
2 tablespoon best-quality
    extra-virgin olive oil

The origins of ciabatta are somewhat mysterious; nobody really seems to know quite where the 'slipper' – as opposed to the 'heel' – of Italy came from. In essence, it is simply a bread dough that is allowed to over-prove, giving it the air holes and slightly loose consistency.

1 Combine the water, yeast and sugar in a large bowl. With your fingertips, stir in half the flour. Then gradually add the rest of the flour, salt and oil, until you have a softish dough.

2 Knead, either by hand or in a mixer with the dough hook, for 5 minutes. Lightly oil the dough and leave it to rise, in a bowl covered with cling-film, for 4 hours.

3 Punch the dough down, divide it into two and shape each piece into 'slippers' on floured baking sheets. Cover again and allow to rise for 2 hours.

4 Preheat the oven to 180°C/350°F/Gas 4. Bake the loaves for 40 minutes, or until they sound hollow when tapped on the bottom.

mayonnaise

makes about 400 ml
(14 fl oz)

1 teaspoon Maldon sea salt
2 egg yolks
about 300 ml (1/2 pint) vegetable oil
lemon juice, to taste

For years I've played around with ratios of olive to vegetable oil to get the right mayonnaise. Finally, reading chef and fellow food writer Rowley Leigh, I realized what I'd known for ages, that the bitterness inherent in all olive oils is somehow enhanced when in mayonnaise. What you need is something almost totally lacking in taste.

1 Combine the salt and egg yolks. While continuing to stir, add the oil, drop by drop initially, until the mix emulsifies to a thick paste. You can then increase the oil to a steady trickle. When the mixture becomes too stiff to stir, add a little of the lemon juice to loosen it.
2 When all the oil is incorporated, adjust the seasoning with salt, pepper and lemon juice.

vinaigrette

dresses salad for 4–6

4 tablespoons best-quality extra-
   virgin olive oil
1 dessertspoon vinegar
1 dessertspoon warm water
salt and pepper

I used to use garlic and mustard in my vinaigrette, but in recent years have moved away from both. It is essential that your preferred combination does not overpower the salad leaves, a problem with too many vinaigrettes in my experience. I vary the vinegar – red wine, cider, rice, or even use lemon juice – for a

change, and sometimes the oil, but generally stick to these quantities. The water helps the vinaigrette to emulsify.

1 Combine all the ingredients in bowl and whisk well.
2 Add the salad leaves and toss.

salmoriglio

makes about 275 ml (10 fl oz)

250 ml (9 fl oz) extra-virgin olive oil
2 teaspoons chopped fresh oregano
1 tablespoon finely chopped new-
   season's garlic
salt and pepper

So simple and yet so effective, this is the essence of Italian cooking – drizzled over grilled fish and meat or on bruschetta.

1 Combine all the ingredients in a bowl, season with salt and pepper, and serve.

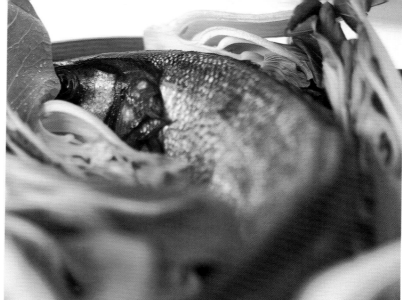

steamed sea bass,

black bean sauce and pak choi

serves 4

1-cm (¹/₂-inch) piece of ginger,
  peeled and thinly sliced
4 spring onions, halved lengthwise
1 sea bass, weighing about 800 g
  (1³/₄ lb)
4 heads of pak choi, trimmed
3 tablespoons vegetable oil

FOR THE BLACK BEAN SAUCE:
3 tablespoons fermented black
  beans, roughly chopped
1 tablespoon soy sauce
1 dessertspoon medium dry sherry
1 dessertspoon rice vinegar
pepper

TO SERVE:
1 dessertspoon toasted sesame oil
1 dessertspoon sesame seeds,
  toasted in a dry frying pan
1 tablespoon chopped coriander
  leaves

*One of the best banquets I ever
attended was a Chinese meal... eight
courses of utter heaven. When I had
finished, I skipped lightly towards the
door feeling I had eaten sufficient,
but not more than. A great deal of
the skill in Chinese food lies in
balance; it is a cuisine that
understands spices implicitly. If you
want an example of the restrained
use of spices, then look no further.*

1 Make the black bean sauce:
combine the black beans, soy
sauce, sherry, rice vinegar and a
generous seasoning of pepper,
together with 2 tablespoons of
water. Set aside.

2 Place the ginger and spring
onions inside the fish's cavity.
Arrange the stuffed fish and pak
choi on a plate in a steamer and
cook for 10–15 minutes, or until
the fish is just cooked. Transfer
the fish and pak choi to a low
oven and keep warm. Pour the
fish juices into the black bean
sauce.

3 Heat a frying pan and, when
hot, add the oil. Seconds later, add
the black bean sauce mixture and
stir to emulsify, cooking the sauce
for about 1 minute. Remove from
the heat.

4 Remove the flesh from the
carcass of the fish and serve it on
top of the pak choi with a
generous scoop of the sauce, a
drizzle of sesame seed oil, a
sprinkling of toasted sesame seeds
and a little fresh coriander.

scallops *with ginger, spring onion and tamarind*

serves 4

1 tablespoon tamarind paste
2-cm (³/4-inch) piece of ginger, peeled and grated
2 spring onions, thinly sliced lengthwise and soaked in iced water
3 tablespoons vegetable oil, plus more for the pan
1 tablespoon toasted sesame oil
12 scallops
salt

If the scallops are really thick, they will sometimes remain cold and uncooked in the middle in the time it takes the exterior to cook perfectly. You can avoid this – and make the scallops go further – by cutting them across into two rounds.

1 Place the tamarind paste in a saucepan with 4 tablespoons of water and heat gently, stirring to extract as much of the tamarind as possible. Set aside and allow to cool.

2 Strain and combine with the grated ginger, drained spring onions and both types of oil.
3 Season the scallops with salt. Get a frying pan good and hot and then oil it lightly. When the oil is hot, fry the scallops over as high a heat as you can manage for no more than 45 seconds on each side.
4 Place the scallops on small shallow plates or, better still, in well-scrubbed scallop shells, and spoon over the tamarind mixture.

condiments,

preserves
and
flavourings

'*The fragrance and taste* (hsiang, hsien)
of many foods are brought out by the use of
supporting ingredients which should merge
into a single flavour.'

HSIANG JU LIN and TSUIFENG LIN,
The Art of Chinese Cuisine

'*Cole and I have cooked dinner every*
night this week. I am inclined to put in far
too much flavouring, as in painting I put
in far too much colour, but I am
learning restraint.'

NOËL COWARD, *The Noël Coward Diaries*

condiments and bottled sauces

How to tell a good marmalade from a bad one... Is there an advantage to making your own piccalilli? What should and should not be on a jar's list of ingredients? Much is made of avoiding preservatives, but sugar is exactly that. And if you don't use sugar, what about the cocktail of other sweeteners used in its place? Should you buy organic and what exactly is unrefined sugar?

Condiments, preserves and flavourings cover a multitude of different ingredients and this chapter aims to guide you towards the better ones. We are supposed to abhor stock cubes, yet quite a number of chefs use them and the practicalities of the kitchen mean for many of us that they are the only choice. Select the best and this flavouring has much to offer, as does soy sauce. Yet the bad examples can leave you feeling less than impressed, distinctly thirsty and a little queasy.

Many of these ingredients are bought infrequently and often you are faced with little choice. How many rose-water brands are on the shelf? Which port or sherry should you go for? In practice, the retailer will have largely made the choice for you, deciding what he or she can sell. Just because something comes in a dinky little jar, however, does not make it superior; indeed quite a number of preserves are so well preserved that the original ingredient has long ceased to feature, the taste being sweet and nothing much more.

Salt we cannot live without, yet the number of brands on offer is huge, their flavour – salt does taste of itself – varying from the distinctly chemical to decidedly of the sea. Determining which one to buy has a huge impact on the flavour of your food. The same can be said of tomato purée, yet how many of us grab a tube, swayed more by the packaging or convenience than the tomatoes that were used to make the contents.

Although many of the following are used principally at the table to season food, they all also have added use as flavourings in their own right during cooking.

ANCHOVY ESSENCE: this bottled purée of salted anchovies was popular in Edwardian times. The high quality of some salted anchovies and the increased availability of good canned anchovies make essence less appealing, but the convenience factor is high.

BLACK BEAN SAUCE: is made by salting black beans and allowing them to ferment. Good examples taste savoury, but without being too strong, and suit meat and fish dishes.

CHILLI SAUCES: there are as many sauces as there are chillies (well, almost) and, although the recipes may vary, essentially they contain chillies, salt and vinegar,

although some contain other ingredients. They tend to be hot, but not particularly flavourful. Their great advantage is that, because of their consistency and because you can add them at the end to taste, they allow you to control the degree of heat you are adding to a dish. If you are a timid chilli user, they are a good means of building up experience.

Popular all over South America and the Caribbean, chilli sauces can also be found throughout many of the Far Eastern cuisines. While the Chinese tend to salt and ferment the chillies for their sauces, sauces in the Caribbean tend to include vinegar and other flavourings, although the chilli element is predominant. In Mexico, the sauce is more of a salsa, the chilli let down with other ingredients, but is still quite hot. Favourite brands include all the Maggi chilli sauces made in Indonesia, Encona West Indian Pepper Sauce and Grammas, more a paste than a sauce but excellent.

FISH PASTES AND SAUCES: are popular throughout Southeast Asia. In the West, the nearest equivalent is probably anchovy paste, although the paste has nothing like the pungency of those used in the East. Most are the by-product of fish that are fermented, the liquid being drained off and bottled. Fish sauce is usually made with anchovies or mackerel fermented in salt. In Thailand it is known as *nam pla*, but each country has its own name for it. Very little is used to achieve the necessary effect, which is not really at all fishy, and most of the brands I have tried are of a generally high standard. Other variations include shrimp sauce (*kapee* in Thai cuisine) and squid paste, and the same observations apply. Although these sauces are strong, their addition to dishes like miso shows that the effect can be startlingly impressive, introducing real backbone to dishes.

HOISIN SAUCE: meaning 'fresh fragrance of the sea', this sauce is based on soy beans, flavoured with garlic, chilli and sesame oil. It also contains wheat flour, vinegar and sugar, and is the basis of the dipping sauce for Peking duck. Cheaper brands tend to taste like Bovril; the better brands having a fuller, rounder flavour that suits poultry and shellfish.

MUSHROOM KETCHUP: these bottled preserved mushrooms produce a thick and meaty-tasting liquid that was popular in Victorian cooking as a way of adding weight to stews. Alternatives are now the easily obtained dried mushrooms, which can be reconstituted in warm water and have a strong meaty taste that is much cleaner and far preferable.

MUSTARDS: most are made from a combination of brown (strong) mustard seed and white (less strong, almost cooling). A great

many of the more commercial brands are bland, providing little heat and a dubious creaminess. One of my favourites is Colman's English Mustard, with its bright yellow colour and fiery taste, but many find it too hot. Dijon is often disappointing, particularly the cheaper brands, while German and American mustards are often quite full-bodied, sweet and quite peppery. Whole-grain mustards, the best known being Moutarde de Meaux, tend to be Dijon in style, the seeds being partly crushed and partly ground. Mild and with a deliciously fruity flavour, you tend to eat rather more than with, say, a hotter mustard.

Mustards are also flavoured with herbs and fruit, citrus particularly. Quality depends very much on the producer, in many instances the 'added value' of the additional ingredient pushing the price up with little discernible benefit. Think of good mustard, with a squeeze of lemon juice, or mustard with freshly chopped herbs. The addition seems better in its fresh form than in the jar.

In all cases you cannot tell from the packaging, you do have to taste. If a mustard is good, it is good enough to be eaten on its own and should have a clean, sharp, smooth flavour and texture. How much fire is a matter of taste. Cost is an indicator; good mustard is not cheap, but then apart from *lapin à la moûtarde* you tend not to use a great deal of it.

Mustard fruits, popular in Italy with boiled meats, are candied fruits in a syrup flavoured with spices and mustard. The best known are the *mostarda di Cremona*, but there are also *mostarda di Carpi* and increasingly *mostarda* from other areas. Sweet and hot rather than sour, they are an acquired taste, but delicious.

OYSTER SAUCE: good brands should be made from oysters, salt and water, but most commercial brands omit the oysters and now also include caramel and cornflour, making them thicker and sweeter. It should give a good savoury flavour without being overtly fishy.

SALT: we eat too much of this vital mineral, but the culprit is unlikely to be you and your cooking; most of our over-indulgence comes from processed foods, from crisps to convenience meals, from biscuits to butter. How much salt you use in cooking is a matter of taste and judgement, but don't think all salt tastes the same.

There are two principal types, rock and sea salt. Rock salt comes from underground, where it has become compacted. The extraction and refining processes vary, but, to my mind, rock salt tastes too minerally and tends to have a chemical flavour. Common table salt is rock salt combined with magnesium carbonate to keep it free-flowing.

Sea salt also varies hugely, but the best examples, like Maldon salt, taste young and fresh, clean and pure, almost sweet. There is something very natural about sea salt. In the Mediterranean, salt pans are often to be found on islands, where the sea water was – and still is, in some instances – captured and allowed to evaporate, leaving salt crystals behind. If these are soft enough, they can be sprinkled directly on to food, providing not just flavour but also texture. Other sea salts to consider are the French *Fleurs de sel* (flowers of salt), the best of which is reputed to come from the salt marshes of Guérande. It is granular and quite grey in colour, but has a delicate flavour.

The size and type of salt crystals do have an impact on its use. Sea salt tends to be soft and easily ground with the fingers, and consequently useful for the table. Large or coarse rock salt is suitable for curing foods and can also be ground in a mill for use at the table.

TABASCO SAUCE: this is made by marinating Tabasco chillies and salt in oak barrels over a number of years. The pulp is then mixed with vinegar, the seeds and skins removed and the resulting liquor bottled. It is hot, very hot, but for anyone chilli-averse, it is a very controllable heat. As with eye drops, you can very easily gauge exactly how much is going into a dish.

TOMATO KETCHUP: primarily tomatoes, vinegar, sugar and garlic, each manufacturer has their own, often secret, recipe that is also likely to include spice extracts. How do you decide on which to buy? The better brands don't lose sight of the tomato, others will be too sharp or sweet, or, if you are really unlucky, both. Brands are sometimes useful, and in this instance mine is Heinz, reputed to be the inventor of the product.

WORCESTERSHIRE SAUCE: a secret concoction of, among other things, tamarind, vinegar and spices, its flavour is strong and meaty, sweet and sour, and should be used only in small quantities. Manufacturers, like its inventors Lee and Perrin's, like to keep their recipe secret, but common ingredients include soy sauce, anchovies and mace. It is essential to shake the bottle before use as a sediment collects at the bottom. Worcestershire sauce is used all over world, even in China and Japan, where it appears on tables with the soy sauce.

preserves

For marmalades, jams, jellies, chutneys, relishes and other sticky items sold in jars (often with twee paper tops), the quality is dependent firstly on the raw ingredient and secondly on how it is handled. Many commercial brands use concentrated or frozen fruit and vegetables, rejected for other higher-grade products. The best preserves use the best fruit; if you want good jam, you need to start with good fruit.

Sugar is generally the main preservative used – in jams and marmalades it needs to be around 60 per cent to preserve adequately – and increasingly among the better producers this will be unrefined sugar. Those jars sold as 'reduced sugar' get their sweetness elsewhere, from apple juice concentrate (rather more unpleasant-tasting than it sounds) or from the growing number of manufactured sweeteners. The manufacture can then be pretty intensive, the ingredients being boiled down to a shadow of their former selves, or handled gently and slowly in open pans.

Balance is all in a jam, or chutney, or marmalade; the sugar is necessary, but you must be able to taste and appreciate the fruit or vegetable. Traditionally balancing the two was the route to a successful jar. Yet modern technology has made things far more complex and preservatives are being introduced – like potassium sorbate, for example, or citric acid – to muddy the waters.

Ironically, a lot of this activity is aimed at producing a crystal-clear jar with a relatively long shelf-life, just what your grandmother was not trying to do, because there was always next year's crop for everyone to look forward to. There are now some examples where the sugar content is low enough for the preserve to require refrigeration after opening.

flavourings

ANCHOVIES, SALTED: their quality is dependent on the anchovy, their size and the salting. The best anchovies are fished off the coasts of Spain and Italy and it is from these countries that I always buy. Even if the fish come from further afield, both cuisines make extensive use of them and they tend to be of better quality. The larger they are, the more meaty their flavour, although smaller ones can be deliciously sweet. In general, the quality of salted anchovies is far superior to those in oil, although there are always exceptions.

CAPERS: country of origin is a help, Italy being top of the list, although most Mediterranean countries harvest them, as do other countries with a similar climate. After that, look for salted capers rather than those in brine or vinegar. They need desalting, but on the whole have more flavour and tend to be more succulent. Caperberries, the fruit, are also sold pickled – hopefully lightly – and they have a crunchy texture and delicate flavour.

DRIED SEAFOOD: I have never been a fan of fish stock, as it is too easy for it to end up glutinous and dull, and I am convinced by the Chinese, who do not really use fish stock, preferring to use a light chicken stock flavoured with dried seafood, such as powdered shrimp, scallops or bonito flakes. A similar result can be achieved using light chicken stock and roasted seafood shells: lobster, crab and prawns for, example.

FLORAL WATERS: mainly rose and orange blossom, these are made by distilling the blossom and then diluting the resulting liquor. Modern distillation methods give much more control over how delicate the liquor is; in the old days, everything was fairly crude. Use sparingly, as the trip from delicately scented to unpleasantly perfumed is a surprisingly short one. Rose water bought in chemists can be old-fashioned rose water, triple distilled and correspondingly stronger. A teaspoon of this is equivalent to one tablespoon of lighter, modern rose water.

FRUIT ESSENCES: vital in many classic cocktails, the likes of pomegranates, raspberries and

strawberries are distilled into essences that add body, complexity and flavour to fruit salads, ice-creams and sorbets, and salad dressings. Telling the good essence from the bad is helped enormously by the list of the ingredients, which should start with the fruit and avoid all mention of extracts and flavourings.

GARLIC: look for tightly packed, firm heads without any green sprouting. If this is present, you need to remove it when slicing, as it tends to taste bitter. Store garlic in a cool, dry, well-ventilated environment away from light. Unfortunately, garlic doesn't actually store all that well, tending to dry out and lose its flavour, so think twice about those long garlic strings. Bottles, jars, tubes, powder and flakes are all to be avoided, as they inevitably taste tired and stale. Look out,

however, for pickled garlic, which is often deliciously mild.

How to prepare garlic

Thinly slice and then chop with a large knife pivoted on its point. Add a little sea salt to the garlic and then, using the flat of the knife, grind it to a paste.

HORSERADISH: you can eat the young leaves of horseradish in a salad, but it is the root that is generally used. Look for firm examples with unblemished skins and no sprouting or greenness, which suggests bitterness. The good news is that horseradish can be frozen; the bad news is that, once grated, it loses its flavour quickly. You can now buy jars of grated horseradish, but more usually what is on offer is creamed

horseradish or horseradish sauce, both of which tend to be over-acidic.

LIQUORICE: extracted from the root of a Mediterranean shrub, this commonly appears as a concentrated black stick of extract. Its flavour is distinctly aniseedy and, although the root's flavour is quite mild, the extract is generally quite powerful. It makes good ice-cream.

MEAT EXTRACT: meat juices concentrated into a paste along with vegetables, flavourings and spices, like Bovril for example, are popular in the UK. They can be added to meat dishes to reinforce the existing flavours, or be combined with hot water to make a savoury drink, or spread on bread, toast or biscuits.

MISO: a Japanese ingredient made by salting and fermenting soy beans (much like soy sauce), the mixture is then combined with a grain like rice or barley and aged for several years. Miso varies in colour and in strength from region to region. The common characteristic is a wine-like pungency. Used widely in Japanese pickles, it is also combined with dashi broth to make miso soup.

Miso comes in three main forms, which can be used to good effect in Western dishes like grilled meat and fish: yellow miso, all-purpose; red, which is very salty; and white, which is smooth and sweet, and is often used in pickles and over grilled meat.

MONOSODIUM GLUTAMATE: abhorred in the West but popular in East, this is the sodium salt of glutamic acid. Completely flavourless, it does enhance the flavour of other foods and was originally extracted from seaweed. It is not bad in itself, but too much can lead to adverse reactions in some people. It occurs naturally in soy sauce, which is the table condiment preferred in the East, as opposed to salt, but is also sold in tins as 'taste powder', and this is often overused in some Chinese restaurants.

MUSHROOMS, DRIED: fresh mushrooms are dealt with on pages 125–6, but most mushrooms can be dried to preserve them. This process also alters their flavour, bringing an intensity and robustness not found in the fresh.

If your intended use for dried mushrooms is to beef up stews, or use in soups, consider the generally less expensive broken pieces. Drying mushrooms levels out their flavours, so even if some of the original mushrooms were not of top quality, the dried versions are generally extremely good. If you want large slices of elegant-looking mushroom in your sauce, then go for the top grade, but realize that you will be paying largely for the appearance.

As dried mushrooms can often harbour insects, which will start to eat the mushrooms, it is a good idea to freeze a new batch, as any insects are usually killed off in the cold conditions.

Before use, dried mushrooms need reconstituting in warm water for about 20 minutes. The soaking water will become packed with flavour, so do not discard it as it is great in stocks, soups and stews. Generally you get a deposit of sediment at the bottom of the bowl. This is dust and grit from the mushrooms, which should be left behind.

As with a great deal of dried food, there are now what are called 'soft-dried' mushrooms, which, when reconstituted, return almost to their former selves. Ceps or porcini are sold this way and can be sautéed or otherwise treated as if they were fresh.

Dried morels may well seem expensive, but a few go a long way. It is worth massaging them a little when reconstituting, as they tend to contain dust and earth. Boletus are the most common dried mushroom and can be ground to a powder that you then dust over a finished dish, or use during cooking. Shiitake are quite smoky in flavour; finely chop them when reconstituted, as they can be tough.

About 75 per cent of the world's morels come from Alaska. Of that 75 per cent, 70 per cent are dried at source. Occasionally the crop fails, which is devastating for the region and has a knock-on effect on global prices.

OLIVES: although olive oil is covered on pages 174–8, both green and black olives are often used as condiments and flavourings. The green olive is unripe, the black one ripe. There are many different varieties of

olive, although they are often aligned with a country: kalamata with Greece, picholine with France, manzanilla with Spain, for example. Olives are all brined, to help rid them of their bitterness, and then combined with olive oil and other flavourings, such as chilli, lemon, cumin and fennel. Texture varies from meaty to quite lean, and the flavour can be acidic, salty or sweet. Personal preference is the deciding factor and, like cheese, there is every reason to request a tasting prior to purchase – after all, an olive is hardly expensive.

Tapenade

Combine 150 g (5 oz) stoned black olives with 6 anchovy fillets and 3 finely chopped garlic cloves, blitz briefly in a blender and whisk in 100 ml (3½ fl oz) of extra-virgin olive oil. Add black pepper to taste and use as a spread, dip or flavouring – it is particularly nice on boiled eggs.

SEAWEED: popular in Asia and on the west coasts of the UK and Ireland, seaweed is rich in minerals, vitamins and proteins, and has a variety of uses – as a seasoning in soups and broths, as well as in salads and stir-fries. Often sold dried, the quality is high overall, particularly any produce bought from Japanese suppliers. In Wales, laver tends to be sold as a wet mass in tubs.

SOY SAUCE (and other relatives such as *tamari* in Japan and *kecap manis* in Indonesia): made from fermented soy beans and wheat or other grain – although some Japanese versions skip the wheat – the fermentation can take several years. The sauce is generally dark in colour and thin, and it is used in place of salt to draw out other flavours. It comes in both dark- and light-coloured versions. Cheaper brands beef up the basic liquor with various additives like MSG (monosodium glutamate), easily spotted on the list of ingredients. In general, the Japanese brands are above average, which is not to exclude Chinese brands at all, but the quality is less evenly high. The flavour should be salty, but with a sweet yeasty taste, nothing too astringent. The various soy-based sauces come with a whole gamut of other ingredients, all of which should be listed. Careful reading will help you be selective. Soy sauce has a relatively unlimited shelf-life. Kikkoman is a particularly well-regarded brand with a distinctive fine flavour.

STOCK CUBES: also come in granules and in liquid form. The flavours vary, from all-purpose to

209

meat, fish, vegetable and chicken. The best way to decide which brand to buy is to make a drink from what you purchase and taste that. Avoid those that have a salty, chemical flavour and look at the list of ingredients. The better brands will use salt, certainly, but also concentrated chicken and vegetable stock, wine vinegar extract, spices and probably something like potato starch, which helps to give body. If you are reducing stock made from a cube, beware that the inherent salt will become more pronounced.

TAHINI: this comes in two forms, light and dark; the latter includes the husks of the sesame seed, the former just the seed. Dark tahini often has a rather unpleasantly bitter aftertaste. There is not a great deal to differentiate the various brands. Tahini tends to separate in the jar. To remix it, sit the jar in bowl of hot water and then stir; this makes the arm-work substantially less tiring.

TAMARIND: usually sold as a block, it is the sticky pulp and seeds from the pod of a tamarind tree. The high tartaric acid present gives tamarind its sourness, similar to lemon and lime juice but balanced with a fruitiness. It makes a great marinade for fish and poultry and is also good in jams and chutneys, not only for the sourness, but also for its high pectin content. To use, soak the block in warm water and squeeze as much liquid out of the block as you can, using your hands.

TOMATO PURÉE: this is concentrated tomatoes cooked down to a pulp and usually sold in tubes. There is not much there apart from tomatoes, so the variety chosen is important, as is the cooking, which should be gentle. Look for an Italian brand, but don't look too hard. You rarely use that much in a recipe and it is not that crucial (did I say that?).

VANILLA: it is now possible chemically to mimic essences, vanilla essence being the most common. As with fruit essences, read what goes into making it and be tough; if it doesn't specifically say it is vanilla essence only, there is a strong possibility they are fudging the issue. Vanilla extract and essence are good; vanillin or vanilla flavourings are bad, the latter a manufactured chemical approximation to the real thing which tastes nothing of the sort. How to tell? Read the label; in order to be pure vanilla it must say so.

The best way to buy vanilla is the way it grows: in a pod. There are three principal styles: Bourbon, Mexican and those that come from Tahiti or Java. The Bourbon has a full-bodied rich flavour; the Mexican is sharper, with a slightly smoky flavour; while the Tahiti and Java style is quite pungent and aromatic. The pod should be pliable, slightly sticky and have a good rich aroma; if it is dry and brittle, you would do far better to buy a natural extract. Vanilla pods freeze well, so if you find a good source it might well be worth buying a few. Store them in your sugar jar and you get exquisitely scented vanilla sugar for use in baking and desserts.

WASABI: a type of horseradish popular in Japanese cuisine. The fresh root is rarely available in the West, so we have to make do with powder or paste. The latter, like mustard, is combined with warm water to form a paste. The paste version comes in tubes or jars and has a hot, clean, sharp flavour.

cooking, from where it spread to Spain, Portugal and Sicily. Think tajines as much as nougat, panforte and macaroons. The first almonds of the season tend to be milky and mild, delicious eaten straight from the tree.

nuts

Nuts are defined as dry one-seeded indehiscent (not splitting when mature) fruit that usually possess a woody wall. Acorns, chestnuts and hazelnuts obviously fall into this category, but the term is also used to cover edible fruit kernels like almonds and cashews. A good source of protein, these ingredients are popular in many different cuisines and in many different areas of the world.

Buying them, however, can be a tricky business; nuts go stale, even rancid, and many a cake has been spoiled by reaching for the out-of-date packet of almonds at the back of the cupboard. Nuts are sold slivered, whole, blanched, unblanched, flaked, ground and chopped. As a general rule, it is far better to buy nuts whole and blanched. The blanching process is a bore to do and best avoided, but the advantage of buying whole is that the flavour is immeasurably better and the task of grinding or chopping is not particularly arduous, provided you have a food processor or blender. Once ground, in whatever manner, the surface area of the nut is greatly increased, so deterioration becomes much faster.

Roasting nuts – far better done under the grill than in the oven (it takes very little time and is easier to keep an eye on things) – generally heightens their flavour.

Look to ethnic stores and health-food shops for variety and high turnover, guaranteeing greater freshness. Look out, too, for the first nuts of the season; a fresh almond is a world away from one months old.

ALMONDS: as widely used in savoury as in sweet dishes, the sweet almond (there is also a bitter variety) is popular in Arab

BRAZIL NUTS: because of their high oil content, Brazil nuts have a short shelf-life, but they provide richness and a faintly sweet flavour.

CASHEWS: one of the more expensive nuts, so make sure that what you buy is the best. Home-roasted cashew nuts are markedly better than those bought ready-roasted. Popular in Indian and Chinese dishes, when well ground they are used to thicken stews and curries.

COCONUT: a so-called 'false nut', this comes in unripe and ripe forms. The former is a green, soft shell with the flesh a jelly-like consistency. A ripe coconut is hard, the flesh being firmer. To buy, look for one heavy in the hand; shaking should result in liquid sloshing about. Pierce the eyes with a skewer, drain the liquid off and drink or discard and place

on a tea-towel to prevent the coconut slipping. Gently crack the outside shell with a hammer and peel away the brown skin with a vegetable peeler. Blitz the resulting flesh in a blender with a little water to form a coconut cream. Coconut cream and milk are sold in tins, useful and time-saving substitutes, but nothing beats fresh coconut.

HAZELNUTS: sweet and rich, these are popularly used in sweets and pastries, but are also excellent in salads, particularly when the dressing incorporates hazelnut oil.

PEANUTS: puréed into a butter, these are useful as a snack. They taste dull as ditchwater until roasted, but are then delicious and can be used for thickening stews, casseroles and curries, as well as in stir-fries.

PECANS: with their high fat content, pecans are inclined to go stale quite quickly.

PISTACHIOS come in various sizes, the larger generally being better and consequently more expensive and more satisfying, given that the nut-to-shelling ratio

is higher. They are good in savoury dishes, like pâtés and charcuterie, and also make fabulous ice-cream and excellent pastries.

WALNUTS: look for light-coloured examples, an indication of quality. Used in both sweet and savoury dishes, walnuts can also be made into a sauce like tarator. The oil is popular in south-west France and is used in vinaigrettes, but I find it too strong, preferring to use walnut vinegar, which is far more subtle.

sugars, syrups and honeys

SUGAR: the scourge of the Western modern diet; so fearful have we become of this ingredient that all reason seems to have been put to one side when debating its pros and cons. Perhaps we should return to the days when honey was used in its place. Sugar is extracted from both sugar cane and sugar beet: the former a

tropical plant, the latter grown throughout temperate Europe. Both sugars are largely manufactured in the same way, the sugar drawn out of the plant and then processed or refined. The key difference between the two is that sugar from sugar beet has to be refined, as left in its natural state the sugar tastes too bitter.

With refined brown sugar, the molasses is removed and then, depending on the type of brown sugar, some molasses or colouring is then reintroduced. White sugars are all refined, the different grades – granulated, caster, icing – determined by the degree of grinding, but the intense whiteness – perceived to be customer demand – is achieved by manipulating the sugar with chemicals and bleaching agents. By this stage, however, most of the flavour has been removed, along with some of the many trace elements present – as in any plant, the make-up is quite complex and can include a long list of vitamins and minerals.

In unrefined sugar the molasses is left in place, together with other trace elements, which seems to make rather a lot of sense. A tasting of refined and unrefined sugars revealed the unrefined versions to have more depth and body; once used in a dish, in my case to make some biscuits, there was much less discernible difference, although it does seem a shame to refine something unnecessarily.

Manufacturers make much of drinks and foods not containing sugar. This may be so, but if there is a sweetness it must come from somewhere and they are usually using one of the chemical substitutes to achieve the same result. Why not just use sugar and be honest about it? Customer concern about calories apparently.

Personally I'd rather have the sugar and worry about the calories than a by-product of the petrochemical industry.

JAGGERY: unrefined palm sugar, it contributes a winey sweetness when used, largely in Indian cookery.

SYRUPS, MOLASSES AND TREACLE: from the refining of sugar we get by-products like molasses, treacle and golden syrup. With its amber colour and gently sweet flavour, golden syrup is reminiscent of butterscotch in flavour and is essential in treacle tart and flapjacks. Treacle is a blend of refinery syrup with molasses and it ranges in colour from gold to jet-black, the latter often referred to as West Indian. Molasses is thick, dark, concentrated and not particularly sweet. Often used in fruit cakes, it can also be used in relishes and chutneys, where it provides a delicious bitterness.

MAPLE SYRUP: tends to be used in a similar way to golden syrup, for flavouring the likes of porridge, pancakes and baked items. It comes in various grades, the list of

ingredients an indication of quality; if corn syrup is listed, I would suggest you put it back – this is maple-flavoured syrup.

HONEY: this sweet sticky substance made by bees from the nectar of flowers has been eaten and used in cooking for centuries. Both the flavour and the appearance are determined by the flower from which the nectar is gathered, but also by the weather and season. Hot weather makes for stronger-flavoured honeys, while spring honey tends to be more delicate than honey made in the summer or autumn.

The quality variation of honey is enormous and buying can be a hit-and-miss affair, made worse by personal preference; honey can taste surprisingly strong, which some find too much. Basic honey is blended by the manufacturer to their specified taste from honeys sourced all over the world; it is often bland and indifferent, heat-treated to ensure cleanliness. Look for information on location, producer and source blossom, which helps to determine quality and flavour, but not always style. Heather honey from Scotland may well be stronger than that from the middle of France. Honey from herb flowers, like rosemary and thyme, tends to be powerfully flavoured, while honey from orange blossom will be quite delicate.

Honey comes in various types: runny honey will eventually crystallize; thick-set honey is runny honey blended with a small proportion of set honey; while honeycomb honey is the purest form, as it is untreated. However, its purity is also a factor of what the bees fed on – fields of chemically treated oilseed rape can still be sold as honeycomb honey. Read the label and taste.

If you are using honey in cooking, runny honey is far easier to handle and tends to be absorbed more easily. Its quite distinctive flavour can be rather powerful, particularly in cakes and biscuits, so use with caution. However, you only have to look at delicacies like halva and baklava to see how effective it can be.

What you buy is a matter of personal preference, but as a guide acacia is delicate and light; clover is thick and full-flavoured; eucalyptus is strong and powerful; heather is rich in flavour and quite strong; lavender is golden,

thick and strongly flavoured; rosemary is fragrant and herbaceous. The list is endless, and remember that the intensity of brands will vary.

My own favourite honey comes from an island off the west coast of Scotland called Colonsay. The island has 100 inhabitants, no intensive farming and is regularly – the islanders might say too regularly – dusted and washed by the winds and rain coming off the Atlantic. The honey is strong-tasting, viscous and very full-bodied. Production is limited and I made the mistake one year of buying only a few jars, and ran out before the next harvest.

alcohol in cooking

A frequently asked question concerns how good wine should be for cooking. A great deal of the subtlety of wine is lost when it is heated, so there is no need to use your best bottle. The opposite can

be said of your worst bottle, however; if you wouldn't drink it, why would you eat it. For most of us, it is a matter of degree. The main aspect to bear in mind is that the wine from the region is likely to suit the dish you are cooking, so look for something relevant; it doesn't need to be the top wine, just drinkable.

The same applies to fortified wines. I did a test, making a Madeira sauce with ten different Madeiras ranging in price from £5 up to nearly £50 and blind-tasting the results with a group of chefs. There was a significant difference between the cheapest bottle and those costing a few pounds more, but no discernible difference further up the scale.

Wine adds richness to dishes and acidity, but should be used with caution, its role being to support not dominate. If you think you need another splash because everything is drying out, you may do better adding a little water; more wine might be too dominant. It is also common for recipes to advise adding red wine early on in cooking, as this can sometimes mean most of its flavour is cooked out by the time the dish is finished; an extra splash at the end

can help to boost its role, but again take care.

Port and sherry are also useful for providing richness: port with game, sherry in soups and sauces. Trifle wouldn't be trifle without sherry and sugar syrups are given a more adult flavour when fortified wines are incorporated.

Spirits are particularly good in marinades, but also work well with fruits. Fruit and nut liqueurs are usefully added to fruit, giving more weight and structure to a dish, even of fresh fruit. Citrus-based liquors are good with strawberries and raspberries; nut, bean and seed-based liquors – like

Tia Maria, Pernod and Crème de Cacao – are good with other fruits, like bananas, pineapple and pears.

Buying liqueurs, spirits and wines can be a frustrating business, however, as you seldom need very much, which means your cupboard ends up being crowded with mostly full bottles. Half-bottles are a good idea, or even miniatures if you really want to economize.

The alcohol in all these drinks is usually more predominant than what is required for the finished dish, which is why you are generally instructed to cook some of it out. Either deglaze the pan,

when the alcohol will evaporate quickly, or if adding it to liquid, like soup, cook it for a few minutes to disperse the excess.

If you are adding alcohol of your own choice, pick something that is complementary: Calvados with apple dishes, Kirsch with cherries, Cointreau with citrus fruits for example. Whipped cream takes fruit and nut liqueur well, as does ice-cream. Coffee, too, can be transformed with spirit, as in Irish coffee, but personally I'd rather have the spirit in a separate glass. The combinations are endless and experimentation with a light hand is advised.

Flaming is a good way of enhancing dishes, either fruit dishes, when it is generally done at the end to help caramelize the sugars, or with a casserole at the start, when it does the same job but the bulk of the cooking is to follow. A beef casserole will have more body if you flame the meat in brandy before you add the bulk of the liquid. Take care when flaming – the flames can reach spectacular heights, but soon die down. If you are concerned, a fire blanket is the most useful way to kill the flames.

directory

The following mail-order companies supply a variety of the foods covered in this chapter:

Carluccio's (020 7240 5710); Clark Trading (020 8297 9937); Fortnum and Mason (020 7465 8666); La Fromagerie (020 7359 7440); Harrods (020 7730 1234); Marchand Le Franc (0870 900 2900); Morel Brothers (020 7346 0046); Take It From Here (0800 137064); Teesdale Trencherman (01833 638370); The Wiltshire Tracklement Co. (0666 840851); Wing Yip, 395 Edgware Road, London NW2 6LN (020 8450 0422) and branches nationwide.

In the UK, health-food shops tend to supply above-average products and have a good turnover. Italian delicatessens are good hunting-grounds, but choose carefully.

Buying loose when it comes to capers, anchovies and olives not only saves money but usually means you can get to take a closer look and even have a taste. Pretty packaging is expensive.

If you are shopping in Middle Eastern shops, do not be surprised to find one, two, even three brands of tahini, nuts like pistachio and several olive oils. Price is a good indication – if something is more expensive, in this instance it is likely to be better.

broccoli *with salted anchovies*

serves 4 as a starter

675 g (1¹/₂ lb) broccoli
6 tablespoons extra-virgin olive oil
8 salted anchovy fillets, roughly
  chopped
1 small red chilli, finely chopped
75 g (2³/₄ oz) Parmesan cheese,
  shaved with a vegetable peeler
1 lemon, quartered

Salted anchovies are well worth seeking out; the flavour often much deeper and more complex than the oil-soaked version. Give them a thorough rinse and dry them before use.

1 Steam or boil the broccoli until just tender. Drain.

2 Make a sauce by mashing together the olive oil, anchovies and chilli. Spoon this over the cooked broccoli.

3 Scatter over the Parmesan and serve with a lemon quarter and the bottle of olive oil, for those who require a little more indulgence.

tahini sauce

makes about 200 ml (7 fl oz)

2 garlic cloves, finely chopped
salt
125 ml (4 fl oz) tahini paste
juice of 2 lemons
a little warm water

This is superb with grilled chicken and lamb, good for meaty fish, like bream, and also good with grilled vegetables. I also spoon it over tomato salad, which makes the dish into a right mess as you start eating, but boy is it good.

1 Mash the garlic to a pulp with a little salt. Combine with the tahini paste and lemon juice.

2 Whisk in enough warm water to form a sauce the consistency of double cream.

salsa rossa

serves 4

1 dried cascabel chilli (or a chilli with a
  nutty and woody flavour), finely
  chopped
1 tablespoon red wine vinegar
1 red pepper
8 tomatoes
2 tablespoons finely diced shallots
4 tablespoons extra-virgin olive oil
salt and pepper

This salsa is good with grilled meats, far better than ketchup with hamburgers and ideal for summer barbecues. Make sure you buy peppers that have a good deep colouring, not something translucent. Variation can come from the chilli used, which should bring its own flavour rather than too much bite.

1 Combine the chilli and vinegar in a bowl and set aside.

2 Deseed and quarter the red pepper. Then, using a vegetable peeler, remove most of the skin. Finely dice the flesh.

3 Plunge the tomatoes into boiling water for 20 seconds, then place in cold water. Skin. Halve and deseed the tomatoes, remove the core and dice the flesh coarsely.

4 Combine all the ingredients together, season and serve.

smoked fish *with horseradish, wasabi and mustard*

serves 4

4 teaspoons olive oil

4 slices of baguette, about 1 cm (¹/₂ inch) thick

2-cm (³/₄-inch) piece of horseradish root

2 tablespoons crème fraîche

115 g (4 oz) smoked salmon

115 g (4 oz) smoked eel

85 g (3 oz) smoked cod's roe

scant 1 teaspoon wasabi paste

2 teaspoons good-quality Dijon mustard

pepper

1 lemon, quartered

Heat – in the sense of chilli-heat rather than temperature – is, for me, one of the most fascinating areas of food. Why does a curry need so much chilli to give of its best? Why does a Bloody Mary taste so much better with Tabasco? Why is smoked fish enhanced with horseradish? Not only does chilli introduce heat and its own flavour, but it seems to have the effect of lifting other flavours. Having three sources of chilli-power on the plate with three types of smoked fish is an opportunity to explore, and eat well.

1 Preheat a hot grill. Drizzle a teaspoon of olive oil over each slice of baguette and grill on both sides until golden brown. Set aside on wire rack.

2 Grate the horseradish and gently whisk it into the crème fraîche. Thinly slice the smoked salmon and cut the eel into 2-cm (³/₄-inch) lengths (it looks more attractive if you do this at an angle).

3 Spread the cod's roe on the toasts and place these in the middle of 4 plates, then arrange the eel and salmon around them, together with neat piles of the horseradish cream, wasabi and mustard. Sprinkle over a generous grinding of black pepper and serve with a lemon quarter.

American-style pancakes
with crispy pancetta and maple syrup

serves 4

225 g (8 oz) self-raising flour, sieved
1 teaspoon baking powder
25 g (³/4 oz) caster sugar
pinch of salt
3 eggs
1 dessertspoon melted butter
about 150 ml (¹/4 pint) full-cream milk
12 thin slices of pancetta
vegetable oil, for frying
maple syrup, to serve

1 In a mixing bowl, combine the flour, baking powder, sugar and salt. Whisk in the eggs, butter and just enough of the milk to form a batter about the same consistency as double cream (you probably won't need all the milk). Set aside.

2 Preheat a hot grill and a low oven. Grill the pancetta until crisp and keep warm.

3 Heat a frying pan and, when hot, lightly oil it. Drop dollops of the pancake mixture into the pan so they make pancakes about 6 cm (2¹/2 inches) in diameter. You don't want them too thick, about 1 cm (¹/2 inch), or they will not cook through. The pancakes will happily keep warm in the low oven until all are cooked.

4 When you have 20–24 pancakes, pile 5 or 6 in the middle of each of 4 warmed plates, top with the pancetta and pour over maple syrup. Serve with lots of coffee.

cucumber relish

makes about 1.5 kg (3¹/₄ lb)

1 kg (2¹/₄ lb) cucumbers
3 onions, thinly sliced
1 red pepper, deseeded and thinly
    sliced
25 g (³/₄ oz) salt
600 ml (1 pint) cider vinegar
350 g (12 oz) jaggery (or caster
    sugar)
6 cloves
1 dessertspoon mustard seeds
4 dried red chillies
3-cm (1¹/₄-inch) piece of fresh root
    ginger

1 Cut the cucumbers lengthwise, deseed and slice thinly. Combine the vegetables with the salt in a bowl and leave for 2 hours.
2 Rinse the salted vegetables thoroughly, drain and pat dry in a clean tea-towel. Transfer to a pan, add the vinegar, jaggery or caster sugar and the spices. Bring to the boil, then lower the heat and simmer for 15 minutes. Turn off the heat and set aside to cool.
3 Clean, sterilize and dry some vinegar-proof storage jars and, when the relish is completely cold, fill the jars with it and seal.

mango, toasted sesame seed and ginger relish

serves 4

1 dessertspoon black mustard
    seeds
juice and zest of 2 limes
2 mangoes
1 tablespoon toasted sesame seeds
1 teaspoon toasted sesame oil
3 tablespoons vegetable oil
2-cm (³/₄-inch) piece of fresh root
    ginger, peeled and grated
2 tablespoons roughly chopped
    coriander
2 spring onions, finely chopped
salt and pepper

1 Combine the mustard seeds with the lime juice and zest in a bowl and set aside.
2 Peel the mangoes, cut the flesh away from the stone and then chop it into 1-cm (¹/₂-inch) pieces. (This need not be too exact, but the chunks should not differ too much in size.)
3 Combine all the ingredients in a bowl, season and serve.

raspberry vinegar

makes about 500 ml (18 fl oz)

3 batches of raspberries, each
   about 250 g (9 oz)
500 ml (18 fl oz) very good white
   wine vinegar

Often the commercial examples of this fruity flavouring are nothing of the sort, but dusty pink bottles of uninteresting acid. Yet, when deglazing a pan, it is that fruity raspberry flavour you seek. It is better to buy the batches of raspberries one at a time, rather than all at once, as they deteriorate so quickly.

1 Gently crush the first batch of raspberries in a preserving jar and pour over the vinegar. Leave for 3 or 4 days.

2 Strain through a muslin-lined sieve and repeat with a second batch of raspberries and the same vinegar, which should take on more colour each time.

3 Repeat a third time with the last batch of fruit, strain and bottle in clean dry sterilized jars and keep away from natural light.

herb and chilli butter

makes about 450 g (1 lb)

2 tablespoons finely chopped
   parsley
2 tablespoons finely chopped chervil
2 tablespoons finely chopped chives
1 teaspoon thyme leaves
1 garlic clove, finely chopped and
   mashed with a little salt
generous splash of Tabasco sauce
400 g (14 oz) butter (at room
   temperature)

1 Mash the herbs, garlic and Tabasco into the butter. Roll up in cling-film to form a cylinder and refrigerate.

2 You can cut the cylinder across into discs and then freeze these, ready for that last-minute steak sandwich when you arrive home from the pub.

preserved clementines
with star anise, cloves and cinnamon

*makes about two 1-litre
(1³/4-pint) Kilner jars*

250 g (9 oz) caster sugar
6 star anise
8 cloves
2 cinnamon sticks, broken into 5-cm
    (2-inch) lengths
6 tablespoons gin
2 kg (4 lb) peeled clementines

*The clementines need to be peeled
very well, with as little pith as
possible left on them. They are great
on their own, or serve them with
cream or ice-cream.*

1 In a saucepan, combine the
caster sugar and spices with 700
ml (1¹/4 pints) of water, cover and
bring to the boil. Stir to ensure all
the sugar is dissolved, stir in the
gin and then set aside to cool.
2 Pack the clementines loosely
into sterilized Kilner jars,
distributing the spices as evenly as
possible, then pour over the syrup.
Leave about 1 cm (¹/2 inch) of
space at the top of each jar and
seal.
3 Place the jars in a large
saucepan and fill with cold water
to come almost, but not quite, to
the full height of the jars, leaving
about 2 cm (³/4 inch). Cover and
slowly bring to the boil. Reduce
the heat and simmer for about 25
minutes. Remove from the pan
and allow to cool.
4 Store the preserved clementines
for up to 5 months.

pistachio and rose water ice-cream

serves 4

100 g (3½ oz) caster sugar
4 egg yolks
375 g (13 oz) full-cream milk
200 ml (7 fl oz) whipping cream
pinch of saffron threads, soaked in a spoonful or two of water
2 tablespoons coarsely chopped pistachios
2 dessertspoons rose water

Serve this delicious ice-cream with a fruit compote or salad; it also goes particularly well with citrus tarts.

1 In a large heatproof mixing bowl, combine the sugar and egg yolks, and whisk until pale. Bring the milk up to boiling point in a saucepan, remove from the heat and pour on to the egg and sugar mixture, whisking all the time.

2 Pour into a clean saucepan, place over a moderate heat and stir, making sure the mixture doesn't catch (particularly at the edges) until thick. As soon as a line drawn with your finger through the custard on the back of a spoon remains, remove from the heat and pour into a clean bowl.

(If it overcooks at this stage you will end up with sweet scrambled eggs. If you are nervous, sit the clean bowl in ice and pour the mixture through a sieve, which will help to catch the overcooked lumps.)

3 Combine the custard with the cream and stir in the saffron and the soaking liquid, with the pistachios and rose water. Transfer to an ice-cream maker or freezer, removing every 30 minutes to stir. Return to the freezer and repeat 30 minutes later. Return to the freezer, stirring once or twice until frozen.

4 This ice-cream will need 10–15 minutes in the fridge to soften before you eat it.

tea, coffee and chocolate

'Tea! Heat and thirst and fatigue and excitement had done their worst for Rose. She was limp and weary and her throat ached. The imminent prospect of a cup of tea roused her to trembling excitement. Twelve cups of tea each Samuel and she had drunk daily for years. Today she had had none – she had eaten no food either, but at the moment that meant nothing to her. Tea! A cup of tea! Two cups of tea!'

C.S. FORESTER, *The African Queen*

Despite their everyday appearance, tea, coffee and chocolate are capable of the most extraordinary finesse. Half an hour spent making and drinking a pot of single-estate Darjeeling is a completely different experience from a rushed mug of tea-bag tea zapped in the microwave; a jug of just-ground Colombian Medellin Supremo a whole world of complex aromas and tastes when compared with the vacuum-packed offering off a supermarket shelf; and as for chocolate, break off a piece of Valhrona Carré de Caraïbe and compare it with a bar of high-street 'chocolate' - they might as well be different foods.

We have come to consume these luxuries without a second's thought, but we are missing out. Some tea -bag tea is good, but nothing in comparison with a fine loose-leaf tea; coffee correctly roasted requires enormous skill and knowledge, it is not something that can easily be automated; and chocolate is one of the world's most extraordinary foods, not something to be snapped up for a few pennies in any corner store.

tea

The teacup was little more than a thimble, the tea a pale golden hue, yet the aroma was bright and green, distinctly refreshing and the flavour almost floral. I thought a packet would do nicely, until I heard the price... I nearly choked. This was Gyokuro, one of the most prized teas in the world. I was at a stall on the edge of Tokyo market, with about 20 teas in front of me. The prices dropped dramatically from the heady heights of 'jewel-dew', but everything was relatively expensive compared to what I was used to paying for tea.

Outside Japan, tea ceremonies are, for most of us, a thing of the past. My one experience was in Singapore, where the whole event lasted one and a half hours, the tea drinking serving to launch a host of subjects to discuss with my companions. I emerged quite restored, stimulated and at ease. Yet, today, a cup of tea is too often a tea bag squashed with the back of a spoon, the object in question binned and the resulting liquor milked to within an inch of its life.

There is nothing intrinsically wrong with tea bags (see page 240 for a list of the UK's best), in their infancy constructed from silk, now more usually fashioned from paper made from Manila hemp. What goes inside them is nearly always a blend – often of up to 30 different teas – the aim of which, as in any blended product, is to produce consistency. Yet, if you are really interested in drinking the best tea, it needs to be loose – not that just being loose makes tea good – and you need to consider the milk question.

Milk serves to soften the tannins in tea, which is one reason why Assam tea, often rich in tannins, 'milks up' well. With lighter, more delicate teas, however, milk tends to swamp any finesse; so with a good Formosa oolong, or green tea (see opposite) the advantages and subtleties are lost. Good tea is expensive; if you are going to explore it, it really is worth considering giving up milk.

Giving up milk in tea

It took me a week and was decidedly difficult at the start, all the harsh notes in every cup of tea I drank coming to the fore. One of the first things that happened was

a reduction in the amount of tea I used. 'One teaspoon per person, plus one for the pot' sailed out the window and a pot of best Darjeeling, which is what I drink when I first get up, now takes a scant teaspoon of tea. The same goes for green teas drunk later in the day. Now, on the rare occasions I am faced with a mug of tea containing milk, all I taste is the strong dairy flavour of the milk.

As for lemon, this is anathema to the serious tea drinker, the citrus flavour all but killing any delicacy that may be contained in the tea. If you are searching for the best in tea, add water, just boiled and only once (water that has been boiled more than once makes tea which tends to be flat and stale).

types of tea

Tea is the leaf of a tree, *Camellia sinensis*, which is pruned to form a low bush as an aid to picking. The harvesting of tea is still very labour-intensive and the plants need high rainfall – sunny pictures of tea plantations are a little misleading, tea-growing areas around the world often being shrouded in mist. The flavour and quality of the tea are largely determined by variety, soil and climate. Also, once harvested the tea leaves are treated in one of three ways, the method determining the type of tea as follows.

Green teas

The leaves are picked and dried (losing about 60 per cent of their water content), heat-treated to prevent any fermentation, further dried and then packed. Common in Japan and China, green tea has little caffeine or tannin, so is good to drink at the end of the day. It is unsuitable for use with milk or lemon, which will swamp the delicate flavours.

Green tea is generally from China and Japan. The Chinese green tea seen most often here is 'gunpowder', so called because the leaves curl up into 'gunpowder balls', only to unfurl when hot water is added. The flavour has a lightly toasted quality and is dry and, at times, quite astringent. Japanese green teas tend to be lighter and slightly more delicate than the Chinese, from everyday teas like Banch and Sencha through to Gyokuro, the jewel of Japanese teas, which, as already observed, costs a small fortune.

Oolong teas

The process is much the same as above, but the leaf partially ferments – usually for a few hours at around 27°C (81°F) – giving more body and weight to the tea. It is often referred to as Formosa oolong (after the old name for Taiwan, where this process was developed), although these teas are now also made in China.

Oolong teas come in two different forms: those from China and Japan, where the process of fermentation tends to be short; and those from Taiwan, where the process is longer, producing a more full-bodied tea. Taiwanese oolong has the advantage of containing very little caffeine and can be light, refreshing and aromatic.

Black teas

After picking, the leaves are dried and then allowed to ferment (encouraged by rolling to damage it), which lends it a characteristic black colour and provides depth and flavour. Black teas come principally from India, China and Africa, the quality varies from finest 'first flush' Indian down to fairly dull teas from Africa, only normally used in blends. See more in 'The grading of black tea' below.

Flavoured teas

There is a final category of tea into which the likes of Lapsang Suchong and Earl Grey fall. These are flavoured (generally black) teas – with smoke in the case of Suchong and bergamot in the case of Earl Grey. Would that the world were so simple. Within each category you will find good and bad versions. Look on the side of a packet of Earl Grey: does it say bergamot oil or bergamot flavouring? The first is probably natural, the second likely to be a 'nature-identical' synthetic – except it is not so identical.

The grading of black tea

Black tea is graded depending on its form, from 'whole-leaf' down to, literally, 'dust'. The gamut runs from 'orange pekoe' (the tip, slightly orange in colour, along with the bud), through 'broken and fannings' (between broken pieces of leaf and dust) down to 'dust' itself. Fine tea can come from all of these classifications, although each produces a rather different style, moving from light and delicate down to full-bodied. As the leaf becomes broken, more surface area is exposed to the water, producing a deeper and more full-bodied liquor.

The world of tea is further complicated by a lack of common terms. From India, for example, the best orange pekoe tea is referred to as 'SFTGFOP' (special finest tippy golden flowery orange pekoe), while the best tea from Sri Lanka will be referred to as 'high-grown', a reference to the altitude of the plantation.

As you move up the scale of quality, specific estates become important, much as they are in the world of wine. In Darjeeling, for example, top estates include Castleton, Goomti, Margaret's

Hope, Jungpana, Seeyok and Selimbong. 'First flush', the name given to the early harvest, commands very high prices, picked as it is in the spring and generally superior to the second flush, picked a few months later – just before the rains. First flush tends to be more delicate and fine, the second flush producing a tea that is more dense and rich.

What to look for you when you buy

If you are buying loose tea, look first to see that the tea matches its supposed grading – that is, 'whole leaf' is what it says. Aroma is crucial, the leaves should smell vibrant and stimulating. If you are buying a packet, bear in mind that a blend labelled Assam, for example, need contain only 51 per cent of Assam tea. If there is a flavouring, make sure it is a natural one (see opposite).

Where to buy tea
Specialist shops will have a far greater range of loose-leaf teas and will offer advice, and probably a chance to smell and sample. Put your nose into three different bins of oolong, for example, and you will have a distinct sense of a common style as well as the variety.

Tasting tea
Tea blenders can often taste 15 or 20 teas at one sitting. All the teas are made in exactly the same way and left for the same time. In the UK, the tasting for blending is often done with milk, on the basis that most tea is drunk with milk.

Colour is always the very first consideration, the tea should have brick-red tones and not be grey or off-brown in colour. The aroma should be bright and invigorating, not dull, insipid or stale. As to flavour, it depends on the tea, but there should be balance, excitement, character and length. From a green tea, delicacy is the keynote; with a black tea, you should expect more body, substance and strength. But all should be in harmony, making you feel relaxed and yet stimulated.

Think of a cup of tea not as something to be drunk on the hop, but something to be savoured and enjoyed, something over which it is worth making a bit of a fuss, if not exactly a ceremony.

How to make tea
Unless you use bottled water, what comes from the tap is likely to be your starting point. Hard or soft, all water will make tea but different types of water gives very different results: softer water produces a richer, more rounded flavour, hard water a more sharply focused tea. The difference is so great that some tea blenders alter the blend depending on the area in which the tea is to be sold.

Boil some fresh water once and make the tea in a warmed earthenware or china pot. Strength depends on taste, and whether you insist on milk or not. Experiment and you'll be surprised how dramatically different and rewarding tea can be without milk and made less strong. Tea needs to stand for about 5 minutes to allow the full flavours to infuse properly.

How to store tea
Stored in dark airtight containers away from heat, tea will keep for several years.

Fairtrade and organic teas
Tea workers have, historically, not been particularly well treated, and the nature of the business – the tea moving from the plantation, through various middlemen and on to the market – means that it is hard to police, control or establish exactly what happens where, when and how. Increasing concern over the welfare of those employed in the industry has led to the emergence of various 'third-party stamps'. These vary, depending on the country in which the tea is sold, but usually aim to specify certain minimum levels of worker welfare and proper reward and, as a general rule, the standard of their product is good, if not exceptional.

The increasing cost of agricultural chemicals has led tea growers right across the world to look at moving over to a less chemical-intensive system of growing. Overall this is good news for the consumer and should be encouraged.

coffee

The moment had come. With a flick of her wrist, Anita turned the switch and 20 kilos of hot glistening coffee beans streamed into the cooling sieve. The air was heady with the aroma of freshly roasted coffee, complex and multi-layered... I counted woody spices, bitter chocolate and a caramelized sweetness among them. The roaster was turned off, the noise and the heat gently subsiding as we gathered a few handfuls of the still-hot beans. Upstairs a kettle had just boiled and we made a cup of the freshest coffee I have ever tasted, from roast to cup in less than five minutes.

We had roasted Yirgacheffe, an Ethiopian coffee that grows wild in the forests and highlands of the Sidamo district. Organic? You bet! The idea of spraying anything on these rambling coffee trees that climb high into the forest canopy is laughable. What we drank was delicate and subtle, rounded and balanced, with a muscatel fruitiness, a smoothness and elegance, and gentle bite at the end. Nothing too overt, simply exquisite.

Coffee is a worldwide commodity, traded much as oil is, and finding the right coffee is a complicated and difficult task, usually made much harder by those who sell it. Packets with terms like 'breakfast' or 'after dinner', 'skilled blending' and 'careful selection' tell you absolutely nothing. 'After dinner' generally means a higher (longer and thus darker) roast. If you like full-bodied coffee, however, strength has nothing to do with the roast but with the ratio of coffee to water – and the so-called 'after dinner' blend might well be perfect for breakfast.

No other food seems open to such variation: type of bean, where it is grown, how and when it is harvested, how it is cleaned. And all of this before it is roasted – to what degree, how long ago – then how is it ground and, finally, how it is to be made. Cafetières may be popular, but there are drip pots, filters, glass balloons, percolators, moka espressos. Even then you have to decide whether to have milk, hot or cold, or not. Two cups of coffee coming from beans from the same tree can taste completely different.

All of this may explain why 90 per cent of the coffee we drink in this country is instant, but what a world to miss out on. Real coffee is as complex and sophisticated as wine, so it's no wonder similar terms are used to describe its taste: 'acid', 'bitter', 'sweet', 'rich', 'mellow', 'smooth', even 'gamy'. So much for meaningless phrases like 'breakfast blend'. If you needed only one reason to go to a specialist retailer, it might be to get an accurate description of what you are buying. Price differentials are nothing like as dramatic as you might imagine.

Types of coffee

All coffee starts life as a bean on a shrub growing more or less between the tropics of Cancer and Capricorn. There are two main varieties of bean. Arabica is the

most important and is generally recognized as the best, although this it not necessarily the case. Robusta, as its name suggests, is a hardy bean and can cope with wider extremes of climate. It is more disease-resistant and requires less care and attention than Arabica. In truth, Robusta is to be found in mass market and espresso blends, where it contributes some background structure.

To get the best from Arabica, it needs to be planted between 700 and 2,200 metres (2,000 and 6,500 feet) – the higher the better – while Robusta likes to live below 700 metres. *Terroir* is not a critical consideration, although it does affect the flavour, as do rainfall, temperature, wind, sunshine. The coffee tree is fairly adaptable, although its not keen on frost and leaf disease can be a problem.

The plants take about five years to develop their root structure sufficiently to bear a crop and will bear fruit for about 10 years before becoming exhausted. Bushes pruned to a pickable 2 metres (6 feet), a coffee plantation in flower is a beautiful sight, snow-white petals blowing lightly in the wind as the fruit turns from green through yellow, to red and

finally black, when they are ready to pick.

The coffee tree flowers and fruits at the same time – and for the best coffee the picker returns several times to the same plant to gather the beans as they ripen. The coffee plant also has a peculiar habit of ripening several times a year. For cheaper coffees the harvesting is mechanized and fairly crude; what you get in your mix will be ripe and unripe, which doesn't bode too well for what you are going to end up drinking.

Growing in pairs, the beans kiss each other on the flat side, protected by the fruit. There are two ways to remove the fruit matter from around the beans. A wet treatment steeps the beans in water to soften the outside, resulting in a slight fermentation

which helps to develop a complexity of flavour. Less privileged coffee gets spread out in the sun, which dries the fruit husks. Whichever means is used, the beans are then sorted, picked over and graded – all of which has to be done by hand... worth bearing in mind when you think how expensive coffee can seem.

With over 40 countries exporting coffee, there is a problem of classification, but broadly speaking coffee production can be divided into three areas. The Caribbean, Central and South America produce the better coffees and, overall, they have good balance, tasting smooth and elegant. East Africa and Arabia, on the other hand, produce coffees with a more pronounced acidity.

If this sounds like a criticism it

is not. Acidity in coffee is similar to wine, it provides a fruitiness. If the acidity is not high enough, the coffee will taste flat and dull; too much and it tastes harsh. Balance is all. If you prefer coffee to be smooth and full-bodied, you would do better to try something from India, Southeast Asia or the Pacific. Classics from this region, like Java and Sumatra, tend to be full-bodied and rich, because of their relatively low acidity. Too little acidity, however, and an unpleasant earthiness creeps in.

Where to buy coffee

With coffee, you must find a specialist retailer, or one that supplies mail order. It is like going into a secret world and, no wonder, you have to trust them. Looking at a bean, you have no idea what its provenance might be.

A good supplier buys the best beans, roasts them in small batches and frequently. His or her job is not easy – the coffee market notoriously changeable. Civil war, frost, drought, currency fluctuations, all play their part and substitution is always a risk.

Roasting coffee requires much skill to get an even result. For the ultimate in freshness, home-roasted coffee – where the bean moves from being roasted to being made into coffee almost simultaneously – is impossible to beat, although it is often difficult to get an even roast. Styles vary enormously. A company in London, Torz and Macatonia, tends to full-roast all its coffees, so the beans have a dark, glossy coating. At the Monmouth Coffee Stores in Covent Garden, however, Anita Le Roy is reluctant to roast further

than the merest hint of a shine, 'I believe passionately in working with the inherent flavours of the bean. The roasting should bring all those characteristics out. If you dark-roast, you start to introduce different, cooked, caramelized flavours. There is nothing wrong with this method, it just isn't how I like to do things.'

The strength of coffee does not depend on the roast, rather on the concentration of coffee. What the roast does, or should do, is enhance the inherent qualities of the coffee. As a rough rule-of-thumb, a light or medium roast is recommended for delicately flavoured coffees. This preserves the acidity and draws out the flavours. These coffees are the ones for breakfast and to have with milk. A dark roast, where the acidity mellows and the delicate flavours are replaced by a slightly bitter caramelized flavour, are better drunk black, as in a typical Italian espresso. We have traditionally gone for a medium roast in this country, but given our enthusiasm for everything Italian the dark version is gaining ground.

Much is made of the deterioration of coffee after it is roasted, the implication being that

been roasted individually. The roasting process caramelizes the sugars in the beans or, as the roasting gets more intense, carbonizes them, producing a bitterness which when done well is extremely pleasant, but if too energetic makes everything unpleasant.

buying small amounts regularly is the best way. Having tested this theory, I can only conclude that, while the coffee does alter, to say it deteriorates is rather dramatic. It mellows slightly, but does not alter that much. Freezing is the best way of extending the life of your coffee, so go ahead and buy largish quantities – for which there is often a discount – and repack in small amounts for the freezer.

Blended coffee

To blend or not to blend? Many speciality coffees are good enough to enjoy as they are, but, as with Scotch whisky, blending can often produce a pleasing balance, drawing out the preferred characteristics of each coffee while maintaining consistency. Although most coffee retailers have their own blends, you can ask them to make up your own preferred style. Ask their advice, highlighting the characteristics you like, when and how you drink your coffee... then experiment, it is the only way.

People can be quite sniffy about blending, believing in the supposed superiority of single-source coffees. Undoubtedly, single-source coffees have a character that will change over time and the roasting has to be more in keeping with individual flavours, but blended coffees, like blended whiskies, also have a character, one that is consistent over time. There is an analogy with sherry, essentially a blended wine. If the blend is good, and you like it, then that may well be the coffee for you.

A few pointers to help. Make sure, if you can, that the beans that go to make up the blend have

Moving from commercial blends to single-source coffees

Most of the coffee you buy from the supermarket will be all, or largely, Arabica; if the label says all Arabica, you are probably on to a fairly good thing. The coffee will, on the whole, taste fine. Which may well lead you to wonder what on earth I am on about. Go now, and buy a small quantity of a single-origin coffee of a similar roast from a specialist coffee shop. Make them identically and then taste. Whether you like the single-origin coffee or not, it will have more character, greater complexity, greater variety – highs and lows – when it is in your mouth. It is also likely to have more length. That is the difference; the next stage is to find a single-origin coffee you like. I generally buy three or four different coffees each time,

drinking one after the other as they run out. As with wine, the same coffee becomes a little dull after a while, even if it is wonderful.

Making coffee

Having got your coffee home, the next question to face is what to make it in. There is a vast array of gadgets on sale, costing from a few pence to hundreds of pounds, but many believe a jug and kettle are hard to beat. It is important, however, to grind your beans appropriately for whichever method you are using, as they all need different degrees of fineness. Note how many mass brands say something along the lines of 'ground for all uses'.

VERY FINELY GROUND –
   for espresso machines and
   paper filters
FINELY GROUND –
   for cafetières and mochas
MEDIUM GROUND –
   for jugs

There is no 'best way' of making coffee, a lot of it is down to preference and lifestyle. Rules to follow with any of the infusion methods, however, are that the water should come in contact with

the coffee at just under boiling point to extract the oils and subsequent aromas. While you can make strong coffee by increasing the ratio of coffee to water, it is not a good idea to reverse the principle if you like weak coffee, as the bitter unpleasant oils become more predominant. Better to make it at normal strength and dilute.

Although it is a matter of taste, there is no doubt that purists will only drink coffee black in order to appreciate the aromas and flavours fully. Milk tends to tone down the characteristics, although many see this as an advantage, particularly in the morning. Whichever route you choose, coffee must be served as soon as it is made, those delicate aromas are already on the wane.

Decaffeinated coffee

There are three ways to remove the caffeine from coffee, none of them particularly pleasant, and undoubtedly a huge part of the

enjoyment of the drinking goes with the caffeine. Better, perhaps, to drink some herbal tea and save the coffee for tomorrow.

In the first, the caffeine is removed using a chemical solvent and there is some debate over the possible harmful effects of the solvent, residue of which will inevitably remain in the coffee. Unless otherwise stated, the solvent method is the most widely used and the cheapest, which makes it popular.

In the second, the removal is achieved by means of water, which leaches out the caffeine from the green beans. The water is then filtered through charcoal and returned to the beans so they reabsorb the flavour constituents.

The last method uses carbon dioxide, which combines with the caffeine.

Caffeine levels in coffee are much misunderstood. Most instant coffee contains quite high levels of

caffeine, Arabica beans contain less than Robusta, and those grown high up even less. Some Arabica beans contain more caffeine than others. If you are concerned about your caffeine intake, my advice is to talk to a specialist retailer, they should be able to balance your concerns with the particular type of coffee you like.

Fairtrade and organic coffee

As with tea, schemes ensuring a more equal distribution of the proceeds from coffee have developed and the buying of such products should ensure that workers are paid at acceptable levels, that basic safety and health care are provided and the coffee being produced in an environmentally friendly way. These ethical concerns notwithstanding, the flavour of the coffee still needs to be assessed in the same way as any other food.

What to look for when you taste

By all means delve into the wine vocabulary, but the trade itself looks at four desirable areas:

ACIDITY: without it, coffee tastes flat, and a little acidity heightens the fruity characteristics. As with wine, some acidity gives focus. Too much, and you end up with a rather thin, metallic flavour.

BITTERNESS: perhaps the most elusive characteristic, bitterness is an inherent part of coffee. Naturally present in some beans, it is also created during the roasting and in the correct proportion is considered an asset, though the bitterness that comes from over-extraction is generally unpleasant.

AROMA: the best coffees exhibit hugely complex aromas, the worst almost none at all. Once you enter the world of speciality coffees, the aroma is often a deciding influence, not in the sense of good or bad, but whether you like a delicate or a powerful aroma.

BODY OR LENGTH: as with wine, when you drink the coffee, consider how long and complex is the after-taste. Is it balanced, or does one particular aspect dominate?

No specialist supplier? What to buy

One option is to buy branded vacuum-packed foil packets or tins. Some very good coffee is sold this way, but not much. Most is mass-produced to achieve consistency, and individual characteristics are lost in the blending. There is nothing intrinsically wrong with these coffees but, like any large-volume product, they tend to be dull. The company is constantly assessing price against quality and, invariably, some of the duller coffees are included in the blend to 'bulk it out'. The best, however, strive to produce for the growing band of quality-conscious coffee drinkers. Finding them, though, is really a matter of trial and error.

chocolate

CADBURY'S BOURNVILLE: this is the chocolate with which I grew up. It has an overt bitterness which then meant that I left it on the shelf rather than gobbling it up. It is fine for cooking, but lacks any real character or finesse.

GREEN AND BLACK'S ORGANIC DARK CHOCOLATE: with an uncompromising flavour that is deep and has medium length, this has a slightly coarse edge for my taste, but it does have character and is full of interest.

LINDT: proudly proclaiming 70 per cent cocoa solids, Lindt has medium length, but is otherwise rather dull.

VALRHONA: universally admired as among the best, although not that readily obtained except from specialist suppliers, these chocolates have a depth of flavour and roundness that is hard to beat. I like them particularly because the bitterness, such an inherent part of dark chocolate, seems so full of character, with a subtle, gentle approach. Complex, with a long aftertaste, these are as interesting to eat on their own as they are used in cooking.

We had just finished supper and the wind outside blew the way it often does at the end of the summer, scattering leaves here and there, early victims of the impending autumn chill. Our main course had been the most perfect fish stew, complete with all the required trimmings of toast and rouille, together with generous portions of freshly grated Gruyère. What was to follow, I wondered, from the kitchen of fellow food writer Philippa Davenport? She reappeared bearing a bowl of the most delicious-looking figs and a bar of chocolate. That was it. Not just any old bar of chocolate, but a hefty slab of Valrhona's Caraïbe, 66 per cent cocoa solids (the remaining 34 per cent being cocoa butter, that is the bean's own natural fat) and all of them from Trinitario beans. A bite of warm, end-of-summer fig, its complex sweetness and gritty-but-forgiving texture followed by the roasted coffee flavour of the chocolate mixed with Trinitario's characteristic sweet tropical fruit flavours – a heaven-sent pud of the best kind.

Types of chocolate

Buying chocolate is not an easy task. To start with, a great deal of what is called 'chocolate' is really nothing of the sort, but a blend of cocoa, sugar and vegetable oil. Ever wondered why your favourite 'chocolate' bar doesn't melt, even on a scorching summer's day? Along with the cocoa content it probably has hefty doses of sugar and vegetable oil, the latter melting at a higher temperature than cocoa butter… There were efforts made to relabel these 'chocolates' as 'candy', which is how they are classified in the US, but without success. Recently EU legislation has changed to allow the vegetable fat in, and consumers must look at the list of ingredients to detect its presence. Purists find all this hard to accept, and you can see their point… Half the fun of eating chocolate is the way it melts instantly on the tongue, an oral pleasure that cannot be gained from any other food in the same way. For nothing melts like chocolate, at exactly the same temperature as our body temperature.

Not that anyone is altogether against the confectionery bars. Life would hardly be the same without

Mars, Snickers and Bounty, but these are confectionery of a decidedly inferior nature to a bar of pure cocoa solids and cocoa butter.

It is commonly understood that the closer you get to 70 per cent cocoa solids in chocolate, the better it is. After that things take a turn for the worse, with bitterness being high on the agenda and a dryness in the mouth being predominant. True, up to a point, but it does rather depend on the cocoa beans in question. There are three principle types: Forastero, Trinitario and Criollo.

Forastero is the workhorse, good and strong but lacking in any real style or finesse. It is primarily used in the less expensive chocolate, providing sufficient kick but no subtlety. Trinitario, on the other hand, has roasted coffee and tropical fruit characteristics that are unmistakable. This is no broad band of flavours, but a distinct freshly roasted coffee flavour, complex and long, the fruitiness an integral part of the extended, gentle aftertaste. Criollo beans give a berry-rich flavour, deep and full of summer, with a rounded almondy finish that is well focused, coupled with a little acidity for real bite. Real chocolate aficionados will only consider eating chocolate made from either of the latter two beans, or a combination of the two.

Is there such a thing as vintage chocolate? There certainly is. The analogy with wine is uncanny in the extreme, the definition being chocolate made from beans from the same year from the same farm and labelled accordingly. Horizontal tastings (across a number of chocolates from the same year) are difficult, however, and it is really not very easy to see how to rate such delectable but fairly expensive offerings.

What to look for when you buy

There is no expertise involved in working out what to buy, you just need to use all your five senses and be able to compare and contrast.

TOUCH: it's a question of melting speed. Place a piece of good chocolate in your hand and it will start to melt within seconds. If you are still staring at solid chocolate after 20 seconds, chances are you're on to a dud.

SOUND: cocoa butter has crystals which produce an ice-clean snap when broken. Any bending or wavering is a bad sign. Clean and pure are the watchwords here.

SIGHT: colour is the first item to consider, which should be bright and clear, ranging from light – through to dark-brown – 'mahogany' is often referred to as a guide. The redder and lighter the colour, the finer the cocoa. Gloss is also important, it should be a tight uniform attractive shine.

Chocolate can develop a bloom on the outside for two main reasons. Firstly, the chocolate was either not handled properly by the manufacturer, or was allowed to get too warm and then cooled down again. The cocoa butter

crystals melt, rise to the surface and recrystallize. This does not adversely affect the flavour or texture, but should be seen as a warning sign – what you are examining has not been stored properly.

The second reason for bloom is to do with moisture and occurs when the chocolate has been stored somewhere moist. Sugar crystals rise to the surface and dissolve in the moisture, recrystallizing later as the chocolate dries. The result is a grey and gritty chocolate, not at all the sort of thing you want to eat.

SMELL: as with wine, smell is vital and again as with wine, too often the warning signs picked up on the nose are ignored. Our noses are complex and able to detect off-smells incredibly well and quickly. With chocolate you should detect a deep rounded complexity, with buttery, coffee overtones and notes of fruit and spice. Sugar dulls these characteristics, so intensity is also important when assessing.

TASTE: spitting is not really an option here, but confine yourself to small quantities if you are tasting more than one type of chocolate. Place it on your tongue and simply allow it to melt. I could

go on about the wonderful floral and other flavours but, in truth, you are looking for an all-rounded complexity, quite a lot of length, which is really an aftertaste with attitude and well-knit flavours. Balance is all-important.

If you are buying from a good retailer they should encourage tasting. As with cheese, the cost of providing tasters is minimal and money well spent if even some customers opt to spend money on good chocolate.

So what are the off-notes? Apart from bloom, mentioned above, a gritty texture suggests the chocolate has not been 'conched' (ground and smoothed) properly, while you can sometimes detect a slightly burnt flavour, which happens if the beans are over-roasted (a technique sometimes used to impart 'character' to dull beans) and finally vanilla flavouring, which will come across as quite chemical in character.

Money invariably plays a part in what you decide to buy, but by following these guidelines, it is relatively easy to establish the difference between good and indifferent chocolate. Some prefer Trinitario beans, others Criollo; some may question the wisdom of spending a little more for a chocolate they find difficult to recognize as being notably different from another. There is no right and wrong in this area, no good and bad, it is a matter of preference. What is not in question, however, is that vegetable fat has no part whatsoever to play in chocolate. There is nothing wrong with it, but it is not chocolate.

All very well, I hear you say, but what do I do when, standing in the aisle of my supermarket, I am faced with bars of chocolate and no information about the type of bean? The percentage of cocoa solids is a good indicator, but not a guarantee, of quality. Around 60 per cent is considered good, 70 per cent even better. More than that, and the bitterness can be too powerful for some, a bit like a double-strength espresso. If the beans are not specified, it's as well to assume they are primarily Forastero. If you are planning to eat it, you might even prefer a chocolate with less cocoa solids. If you are planning to cook with it, my advice is to go for a high proportion of cocoa solids, given you are going to be diluting the chocolate with other ingredients.

The better brands tend to be French and Belgian, and some of the better supermarket own-brands will be made in these countries.

Milk chocolate

Milk chocolate, as the name implies, is chocolate incorporating milk solids. For many, this is the preferred way of eating chocolate and all the notes above on tasting apply equally here. There is an analogy with tasting tea; most tea blenders taste the tea with milk. In milk chocolate, the cocoa solids percentage should be more like 40 per cent, with all the other characteristics somewhat diluted, but still present.

Most cheap milk chocolate has around 20 per cent cocoa solids and up to 5 per cent vegetable fat is allowed. Sugar makes up a significant proportion, and up to 50 per cent is admissible. Sound like a rather dull cocktail? It is, so a whole load of flavourings get hurled in to make them taste of something.

White chocolate

White chocolate varies, depending on how good the quality is. If it is top-of-the-range, it contains only cocoa butter, no solids. At the bottom end of the scale all the additives used in low-quality milk chocolate will be there.

Fairtrade and organic chocolate

What is Fairtrade chocolate and what of the quality? As with tea and coffee, cocoa growers and workers are not the best paid in the world and the conditions they work in often don't score high marks either. Fairtrade chocolate aims to ensure a better deal in terms of both pay and working conditions. Quality is reasonably high, certainly above average, and it is well worth considering alongside the better chocolates.

There is a growing number of organic types of chocolates, too, which are also worth considering. The higher price and greater care required in growing and manufacturing the cocoa beans means there is an incentive to make and sell a better chocolate in order to make sufficient returns.

Drinking chocolate

Drinking chocolate should be what it says, chocolate made liquid so it can be drunk. One of my mother's earliest childhood disappointments was the realization that drinking chocolate was not how she expected it to be. Having been told the story when I was young, it was some years before, sitting down to a cup of the real thing in Barcelona, I realized just how disappointed my mother must have been – it was a revelation. That there were perfectly cooked *churros* to go with it only heightened the sense of occasion. What we have most of the time is a so-called instant version, over-sugared and containing emulsifiers and flavourings. Buy chocolate flakes and make the real thing, the difference is phenomenal.

directory

Tea

GOOD TEA-BAG TEA: Twining's English Breakfast; Jackson of Piccadilly's Irish Morning, Tetley Gold.

LOOSE LEAF: Twining's English Breakfast, Ceylon and Assam; Whittard's English Breakfast, Ceylon and Assam.

GOOD RETAILERS (MOST OF WHOM DO MAIL ORDER) INCLUDE: Algerian Coffee Stores, 52 Old Compton Street, London W1V 6PB (020 7437 2480); Layton Fern, 27 Rathbone Place, London W1P 2EP (020 7637 2858); Harrods, Knightsbridge, London SW1X 7XL (020 7730 1234); H. R. Higgins, 79 Duke Street, London W1M 6AS (020 7491 8819); Newby Teas (0800 136662); Tea House, 5 Neal Street, London WC2H 9PU (020 7240 7539); Whittard's, various branches (020 7924 1888).

Coffee

GOOD COFFEE RETAILERS THAT ALSO DO MAIL ORDER INCLUDE: Algerian Coffee Stores (as above); Bettys and Taylors By Post of Harrogate (01423 886055); Harrods (as above); H.R. Higgins (as above); Monmouth Coffee House, 27 Monmouth Street, London WC2H 9DD (020 7379 3516); Valvona and Crolla, 19 Elm Row, Edinburgh EH7 4AA (0131 556 6066); Whittard's, various branches, (020 7924 1888).

FURTHER READING:
Coffee: A Connoisseur's Companion by Claudia Roden (Pavilion, £9.99)

RECOMMENDED VISIT:
Bramah Museum of Tea and Coffee, 1 Maguire Street, London SE1 2NQ (020 7378 0222).

Chocolate

RETAILERS: L'Atelier du Chocolat, (020 8311 3337); Fortnum & Mason, 181 Piccadilly, London W1A 1ER (020 7734 8040); Harrods (as left); Monmouth Coffee House (as left); Villandry, 170 Great Portland Street, London W1N 5TB (020 7631 3131).

The Chocolate Society is on 01423 322230 (there is also a shop in London, 020 7259 9222).
The annual International Festival of Chocolate is held in London, usually in November. Call 020 7352 9015.

tea, coffee and chocolate recipes

chicken mole *with chilli and chocolate*

serves 6–8

2 cascabel chillies
2 costeno amarillo chillies
2 pasado chillies
2 kg (4¹/2 lb) chicken thighs
salt and pepper
2 onions, chopped
3 garlic cloves, finely chopped
2 tablespoons sesame seeds
450 g (1 lb) chopped tomatoes
100 g (3¹/2 oz) flaked almonds
3 tablespoons vegetable oil
4 star anise
4 cloves
4-cm (1¹/2-inch) piece of cinnamon stick
45 g (1¹/2 oz) best dark chocolate
1 bunch of coriander, roughly chopped

'Mole' simple means sauce and in this sense the meat is cooked in the sauce, rather than the sauce being served as an accompaniment. The chocolate lends the finished dish a voluptuous roundness, transforming without altering. This recipe is Mexican in origin, the land of the Aztecs and Mayans, who gave us chocolate... or, at least, gave it to some – women were not allowed chocolate, nor indeed were those at the bottom of the pecking order. If you wanted chocolate, not only did you have to be male, you also had to be part of the military, royalty, a top merchant or one of the clergy. Chillies are primarily used for flavouring, the heat is secondary. If these chillies are hard to find, substitute others.

1   Cover the chillies with hot water and allow to soak for 30 minutes. Remove the stems and roughly chop the chillies (remove the seeds if you don't want too hot a dish).

2   Put the chicken in a saucepan, cover with cold water, season with salt and bring to the boil. Simmer gently for 45 minutes.

3   Drain and reserve the liquor, remove the skin from the chicken and discard.

4   Combine the onions, garlic, sesame seeds, tomatoes and almonds in a food processor and blitz to a purée.

5   Heat the oil in a frying pan and, when hot, add the star anise, cloves and cinnamon. Sauté for 30 seconds, or until they give off a sweet aroma. Pour in the onion purée and sauté for 5 minutes, or until the sauce starts to separate.

6   Pour in the reserved stock and the chocolate, lower the heat and cook slowly, stirring, until the chocolate melts.

7   Slide in the chicken pieces, season with salt and pepper and continue to simmer over the lowest possible heat for 30 minutes.

8   Sprinkle over the coriander and serve.

petits pots au chocolat

serves 6

125 g (4½ oz) chocolate
350 ml (12 fl oz) single cream
1 teaspoon lapsang souchong tea
scant grating of nutmeg

This is a simple chocolate fix, an ideal way for a final blast of luxury at the end of an elaborate dinner. You can set it with egg yolk, much as crème brûlée, but I find the result is simply too rich.

1 Grate the chocolate into a bowl.
2 Combine the cream, tea and nutmeg in a saucepan and bring to the boil. Set aside to infuse for 5 minutes.
3 Strain over to the chocolate, stirring with a wooden spoon until it has dissolved.
4 Pour the mixture into espresso cups and chill for about 3 hours before serving.

mint tea

...or any other herb tea for that matter... is a world away from manufactured, if made with some fresh herbs. Try stuffing a pot with mint leaves and pouring boiling water over them. Compare it with a cup of mint tea made from a tea bag, if you are in any doubt.

coffee granita

serves 6–8

1 litre (1³/4 pints) freshly made
    espresso coffee
5 tablespoons sugar
200 ml (7 fl oz) whipping cream

Incredibly refreshing, this is iced coffee turned into an art form. It is perfect for a hot Sunday lunch, when a celebration requires something elaborate, but nobody wants to feast on heavy food.

1 Put the coffee and sugar in a saucepan and gently heat until the sugar has dissolved – you may need more sugar to taste, so check. Remember, too, that because it is to be eaten chilled, the sweetness will be less pronounced.

2 Pour into a plastic tray and freeze, stirring every hour, so the crystals don't get too big.

3 To serve, remove the tray from the freezer about 40 minutes before serving. Break up with a wooden spoon and place in 6–8 iced long-stemmed glasses. Whip the cream, add to the glasses and serve.

Elizabeth David's very indulgent coffee ice-cream

serves 4

225 g (8 oz) fresh medium-roasted
   coffee beans
600 ml (1 pint) single cream
3 egg yolks, lightly beaten
strip of lemon zest
100 g (3½ oz) caster sugar

This is termed 'indulgent' because it requires so much coffee, but it really is worth it. You can make a second batch from the same beans, but it has nothing like the intensity. How could it, when you have simmered all those deliciously complex flavours out of the beans and into the cream?

1   In a mortar with a pestle, bash the coffee beans to break them up.
2   Place in a saucepan with the cream. Bring the cream almost to boiling point, remove from the heat and pour over the egg yolks in a heatproof bowl. Return to the saucepan along with the lemon zest and the caster sugar and replace over a low heat. Continue to cook, stirring constantly until the mixture starts to thicken.
3   Strain into a bowl through a fine sieve and place in the freezer. After 1 hour, stir the mixture to prevent crystals forming and replace in the freezer. It will take about 3 –4 hours to freeze solid, so stir every hour or so.
4   Rinse the coffee beans thoroughly under cold water. You can make a second batch of ice-cream with the same beans, although you will need at least 2, if not 3, more egg yolks.

Earl Grey sorbet

serves 6–8 (or 8–10 with biscuits)

250 g (9 oz) sugar
2 teaspoons Earl Grey tea
juice and zest of 1 lemon
juice and zest of 1 lime

This sorbet highlights the curiously elusive flavour of bergamot, an essential ingredient in Earl Grey tea. Transferring the aroma of flowers into food is not an easy task – you need think only of cheap Turkish delight and nasty rose water – but here the sorbet has all the freshness of the original tea. Serve with a mixture of other sorbets or rich butter biscuits.

1   Place 850 ml (1½ pints) of water in a saucepan with the sugar. Cover and bring to the boil. Simmer for 5 minutes. Remove from the heat, add the tea and set aside to infuse for about 15 minutes.
2   Strain into a bowl. Add the lemon and lime zest and juices and set aside to cool.
3   Freeze for several hours, stirring occasionally, or put in an ice-cream maker until set.
4   Allow to soften before serving and scoop into balls.

index